HENRY SWANZY

THE SELECTED DIARIES

ICHABOD 1948-1958

Henry Swanzy in the studio

HENRY SWANZY

THE SELECTED DIARIES

ICHABOD 1948-1958

INTRODUCED AND EDITED BY

CHRIS CAMPBELL

MICHAEL NIBLETT

AND

VICTORIA ELLEN SMITH

PEEPAL TREE

First published in Great Britain in 2023
Peepal Tree Press Ltd
17 King's Avenue
Leeds LS6 1QS
England

© 2023 The Estate of Henry Swanzy
Chris Campbell
Michael Niblett
Victoria Ellen Smith

ISBN13: 9781845235611

All rights reserved
No part of this publication may be
reproduced or transmitted in any form
without permission

Printed in the United Kingdom
by Severn, Gloucester,
on responsibly sourced paper

CONTENTS

Introduction — 7

The Diaries — 25

Appendix — 197

Acknowledgements — 242

Index — 243

INTRODUCTION

Writing in a letter to his friend, Diana Athill, in 1979, the BBC producer and editor Henry Swanzy responds to an earlier enquiry from Athill as to whether he was "contemplating writing something about *Caribbean Voices*" with the news that he had been "in the thick of typing out vast chunks of diaries [that he had] kept since 1945." Swanzy asks whether Athill's company, André Deutsch, would be interested in publishing the manuscript he was putting together. "The book would have to be rather long and solid," Swanzy admits, "a picture of a whole community at a vital moment in time. For to make it actual, it would be a social picture, as much as a literary one. [...] It would also need a vast amount of work." Swanzy's notes later record a reply from Athill in the negative: "No interest outside [the West Indies]." The diaries were given the title "Ichabod" by Swanzy, a Biblical name deriving from Book 1 of Samuel 4:21 and used as an expression of regret ("And she named the child Ichabod, saying, 'The glory is departed from Israel'"). The diaries would remain unpublished in Swanzy's lifetime, although he continued to work on them in the hope that they would one day find a readership.

This edited volume of Swanzy's diary entries from 1948 to 1958 makes available a small but significant selection of this remarkable life's work. The diaries themselves truly are "vast," as Swanzy acknowledged: fifteen volumes, each between 400 and 800 pages long, documenting his personal and professional experiences across the decades. They describe his encounters with Caribbean and West African writers such as Una Marson, George Lamming, Edgar Mittelholzer, V. S. Naipaul, Cyprian Ekwensi and Efua Sutherland; his dealings with the BBC and with literary agents and broadcasters in the Caribbean and Ghana; and his meetings with nationalist leaders such as Michael Manley and Kwame Nkrumah. The diaries also document his homelife and contain a wealth of observations on contemporary cultural and political events, from anticolonial insurgencies and the crumbling of empire to the latest plays in the West End and changing tastes in fashion.

The diaries shed light on Swanzy's involvement in the pioneering literary radio programme *Caribbean Voices*, as well as the programme's significant influence on the development of Caribbean letters. They also reveal Swanzy's work on the BBC's West African output, where he was the first producer of *Caribbean Voices*' sister programme *West African Voices*, broadcast on *Calling West Africa*. In addition, the diaries record his role in the establishment of the Gold Coast Broadcasting System and, in so doing, provide a first-hand account of the transition from colonial rule to independence in Ghana. More generally, Swanzy's record of his almost daily encounters with a whole host of writers and artists illuminate the complex relationships that existed between the BBC and its correspondents and contributors in the colonies. Swanzy's contemporaries were in no doubt as to the importance of his contribution to the fields of Caribbean and West African letters. Writing in his essay "A Way of Seeing" in 1960, the Bajan novelist George Lamming observed of his time in London and of the postwar developments in Caribbean literature:

> Our sole fortune now was that it was Henry Swanzy who produced 'Caribbean Voices.' At one time or another, in one way or another, all West Indian novelists have benefitted from his work and his generosity of feeling. For Swanzy was very down to earth. If you looked a little thin in the face, he would assume that there might have been a minor famine on, and without in any way offending your pride, he would make some arrangement for you to earn. Since he would not promise to 'use' anything you had written, he would arrange for you to earn by employing you to read. No comprehensive account of writing in the British Caribbean during [the 1950s] could be written without considering his whole achievement and his role in the emergence of the West Indian novel. (1992: 67)

Cyprian Ekwensi, meanwhile, writing in *West Africa* in March 1959, declared:

> Time will one day tell of the work of Henry Swanzy, man of energy, whose foresight has given a flying start of the Commonwealth literary scene to so many writers from the Caribbean and West Africa. [...] *Voices of Ghana*, an anthology of literary contributions to the Ghana Broadcasting System, is the monument Swanzy has left as evidence of his energy and success while he was in Ghana. (1959: 273)

Swanzy's diaries reveal the minutiae of his day-to-day efforts in promoting and assisting writers from the Caribbean and West Africa. But they also lay bare some of the underlying tensions and contradictions of his position. For in an age of anticolonial struggle and growing demands for an end to empire, he remained a member of the metropolitan elite and, as he put it, a "colonial gentleman" or "CMG = Colonial Made Gent" with an inclination to go "scuttling for cover among the faded upper-middle-class, to which I think I belong."

Swanzy in London

Born in 1915 at Glanmire Rectory, near Cork, in Ireland, Swanzy was the eldest son of Rector Samuel Swanzy and his wife Joan (née Glenny). Following the death of his father in 1920, Swanzy moved to England with his mother and siblings. He was educated at Wellington College and New College, Oxford, where he studied modern history. After travelling widely in Europe during the 1930s, he became an assistant principal at the Colonial and Dominions Office (1937-1940), before securing the position of Producer in the General Overseas Service at the BBC in 1940. During the Second World War he was refused for military service on health grounds and worked as a Fire Warden throughout the Blitz.

Working in London in the 1940s at the BBC and, from 1944, as editor of *African Affairs*, Swanzy became an important presence in literary and media circles. He moved into a flat with the future publishing magnate George Weidenfeld. Recalling their time together in his autobiography, Weidenfeld hails Swanzy's dissenting mind and acute grasp of contemporary politics and culture:

> At one point I shared a bachelor flat behind broadcasting house with Henry Swanzy, who, perhaps more than anyone since, intuitively grasped my failings and appraised such virtues as I might have. Henry was a stern but well-meaning critic. He had a double first from Oxford, was a good athlete and was widely read, but he was anything but a conformist. He worked as a talks producer, and I had to deliver much day-to-day comment on European politics to him. He later became a widely acknowledged expert on colonial Africa. Earlier than most students of Britain's African colonial burden, he warned the British Government about the deep flaws in its colonial policy. Henry Swanzy was an underrated genius – for decades he cried in the wilderness. Many of his good ideas for reform were tacitly adopted, but he never got enough credit for what he did. (1995: 148)

It was in this period, too, that he first met Diana Athill, whose own recollections of sharing living space with Weidenfeld and Swanzy are revealing in their own way:

> The flat was the top two floors of a stately house in Devonshire Place, one of the streets traditionally inhabited by England's most expensive doctors who had left a temporary vacuum in the neighbourhood when carried away by the war. Marjorie and I had the top floor, which included the kitchen. George Weidenfeld and Henry Swanzy had the floor below us [...]. The men's floor had an enviable bathroom, all black glass and chrome, given extra distinction by containing a piano on which Henry often played moody music [...]. Neither Marjorie's parents nor mine

questioned the propriety of our ménage – but whether this was because they chose to believe us unshakably chaste, or because we avoided mentioning George and Henry, I no longer remember. The two of us who ended up in bed together were Marjorie and George. (2000: 12-13)

In addition to his connections to the publishing world, Swanzy's personal life brought him into the orbit of artists associated with the village of Great Bardfield in Essex. In 1945, he became engaged to the artist and engraver Tirzah Garwood. Garwood was known for the originality of her print-making and designs, as well as for her oil paintings, which typically blend a whimsical style with startling, uncanny moments. She had been married to painter and war artist Eric Ravilious, with whom she had three children. Swanzy's diaries record his life together with Tirzah and her children in London, as well as, tragically, her battle with cancer and death in 1951. Swanzy's account in the diaries of the latter stages of Tirzah's illness are some of the most moving examples of his prose.

Swanzy continued to work in London during the late 1940s and early 1950s, producing programmes for the BBC's West African Service and assuming the helm of *Caribbean Voices* in 1946. In 1952, he married Henriette Van Eeghan, with whom he had two sons and a daughter. In 1954, Swanzy and his family moved to Ghana after Swanzy was seconded to lead the new Programmes Section of the Gold Coast Broadcasting Service. They returned to England in 1958, after which Swanzy continued to work for the BBC's external services. By 1971, he was the senior script writer for central talks and features. He remained there until his retirement in 1976. He died in March 2004, aged 88. In summing up his own life at the end of his CV, Swanzy wrote: "An odd passage through life, which might explain something to the alert. The key, I think, has been my sympathy with the different peoples brought into contact by an imperial structure, perhaps too much linked by politics and economics, and not enough by art and culture."

Swanzy and Caribbean Voices, 1946-1954

Caribbean Voices was recorded and edited in London and broadcast weekly to listeners in the Anglophone Caribbean through the BBC's General Overseas Service. It was one of a number of programmes under the umbrella of the *Calling the West Indies* series. As programme assistant on this series, the Jamaican writer and journalist Una Marson began "weaving readings of published works by Caribbean writers and reports of cultural events into her broadcasts" (Donnell: 2011, 29). The success of this format paved the way for *Caribbean Voices*, which initially ran for twenty minutes on Sunday evenings, under the stewardship of Marson.

Following Marson's return to Jamaica in 1946, the writer Mary Treadgold took temporary charge before Swanzy assumed the helm, overseeing the extension of the programme from twenty to thirty minutes.

As is now generally well recognized, *Caribbean Voices* played an integral role in the development of Caribbean literature. Gail Low summarizes the function and influence of the programme thus:

> [It] contained both creative work, read by West Indians resident in London, and critical reviews and commentaries undertaken by English critics [...]. This tied the literary world of the English-speaking Caribbean to that of London. [...] Swanzy looked and paid for original and unpublished material, and *Caribbean Voices* became especially important for the development of regional creative writing, cultivating strong links with regional literary journals such as *Bim*. (2011: 97-98)

Swanzy's role in selecting and shaping the material he received for broadcast has been widely remarked upon. An Irishman with an understanding of colonial politics, he was sensitive to the possibility that the London-based *Caribbean Voices* might be construed by its listeners as a form of metropolitan interference. Yet although he was keen for the programme to avoid, as he put it, imposing "alien standards" on "a regional culture which ought to develop of itself", he nonetheless "made no secret of what he did want from contributors" (Swanzy, 1948a; Nanton, 2000, 66). Swanzy was particularly eager for any work that he broadcast to reflect Caribbean culture and landscape. In an oft-cited letter to Gladys Lindo, the BBC's literary agent in Jamaica, Swanzy complains of a batch of manuscripts that he has recently rejected that they "all have something in common, and that is a complete absence of local colour" (Swanzy, 1946). Swanzy's promotion of local colour went hand in hand with what John Figueroa has described as a reluctance to air Caribbean writing on "subjects of universal interest" (2003, 64). As Low observes, despite Swanzy's "own disavowals about the Caribbean picturesque or topographical," there is evidence that "Caribbean folk culture possessed some exotic appeal for [him]" (103). Indeed, Swanzy had an especial interest in depictions of the lives and struggles of the working-classes, which, he felt, possessed "a charm and vitality [...] missing from depictions of middle-class lives" (Low, 103).

Amongst Swanzy's other preferences were a taste for stories that were unsentimental and a lack of enthusiasm for writing by middle-class women focusing on domestic, intimate themes (French, 2008, 86; Low, 103). These preferences filtered down to Lindo and her husband, Cedric, who were responsible for choosing which of the submissions were to be sent on to Swanzy in London. His preferences also seem to have been recognized by many of the potential contributors. At one point, Swanzy was moved to complain to the Lindos about manuscripts that seemed "written to order", suggesting his criteria for inclusion on the programme was in some measure shaping the terms on which writers sought entry into the literary field and access to the prestige that came with being broadcast on the BBC (Swanzy, 1948b).

In this connection, it is worth highlighting the significant seam of recent scholarship on *Caribbean Voices* that has focused on the editorial treatment of women writers. Of the 372 contributors who featured on the programme over the fifteen years of its existence, 71 of these were women (Nanton, 2003: 66). As Alison Donnell has argued, given that "the *Caribbean Voices* programme is so emphatically and repeatedly linked to the success of Caribbean literary authorship, it is all the more regrettable that nearly all of the women writers whose work it broadcast remain unknown to readers and even researchers of Caribbean literature today. Talented writers such as Eula Redhead, Inez Sibley, Marjorie Brown and Edwina Melville remain unremarked upon" (2011: 30). Donnell's own important work (along with that of the contributors to her *Caribbean Literary Heritage* project) has done much to rectify this situation in recent years. We hope that the interactions the diary records between Swanzy and many such women writers can contribute to this critical and restorative task. Swanzy's responses to the work of Redhead, for example, emphasize the gendered tastes and assumptions informing his editorship. At various points, he refers to Redhead's contributions as "simple folklore," "agreeable, childish fantasies," and "little Anancy tales." As Donnell shows, while many of Redhead's stories certainly drew on Caribbean folklore, they reworked it with "considerable skill," deploying complex formal devices and stylistic techniques (2015: 92). Swanzy's comments, however, downplay the literary qualities of Redhead's prose in line with a general tendency on *Caribbean Voices* to frame women's writing "as connected to authenticity, affect, and intimacy": women writers are viewed as conduits for 'authentic' folk beliefs, rather than as literary innovators in their own right (Donnell, 2015: 90).

If Swanzy's editorial gatekeeping on *Caribbean Voices* often betrayed his own biases and sympathies, nonetheless he was keen to foster independent networks between emerging writers from the Caribbean and West Africa. He opened his home in Bishop Stortford to many of these writers by hosting Thursday evening get-togethers, or, as he referred to them in his diary, his *"causerie de jeudi"*. The first Thursday get-together took place on 25th October, 1951, and was attended by Edgar Mittelholzer (Guyana), Sam Selvon (Trinidad), George Lamming (Barbados), John Figueroa (Jamaica), Denis Williams (Guyana), Davidson Nicol (Sierra Leone), Cyprian Ekwensi (Nigeria), Solomon Adeboye Babalola (Nigeria), and Peter Abrahams (South Africa). He offered beer, cider, ginger wine and orangeade. A few weeks later he added gin to the drinks options "as an inducement."

These social gatherings enabled Caribbean and West African writers to get to know one another. But more than that, they were designed to create a sense of community amongst young men and women who were a long way from home; and to provide work-in-progress sessions for writers wishing to develop their skills. The Jamaican writer Andrew Salkey recalls that "Henry not only became our patron but our friend. He held tutorials at his house… And took a very close compassionate look at our work. I think this has been invaluable in getting the writers started" (qtd. in Nanton, 2000: 68). Those Caribbean writers whose careers Swanzy helped to launch included Sam Selvon, George Lamming, John Figueroa, Kamau Brathwaite, Wilson Harris and the Nobel Prize winners V.S. Naipaul and Derek Walcott. Swanzy's connection to these figures is now well-known. However, the diaries also bring to light the extent to which his work on both *Caribbean Voices* and *West African Voices* brought together a wider network not only of writers, but also of actors, dancers, and singers, who regularly featured as readers on the programmes or at the very least passed through the recording studios. The diaries emphasize the degree to which artists such as Pauline Henriques, Orlando Martins, Beryl McBurnie, Rudolph Dunbar, Ben Enwonwu, and Edric Connor contributed to the larger cultural and artistic discussions with Swanzy out of which the programmes arose.

The emphasis placed by writers like Salkey and Lamming on Swanzy's importance to the development of Caribbean letters, as well as the large amount of archival material available on *Caribbean Voices*, has led to Swanzy receiving significant attention from scholars of Caribbean literature in recent years (see, e.g., Nanton, 2000; Donnell, 2011, 2015; Low, 2011; Griffith, 2016; Proctor, 2015). But in the late 1940s and early 1950s he was better known to Africanist scholars due to the immense amount of research that he put in to writing the lengthy "Quarterly Notes" for the Royal African Society's journal, *African Affairs,* which he edited for ten years from 1944. As Philip Nanton argues, Swanzy had "editorial skills, considerable knowledge of Africa, as well as effective promotional skills and a direct, deep and learned understanding of literature" (2000: 65). It was perhaps this that in 1954 led the BBC to invite Swanzy to lead the new Programmes Section of the Gold Coast Broadcasting Service.

The Ghana Years: 1954-1958

In March 1953, Swanzy had a conversation with John Grenfell-Williams in which Grenfell-Williams encouraged him to consider various overseas posts such as Head of the Western Region in Ibadan, Nigeria or Head of Programmes for the newly established Gold Coast Broadcasting Service.

Swanzy believed that the Head of the Colonial Service was attempting to lure him away from the BBC so that "JGW" could "become the one and only African 'expert'" (3 Mar. 1953). However, Grenfell-Williams was of the opinion that broadcasting in colonial Africa was "about to come into its own" and so the advice may have been more genuine than Swanzy's suspicions allowed him to believe (1951-52: 217). Swanzy had been seeking employment in Africa for many years and felt that working for the Uganda Broadcasting Service in Entebbe under Andrew Cohen was the most interesting avenue to explore. But, as he recorded in his diary, the timing was not convenient "with Henriette in the family way." He went on to write:

> But I *must* get out sooner or later, with JGW taking everything that is going, the literary programmes are at the bottom of the barrel, the African Society tottering along with a hundred generals and one private... (4 Mar. 1953)

In January 1954 Swanzy visited Uganda as part of a six-week tour to East Africa for the BBC. Whilst there, he took an interest in how the new radio station was developing. "It is all rather intoxicating," he noted, "the creative side of colonialism, the belated effort which should have been made after the end of the first war" (2 Jan. 1954). Seeking a way to involve himself in "the creative side," he suggested to the British radio personnel in Uganda that he make a literary programme in London that would be relayed to them. They showed little interest and there was no further mention of him taking secondment to Uganda.

However, later the same year the opportunity did finally present itself for Swanzy to work in Africa. James Millar, Senior Administrative Assistant with the BBC Empire Service, had recently been appointed Director of Broadcasting for the Gold Coast Broadcasting Service (GCBS) and he was looking for BBC staff to head various departments. Swanzy was offered Head of Programmes, one of the posts that Grenfell-Williams had suggested to him. On 10th June 1954, Swanzy recorded the moment in his diary:

> A key day in my life. At 11 in the office of JGW, James Millar casually asked if I would come to the Gold Coast for two tours, as Head of Programmes... A new place, which I only know on paper, at a historic moment, the first handing-over of power in British Africa.

This was the opportunity that Swanzy had been waiting for and at a time when the Gold Coast colony was preparing to become the independent nation of Ghana on 6th March, 1957. A few weeks after Millar's verbal invitation, Swanzy wrote him a letter titled "Preliminary Thoughts on a

Radio Service as Support for a Young Nationalism." In this important letter, Swanzy enthusiastically explains how he envisaged the first phase of GCBS programming. When considering what would make radio popular, he explored ideas on modern and traditional music, entertainment and information, Ghana's history before the arrival of Europeans in the fifteenth century, world religions and, naturally, a programme of original literature by Ghanaian writers. In developing his thoughts, Swanzy evidently drew on his experience of programme making for the BBC's West African Service. However, as the title of his letter to Millar suggests, he was also acutely aware of the responsibility he held in overseeing the development of programme content that would be appropriate for the specific political milieu and unprecedented nature of Ghana's imminent transition out of colonial rule.

Swanzy's letter also demonstrates his continued concern for navigating the complex relationship between programme content and political milieu. "The only difficulty," he concludes, "is the fact that any appeal to tradition will only encourage separatism." He knew that celebrating the Gold Coast's rich oral histories and varied cultures would be crucial to the success of GCBS as it would enable audiences to recognise themselves in radio, but he was equally sensitive to the need for a radio service that reinforced a collective national identity. As such, Swanzy saw the cultivation and reinforcement of an emergent literary nationalism as a key ingredient in the move toward inevitable political independence. And so, in seeking to nurture tradition whilst enabling unity in a nationalist culture, he developed his plans for a flagship literature programme for GCBS. Swanzy outlines his position on this in the "Preliminary Thoughts" letter: "An aspect of the cultural situation which, I believe, offers great opportunity in an independent radio system is a definite policy for encouraging creative writers." This would be achieved at GCBS through a combination of Swanzy's existing relationships with Ghanaian writers from the BBC; the receptiveness of listeners in the Gold Coast, "one of the most 'radio-minded' of all the colonies" (Bloom, 2014: 136); and the firm commitment of Ghanaian programme makers to not only broadcasting but also writing original literature.

The Gold Coast Broadcasting Service was established in 1953, but radio had been in existence in colonial Ghana since the 1930s when Station ZOY – named by adaptation of its call sign ZD4AA – was initiated by Governor Arnold Hodson. Initially the station relayed BBC programmes from London that were intended to expose the colonised to the culture of the coloniser. The transformation of Station ZOY into the Gold Coast Broadcasting Service began in earnest from 1951 when the future first leader of independent Ghana, Dr Kwame Nkrumah, and the former first Director-General of the BBC, Lord John Reith, met in London. It was during this meeting that Nkrumah initially proposed the development of an independent, comprehensive broadcasting service for Ghana. In the late 1940s, the colonial government had begun inviting Ghanaian programme makers to attend Programme Production Skills courses at the BBC with a view to more programmes being developed at Accra's Broadcasting House and at sub-stations across the country. As his diaries evidence, Swanzy met and worked with a number of those who underwent training in London such as Ben Gadzekpo, Joseph Ghartey, Florence Prah and Marian Smith-Mensah.

Having been appointed as Head of Programmes to GCBS, Swanzy arrived in colonial Ghana on 15th November 1954 and immediately started working with Ghanaian staff to significantly increase the amount of locally-generated material that GCBS produced. Over the coming months these programmes included music request shows, *Radio Doctor*, *Women's Half-Hour*, the documentary series *Work in Progress*, the newsreel *Window on the World*, the fortnightly discussion series *Seconds Out*, the broadcast of religious services on *Sunday Magazine*, *Good Neighbours* about other West African countries, the variety show *Everybody Loves Saturday Night*, the arts programmes *Sound Judgement*, *Akan Theatre* (later *Ghana Theatre*) and the literary programme *The Singing Net* (see Smith, 2018: 14). In terms of the latter, it took Swanzy less than three months from his arrival in Accra to develop GCBS's pioneering literary programme from concept to broadcast, including identifying creative writers and readers, editing individual pieces, preparing the first script, and recording it for transmission.

The process began with Swanzy organising more than forty "letters soliciting contributions to the projected literary programme, *The Singing Net*" (27 Nov. 1954). A list of potential authors was initially prepared by the Ghanaian dramatist and poet Efua Sutherland, who knew Swanzy from the BBC where she contributed to *West African Voices* through her own writing and as a reader, as well as being published by Swanzy in *African Affairs*. Entries in Swanzy's diary suggest that Sutherland's list included a number of writers that he already respected such as Michael Dei-Anang and Kobina Sekyi. However, he noted that the only authors from the original list that made any significant impact in shaping *The Singing Net* were Albert Kayper-Mensah and Sutherland herself (20 Oct. 1957). It was after the 8pm BBC news on 28th January 1955 that the GCBS Announcer informed listeners for the first time that they would now hear literature written and performed by their own writers, broadcast from their capital. Swanzy's critique of the first episode was that it "passed off quite well, although rather too much crammed into fourteen minutes" meaning that, in the words of Frances Quarshie-Idun, it had "too many words and too much Swanzy" (28-9 Jan. 1955). With him stepping back in subsequent programmes and Ghanaians stepping forward as contributors, readers and presenters, *The Singing Net* soon became popular and received sufficient poetry and prose pieces to air once a week for the next 11 years.

Literary contributions to GCBS came through regular unsolicited submissions, competition entries, and Swanzy's efforts to elicit contributions from the station's own broadcasters and extended literary networks. The programme featured established and emerging Ghanaian writers such as Frank Parkes, Henry Ofori, Atukwei Okai, Cameron Duodu, Efua Sutherland, Andrew Amankwa Opoku, Geormbeeyi Adali-Mortty, and Albert Kayper-Mensah. Both Okai and Duodu, for example, have spoken about how listening to early broadcasts of *The Singing Net* encouraged them as young writers to submit their work for broadcast. Swanzy also recognized, as he had done with contributors to *Caribbean Voices*, that young writers needed a means of making money that allowed them to spend time writing. Consequently, he ensured that several of the contributors to *The Singing Net* were employed by GCBS as broadcasters. In addition to salaries, the broadcasting service also paid writers for each creative piece that was broadcast on air and so Swanzy encouraged those with literary talents to contribute regularly.

There are no known recordings of *The Singing Net* or *Ghana Theatre* and so evidence of what they included, what format they followed, and how literature was received by Ghanaian audiences must be pieced together from secondary sources. These include newspaper reviews of the programmes; private papers and testimonies of Ghanaian writers and broadcasters; Swanzy's diary and other writings; and the anthology *Voices of Ghana: Literary Contributions to the Ghana Broadcasting System 1955-57* (1958), which Swanzy compiled and published through the government's printers in Accra as a conclusion to his time in West Africa (see Smith, 2018: 1-46). It is remembered that *The Singing Net* was fourteen minutes long, it either focused on a single writer or a single theme, and it aired weekly on a Sunday evening. It was further developed with the addition of music to accompany some of the literary performances. On 17th April 1957, the *Daily Graphic* printed an article titled "At Last! Radio Ghana has done it" in which the critic encouraged readers to give more time to listening to radio and, in doing so, complimented the use of music to support Adali-Mortty's "first-class" performance of Kayper-Mensah's *The Ghosts* (Swanzy, 1957: n.p.).

As was the case with his editorial gatekeeping on *Caribbean Voices*, Swanzy's role as literary editor on *The Singing Net* was contradictory and problematic. From diary entries and statements made by those who worked on and contributed to GCBS programmes, the tensions surrounding his position are clearly evident. Whilst capable of deferring to writers on matters concerning their work, he had little compunction in making unilateral editorial decisions when he saw fit. Cameron Duodu has spoken candidly on a number of platforms about the moment he heard his first short story aired and discovered that Swanzy had dramatically changed the ending without seeking the writer's consent (see Campbell, 2018). "He had midwifed several West Indian writers on to the BBC's Caribbean programmes," writes Duodu, "and he was in the Gold Coast to tell the Cameron Duodus too what they could write!" According to Duodu, Swanzy explained his motivation by declaring: "Look, Mr. Diwodu, we have to take the whole population into account when we broadcast things, you know, and we can't take the risk of broadcasting examples of bad behaviour, in case it influences other people to imitate it and act likewise, you know?" (Duodu, 2013: 74). Despite their disagreement about the value judgement that Swanzy had imposed on Duodu's *Tough Guy in Town*, Duodu wrote an article for the *Daily Graphic* on the occasion of Swanzy's departure from Ghana on 9th April 1958. In this article, he refers to Swanzy as the "brilliant boss of the Programmes Section of Radio Ghana." He states that Swanzy "had made programmes what they are today. From a remote, high-flung institution cut off from the people it serves, Radio Ghana has now grown to become a household word for the people to whom it belongs." The article praises Swanzy's skill as a literary reader, his vision in developing programmes in line with the aspirations of GCBS and the "great boon to Ghana writers" that he provided by publishing *Voices of Ghana* (1958: 5).

Ichabod

"After all, I have not been a total failure." These are the words with which Swanzy sums up his time as Head of Programmes at GCBS on the day he left Ghana in 1958. The sense of ambivalence, the mix of pride and self-doubt, and the melancholic tone are all typical of Swanzy. His decision to give the name "Ichabod" to his diaries, with its connotations of regret for departed glory, is entirely in keeping with his perception of his own life and career. Any objective evaluation of Swanzy's contribution to literature and broadcasting might not share his rather melancholy self-assessment, but one poignant thread running through the diaries is his palpable sense of a life defined by missed opportunities and a general lack of recognition.

The last couple of decades have most certainly brought that recognition, with a range of critical studies and documentaries illuminating Swanzy's life and work. Many of these have drawn attention to his problematic position as a literary and cultural gatekeeper, simultaneously attempting to foster independent artistic networks in the Caribbean and West Africa yet forever in danger of imposing metropolitan standards and values. As his diaries make plain, Swanzy was painfully aware of the vexed nature of his position. Indeed, in the post-war context of the crumbling of the British empire and the explosion of anticolonial nationalisms, his sense of himself as caught between a series of irreconcilable forces is, at times, acute. Swanzy's diary entry for the 19th of October 1948 provides something of a microcosm of the contradictions he felt forced to negotiate. In it, he describes a missive from the BBC hierarchy, advocating "selection, relevance, very close co-operation with Government departments. In particular, news must be 'carefully balanced' presenting the 'British way of life'. There must be only a 'British view', not 'British views'. [...] 'We must not in any way shrink from giving full expression to the British view, and to assist by all means in our power the national Effort. Only in this way shall we be framing our programmes in the national interest.'" The missive infuriates Swanzy, not only because of its content but also because it highlights to him the limitations and hesitations of his own position. "I was in a rage all day. [...] Rage at myself above all: neither artist nor man of action, neither African nor European, neither Communist nor Conservative..." Swanzy's rage is telling: a "Colonial Made Gent" he may have been, but he was also, as Lamming put it, a "kind of maverick." Unable to fully escape the institutional orthodoxies of his class, schooling, and workplace, he was nonetheless always ready to question and contest such orthodoxies.

Notes on editorial procedure

Editing Swanzy's diaries has been no easy task; indeed, as he predicted in his letter to Athill, it has required "a vast amount of work." It bears re-emphasizing just how copious the diaries are: 14 volumes stretching from 1945 to 1983, with a fifteenth serving as a retrospective account of Swanzy's life from 1915 to 1945. Swanzy originally wrote the diaries in long hand before subsequently typing them up in the late 1970s with an eye to publication – as the letter to Athill cited earlier makes clear.

Swanzy's daily entries each contain a wealth of detail relating to his personal and professional life. Indeed, the personal and professional are often deeply entangled in his writing: a single entry, a single sentence even, will move from, say, a comment on his work in the recording studio to musings on his dinner to an observation on global political developments. In trying to produce a critical edition of the diaries that is accessible and readable, we have generally sought to foreground Swanzy's professional life in our editing. However, in order to retain the tone and texture of the diaries, significant personal incidents and relationships are included, as are many of his references to contemporary world-historical events and the mundane matters of homelife. It is worth noting that sometimes such references reproduce contemporary views and attitudes that Swanzy takes for granted, but which might strike readers today as troubling or strange. In particular, some of the language around race, gender, and sexuality is problematic. It may also suprise some readers the degree to which identifying as a communist in institutions such as the BBC was relatively normal at the time, even though those institutions themselves were vehemently anti-communist.

Given the concern in much recent scholarship with Swanzy's editorial decision-making we are very much aware of the irony of our position as editors of this volume and the questions that might be raised about our own principles of selection and exclusion. Our decision to focus on the years 1948 to 1958 stems in part from the perception, widely held amongst critics, that this was the highpoint of his professional life. His work on *Caribbean Voices*, *West African Voices*, and at GCBS was of signal cultural import, and his record of this time and his encounters with a vast array of writers, artists, actors, scholars, politicians, and activists is most likely to appeal to both a general readership and scholars of Caribbean and West African literature. Readers will see that our selections from Swanzy's diary entries for the period 1948-1954 occupy a greater proportion of this critical edition than those recounting his time in Ghana. This is in part because his entries for the Ghana years tend to be more succinct in and of themselves, but also because they do not quite contain the same density of social and interpersonal detail that typify Swanzy's writing when ensconced in the more familiar surroundings of London. It is our hope that at some point in the future, the full span of the diaries will be made available.

In editing individual diary entries, we have used ellipses in square brackets [...] to indicate where we have omitted text (although for ease of reading, we have not used such ellipses when omitting material at the beginning or end of entries). Ellipses not in square brackets are Swanzy's own punctuation. After producing his typescript of the original diaries, Swanzy made a series of minor revisions and edits in longhand, occasionally striking through the odd line of text (for the most part, it seems, in a valiant but doomed attempt to reduce the word count in light of his difficulties in getting the volumes published). At times in our editing of the diaries we have found it necessary to restore these strikethroughs for reasons of clarity or literary interest. In the course of the period covered by this critical edition, Swanzy takes a number of trips for both personal and professional reasons. In general, we have omitted a large portion of the entries relating to these for reasons of space and the particular focus of this critical edition. (Future scholars may well want to examine Swanzy's trip to, for example, Nigeria in 1949, which is recounted in a slightly different idiom to the rest of the diaries.) One exception is Swanzy's first and only visit to the Caribbean in 1952, the diary entries for which we have reproduced in detail because they are so closely tied to his work on, and the artistic networks surrounding, *Caribbean Voices*.

During the course of the diaries, Swanzy makes reference to a huge number of colleagues, acquaintances, and correspondents, not least the many writers and readers who contributed to *Caribbean Voices* and *The Singing Net*. Where possible, we have tried to provide the reader with some brief biographical information on these figures in our Appendix (names starred * in the text can be found alphabetically in the Appendix).

Chris Campbell
Michael Niblett
Victoria Ellen Smith

WORKS CITED

Athill, Diana. 2000. *Stet*. Granta.

Campbell, Chris. 2018. "The Case of Cameron Duodo's 'Tough Guy in Town.'" *Obsidian*. 44.2: 200-215.

Donnell, Alison. 2011. "Heard But Not Seen: Women's Short Stories and the BBC's *Caribbean Voices* Programme." In *The Caribbean Short Story: Critical Perspectives*. Eds. Lucy Evans et al. Leeds: Peepal Tree Press. 29-43.

—. 2015. "Rescripting Anglophone Caribbean Women's Literary History." In *Beyond Windrush*. Eds. J. Dillon Brown and Leah Reade Rosenberg. Jackson: University Press of Mississippi. 79-96.

Duodu, Cameron. 1958. "He Helped Build Radio Ghana." *Daily Graphic* (9 April), 5.

—. 2013. "Why Chinua Achebe Mattered to Us All." *New African* 530 (July): 70-74

French, Patrick. 2008. *The World is What it Is*. London: Picador.

Grenfell-Williams, John. 1951-52. "Broadcasting in the African Colonies." *The B.B.C. Quarterly* 6: 217

Griffith, Glyne A. 2016. *The BBC and the Development of Anglophone Caribbean Literature, 1943-1958*. Palgrave.

Low, Gail. 2011. *Publishing the Postcolonial: Anglophone West African and Caribbean Writing in the UK, 1948-1968*. New York and London: Routledge.

Nanton, Philip. 2000. "What Does Mr. Swanzy Want – Shaping or Reflecting?" *Caribbean Quarterly* 46 (1): 61-72.

—. 2003. "London Calling." *Caribbean Beat*. 63: 66-71.

Procter, James. 2015. "Una Marson at the BBC". *Small Axe: A Caribbean Journal of Criticism*, 19.3: 1-28.

Smith, Victoria Ellen. 2018. "Introduction to the 60th Anniversary Second Edition – Three Years Catch in *The Singing Net*: creating *Voices of Ghana*." *Voices of Ghana: Literary Contributions to the Ghana Broadcasting System, 1955-57*. Ed. by V. E. Smith (James Currey, 2018), 1-46.

Swanzy, Henry. 1946. Letter to Gladys Lindo, 13th August. Henry Swanzy Papers, held at the Swanzy, Henry. 1948a. Letter to Mr. Debysingh, 18th October. Henry Swanzy Papers. No pag.

Swanzy, Henry. 1948b. Letter to Gladys Lindo, 20th September. Henry Swanzy Papers. No pag.

Swanzy, Henry. 1957. "At Last! Radio Ghana has done it." *Daily Graphic* (17 April). University of Birmingham. No pag.

Weidenfeld, George. 1995. *Remembering my Good Friends: An Autobiography*. Harper Collins.

Writing in the UK, 1948-1968. New York and London: Routledge.

ICHABOD:

[FROM VOLUME 2:

2ND JANUARY 1945 – 3RD JANUARY 1948]

1948

1 January. Start the New Year with a nasty cold, and stagger to the office in the afternoon to meet a young French geographer called Savonnet, an emissary of *Présence Africaine*. This proves rather disappointing, typical Left Bank production. Perfunctory, messages from OK names (Gide, Sartre, Camus), a great deal of hot air about Negritude, only one good piece of direct writing, so far as I could see, an account by one Abdoulaye Sadji of a mulatto girl in Dakar, whom he does not seem to like…There were, however, some penetrating reviews signed JH (Howlett?), in particular of Richard Wright, who figures *outre Manche* as "the great American writer", but who, if he were white, would be relegated to where he rightly belongs, the Boots catalogue.

3 January. John Fig [John Figueroa]* reads another remarkable piece by [George] Lamming,* "The Islands". This is the densest talent so far seen in the fishing net of Prospero.

[From VOLUME 3: 4th January 1948 – 1st January 1951]

4 January. At least at this bad time, the family are rallying round. John was surprised to find that I have written poetry. Tirzah is very much softer and more gentle in this illness than she has been in the past. She even seems not hopelessly put off by the beard I have grown. There is something indescribably appealing about her, as she stands in her red sweater and blue bloomers, with a faint line of white in between, to complete the tricolour.

7 January. James Gray [*African Affairs*] gave me a very fine luncheon at the Devonshire Club. I don't remember much of what we talked about, it was that kind of lunch, but I told him that *Libertas* had foundered, and he told me that *West Africa* was created by Lord Milner, to find a job for Albert Cartwright, whom he had jailed in South Africa for being pro-Boer. Walking back through the streets I thought of a definition of my plight, and the plight of those like me: *Too strong to follow, too weak to lead.*

9 January. My first "summary" of work in progress on *Caribbean Voices*, in which I tried to cover the most significant items in 1947. Thanks to Tony's [Tony McGlone, a colleague of Swanzy's at the BBC] excellent filing, and my own notes, it did not take too long to string it together. I hope that it will help. At least, there is nowhere else, except perhaps in the columns of *BIM*, where you can find such a *compte rendu*. The cash comes from the BBC (so little!). The credit comes from the little magazine. It allowed me the necessary equanimity to put up with very cavalier treatment from Sir John Chancellor, a fierce little ex-Governor of Mauritius, who came in ostensibly to record a New Year Message. In fact, he tossed me some gossipy notes he had written on the back of an envelope in the train, with a request to "knock them into shape." Such an attitude justifies the cruel remarks about 200 [Oxford Street, the BBC studios] made by Orwell, "wretched hacks". In the lift going down, the nasty little man drove the lesson home, by enquiring whether Haley worked in the BBC. "He was an office boy under my son, when he was Head of Reuters". Grrr. One does not, I must say, generally have to put up with such bad manners.

13 January. At least, there is one sop to my pride, hurt by the BBC. A cable from Mrs [Gladys] Lindo*, asking for the summary script of the survey of 1947, for publication in the press. One grasps at such straws. A long talk with Lewis at the RAS [Royal African Society], where the auditors reveal an increasingly serious financial situation.

15 January. In bed all morning, my ganglions all a-jangle. I did not realise how much my nervous system was affected, until I struggled back to Oxford Street, to produce Pauline [Henriques]* reading a story from Jamaica by Inez Sibley,* "When the New Prophet Came", rather good, direct and honest, like everything by this writer. It was really the scenario of Pasuka's ballet, *De Prophet*, the Shepherd who was due to ascend to Heaven from August Town, near Kingston. At the studio, I felt a queer weakness, as though from the heart, and unpleasant cramp round the ribs, which Tirzah says comes from the salts.

16 January. I had to spend all day at home, giving up a meeting with Arthur Calder-Marshall,* a possible critic for *Caribbean Voices* (thanks to his excellent book *Glory Dead*). Even sadder, I have also to call off attending a Fabian Conference at Pasture Wood, the Webbs' old house at Dorking. As a bad alternative, I read Rhodes' speeches, which are appalling, and dithyrambs from Basil Williams. Q [Swanzy's mother] and Aunt Lily looked in during the afternoon, Q full of Aunt Mary's funeral.

20 January. Back at work, still with a swollen jaw. I had to come, because Calder-Marshall was due to call. Needless to say, JGW [John Grenfell Williams]* annexed him, and whisked him away to coffee in the canteen, where he fed him with the wrong remarks about Caribbean literature. The main thing is that Calder-Marshall was interested enough to take on the job of occasional criticism of short stories, immediately after broadcast in the same programme.

Later in the day, our new Controller came round, Major General Sir Ian Jacob, a nice, unpretentious man, with grey hair and spectacles, a member of an old Anglo-Indian family originally from the Scottish border. I was feeling muzzy from the jaw, and behaved oddly. I remember saying that I was cast adrift, or rather, locked tight, in this prison, no contacts, no functions, a Brahmin to the outside world. Mem: by all accounts the Fabian conference, which I missed, was a fiasco, with the Nationalists, type Nkrumah and Kenyatta, finally turned nasty.

27 January. At 200, JGW introduced me to Robert Herring, the editor of *Life and Letters*, back after nine months in the Caribbean. An amiable, soft, brown-eyed man, the typical man of letters, fast disappearing from the scene. When I mentioned him later to Tirzah she remembered him as an arrogant young man-about-town, with a book called *Adam and Eve at Kew*, which [Edward] Bawden illustrated. He talks of "Dylan [Thomas] and Stephen [Spender]", and in Jamaica seems to have cultivated the 'right' people: Clare McFarlane,* George Campbell,* Wycliffe Bennett,* Vivian Virtue,* and all the tribe of Parnassus, among their native woodnotes wild. Inspired by his elegance, and charm, I went out to Fortnums, and bought some titbits for Tirzah from an old gentleman in a morning coat: beef tea of pre-war strength, *marrons glacés*, crystallised strawberries. Then to Boots in Piccadilly, for a worm-powder for Annie [Ravilious].

29 January. At 200, Arthur Calder-Marshall records his first critique for *Caribbean Voices*, a general pep-talk to establish his own position. (There must be few who remember *Glory Dead*). He is nice, shaggy-browed, shoe-contemplative, *strange* (to quote Coleridge). One thing that endears him, he is a sworn enemy of Noel Sabine, whose one disinterested act, he said, had been to threaten to shoot himself, after he had been turned down by the girl who subsequently married Frank Pakenham. He even pursued her to East Africa in a plane. After the recording, he gave me a drink, but I had to hurry off, to meet two young Mauritians, radiomen, sent here for training. At tea, Mary Treadgold* told me that Edric Connor* has conceived a passion for her. He has refused a part in a film, because he had to play a eunuch.

30 January. A crowded day. In the morning, a talk with Lewis Hastings, full of the 'African hinterland' of Western Union. He wants to have details about Davidson Nicol,* whom he has invited to speak on the same platform, as the Tory MP, Dodds-Parker, the friend of [Sir Charles] Ponsonby.* Lunch at the MM Club with Kenneth Little, increasingly authoritative – he addresses the Colonial group in the Commons on general questions of race – but also quite agreeable. When we came out, we saw posters, *Gandhi Shot Dead*. I went back to my desk, and dug out the verses I wrote in 1942 or 43, when it was thought he would die, and took them down to Red Continuity, where John Arlott was recording a commemorative programme, over lunch, with sandwiches and whisky. To my surprise, he liked it, and even read it, placed between beautiful Indian dirges. As it is the one and only poem I ever wrote, apart from the special, topical pieces for Newsreel, that were broadcast or published (even paid for), I feel that I should note it here.

GANDHI DEAD

World hater, lover, none the less
He has the world in keeping now,
Is one with lands that round him press,
And pack that enigmatic brow
With the perpetual silent shade
He sought beneath the village tree,
Out of the sun where flowers fade –
And sought in vain from History.

Nor can we here, in doubt ourselves,
As English, follow all his thought.
The engineer in silence delves,
Diviners move another sort
Of mystery to where the wells
Of earth produce their living streams,
Where distance brings enchanted bells,
And nothing is, but only seems.

For him the West will still remain
Indifferent, but Eastern soil
Gather in its arms again
A son achieved with so much toil.
The secret here we only guess,
And point at, yet not understand,
But know his life and words express

> Embodiment of Indian land.
>
> And feel, entangled in this world
> Of problems, Gandhi not the least,
> There lay in him a wisdom furled,
> Answering West as well as East.
> For him inexorable modern Fate
> Retrieves from all his later homes.
> And we, in part, in love or hate,
> Must follow where his spirit roams.
>
> And follow vaguely where the height
> Fuses the many into one,
> Where snows may lie, and evening light
> Dapple Mount Everest alone;
> Where, poised on knife-edge of the truth,
> Binding today with long ago
> We climb to find another youth,
> And drink the waters of the snow.

Arlott, needless to say, saw fit to make a correction. "Gandhi not the least" became "Gandhi not least". But all the same I am grateful, remembering my aspirations years ago.

31 January. The Gandhi poem went out in the North American and Pacific Services, as well as the Eastern, so one has had one's little contact with the world spirit. Back at the ranch, Gordon Bell* read, A.E.T. Henry's* amusing "Electioneering in Jamaica", after long rehearsal. He (Gordon) is returning to Barbados next week.

5 February. This month for *Calling Mauritius*, Georges Rozan has collected two excellent talks: a report from Paris, by a young man called Leroy, who sported a Cambridge Wanderers scarf and a personality piece by a modest Indian called Abel Lawrence, who was a prisoner-of-war and now works in the London Telephone exchange. I gave drinks and lunch to Leroy, and Mlle. Labat, the narrator, a young person over from Port Louis for radio training. It looks as though one might well launch a second cultural programme; but it would be necessary to have someone from the French Service to hold a watching brief.

7 February. Saturday. John Fig and Pauline [Henriques] read excellent stories from Trinidad and Jamaica: "Stones of Darkness" by C. L. Herbert,* and "The Goat" by John Mansfield. The RPA asked for a script, a practice

which is becoming quite common. Is there any chance of presenting some of this work on the Home air? There may be a chance, now that the prep school master, George Barnes, has left the Third. In the afternoon, gardening, walking, in Belsize Park.

17 February. Four guineas arrive for "Gandhi Dead" from Miss Alexander, my first, and probably my last, earnings from poetry. Gordon Woolford* reads his reminiscences of childhood in Belgium, *Black Velvet and Lace*, brought up by a mother, fled from the appalling father. At noon, he discusses it with Calder-Marshall. For lunch, the Irish poet Harry Craig, who quotes Gaelic to me, and stirs old longings of the beautiful, closed world, which should have been my birthright. Finally, the *Listener* asks urgently for A. E. T. Henry's Pickwickian piece on electioneering in Jamaica.

20 February. All day at work on *African Affairs*. It is as well that the BBC, in its infinite wisdom, gives me so little to do. Outside, it is becoming very cold again, and the incautious buddleia is blackened.

24 February. Sam Morris* reads rather a good story by Samuel Selvon,* the young Trinidad journalist who wrote the poem about "Harry's little car", which still lodges in my brain. It was called "The Great Drought," and revelled in curious local phrases and rhythms. "Too besides" seems a regular construction, as well as figures like "their eyes made four". Apart from this, the day was largely passed typing the notes.

1 March. Tea with George [Weidenfeld], whom I found preoccupied, but still a marvellous good tempered, ebullient *burschen*. He is having an affair with Vivienne Mosley, the daughter of Oswald, which he finds surprising, but I do not. If George were not Jewish, he would have been 105% Fascist, Italian style.

2 March. I wrote a piece for RNR on the ugly little riot in the Gold Coast, which Rees-Williams blames on "Communists", when it is really concerned with market prices and market mammies and used by the Convention under [J. B.] Danquah, for Nationalist ends. The Fabians, whom I saw at lunch-time, agree with this diagnosis. It is pleasant to talk about something one knows some things about; even though perhaps unwise to mention "the resentment aroused by the trading policies of the UAC."

5 March. The last *News of the Colonies*, No 64, meaning that it has now gone out for five years, with scarcely a break. It was sad to say goodbye

to my good friend Keith Hamilton Price, a gentleman, if ever there was one, and very gloomy, poor dear, about his prospects, with the acting school failing to come off. At lunch at the MM Club, I met a very sympathetic lady, a dark-haired pianist called Joyce Kennedy, whose husband, a tea planter in Ceylon, committed suicide. In the afternoon, endless confabulation about the Royal African Society's future. The trouble is that it is desperately under-capitalised, founded on a string by Mrs Green, in memory of her friend Mary Kingsley, and never attracting a patron, least of all the Tory MPs and big businessmen on London Wall, who think that, because their firms (mines, explosives, textiles) contribute £100 a year, they have a right to say exactly what should be said. Andrew [Cohen] was there, biting his nails and whispering, and George Turner, watchful and stony eyed, so perhaps there may be a little hope. In late afternoon, a flap at 200. Creasy, the egregious Governor of the Gold Coast (his brother is an Admiral and a Sea Lord), is angry about the piece I did on the riots.

8 March. A bad day at the office. It started with the Mauritius recordings. After M. Pierrot, an amiable old schoolmaster with a violet ribbon in his lapel, I had words with Madeleine Labat, the little announcer, here for training. She brought a very bad script, my rough brief cobbled together, verbatim, with unchecked facts. Although I was on the point of asking her to lunch, she refused to correct it, and Mary Hicks, never a friend of mine, led her away in tears. To make matters worse, in the afternoon Andrew Cohen rings up in peremptory fashion, to see the offending Gold Coast script, admitting, it must be said, that Creasy, who has been a Private Secretary all his life, was very "jittery". How jittery, JGW told me soon afterwards. Last Sunday, about a dozen cables came in, protesting against a "heartless" News broadcast. In the riots, there had been 22 dead, and the Announcer (Richard Wessel) had commented on this number, when reading Rugger results. "22-6. They must have been watching the Gold Coast pretty closely". Of course, what he had actually mentioned were the *goal posts*. To make matters even odder, the figure he gave had not been 22 at all, but 28. All this suggests that the old Liberal shibboleth, too faithfully followed in our Overseas broadcasts, that comment is free, facts sacred, is wrong. A report to Accra on trade unions is not the same as a report to Manchester, since communication involves a listener, as well as a speaker.

11 March. At the bus stop at Swiss Cottage, they have put an inspector, to control the jostling foreigners in the queue. "We British." Out of the beautiful morning, into the dank vaults of 200, for Pauline to record a bad story from Jamaica about obeah, which will be duly rent by Calder-

Marshall. She is part of a new group of Coloured actors (Edric Connor, Orlando Martins*) and I pass on names that might help: Lovedale, Fiawoo (The Fifth Landing Stage), Mbonu Ojike, the Nigerian. Lunch with Willy Edmett,* who looks poorly. A long session, over two hours, with Camacho and Willams, a Bush House script writer, who has manufactured a simple ABC of West Africa, in place of my elliptic and cynical picture.

12 March. The latest complaint from the Gold Coast is that a Forces Favourites programme contained a coded message to the revolutionaries: *Now is the hour...*

15 March. Edgar Mittelholzer,* the West Indian novelist, looks in for a moment. A tall, bony man, with a wide brow, lined face, and skin freckled like a blackbird's egg. He spoke very rapidly, obliquely, in a curious slurred voice, as if dictating. What he had to say was not pleasant – Trinidad Rediffusion gave up broadcasting the *Voices* last November, replacing them by a religious programme. Never mind, one can still help people like Mittelholzer, even on our inadequate budget and inadequate fees, for stories and for reading. I fear that he will not make a very good reader, with his snatched diction. "Oh definitely", as he says. What he wants is time to get some of his many manuscripts published, following *Corentyne Thunder*, which was swallowed up in the war. I asked him a stupid question, what he thought of London. "The solidity of the houses". Went to Studio 2 in the evening, angered by a particularly cruel report, in colour, of an American couple, Mr and Mrs Harington, with discontented faces, who "battle the fearsome swordfish, the mighty mackerel of the deep", in green water off the coast of Chile that suddenly became a "fury of red". Perhaps Edgar M. might like this? He seems to have strong views on the superman and the dangers of being "soft". And he comes from the same continent, South America.

19 March. John Fig makes a good reading of not very good pieces by Bunting (in Jamaica) and [Barnabas] Ramon Fortune* (Trinidad). Over the phone, [George] Padmore of all people rings up to say that the Gold Coast piece "does me honour".

24 March. Edgar Mittelholzer came in to do some reading, poems for Easter and a short story by Ernest Carr.* This is the only way that I can really help him, even though the fees are derisory. He showed me some of his manuscripts, five short stories (and two novels at his digs) beautifully typed and corrected, rather like himself, lean, unbending, clipped, humourless. He told me something of his life: clerk, employee in an agricultural bank, cinema inspector, harbour official, merchant

seaman, gunner. He had written no less than twelve novels, before one was accepted by Eyre and Spottiswoode in 1941. (This was *Corentyne Thunder*.) I am much afraid that he may break his proud heart here, as he waits for a break. But he conveys such a sense of purpose, of dedication, that he may just possibly succeed. The Kellys were out in the evening, but Peter Blackman* came, another aspirant, the little Barbadian, with the good round head, to which the sparse curls are fixed as though by glue. He has been left with his two children by his Cockney wife, and has returned to clerking, full of bitterness about the Labour politicians who once patronised him. No wonder he quotes the Communists, with great frequency, Tirzah was polite, but nearly fell asleep.

2 April. Edgar Mittelholzer, importunate, for good reason, poor devil. He rang up yesterday, and called this morning. One must really use some of his work, to boil the pot.

3 April. Saturday. Sam Morris reads some more of the work of the Grenadan [sic] lady Eula Redhead,* simple folklore, and something, about *maljo*, (mauvais yeux). John Fig followed, with an actress called Carmen Manley, rather pretty, related to the well-known politician. She deputized for [Vivette] Hendricks*, and read some Jamaican poets, not of the professional Parnassus, Louise Bennett* the diseuse, Roger Mais*, the violent novelist, Harry Milner an Englishman, and Figueroa himself. We ended with lunch, and Frank Singuineau,* so nice, but so bad. In the afternoon work on the trees, two figs, two lilacs, one almond, one plum, one laburnum, a buddleia bush, a syringa. Disturbed by Davidson Nicol, who always disturbs me, with his sense of the world as a ladder on which we should always be climbing, climbing. He manages to disturb Tirzah too, at least she hit me hard in the eye, on some disagreement, wearing a vest or something of the kind.

10 April. Saturday. A morning given up to E. Mittelholzer. He read his own "Burglar", rapidly and without much timing. His interpretation of his own poems, "Island Tints," was so flat that, much against my will, I took over and read them myself. He took this, on the whole, in very good part. After all, the same voice for prose and poetry is a bit dull in the same programme. And I don't think he has a great regard for verse, even when written by himself. Of course, in this kind of operation the main thing is that he is paid better. Work in the garden, tearing the clinging convolvulus from the lilac. As it is London I was as black as a nigger minstrel by the time I had finished. At 18.00, back in 200, recording Arthur Calder-Marshall, whose views on the Jamaican number of *Life and Letters* are exactly my own. Afterwards, in the

Marlborough Arms, a literary conversation. He told me that his affairs had been put in the hands of the Society of Authors. "I have got so tangled up... Income Tax and so on".

17 April. After lunch, I went to a course on adult education in West Africa, held at the Mary Ward Settlement in Bloomsbury. The warden, Walkinshaw, was still there, with his great grey head, and bemused air, as though not knowing what was going on around him. He remembered my face from ten years ago, when, very lost, my application for residence was turned down through Richard Tambling. I asked what had become of the latter, and learned that he had gone to that refuge of the highly educated, the Army Film Unit... The chairman of the conference was A. G. Fraser, the great headmaster and founder of Achimota, a spry 75 years old. With him about ten other Europeans, including Fred Irvine, just back from Accra, and R. R. Young, the pioneer in Sierra Leone. The Africans were for once three times as many, including the Nigerian economics student Fidelis Ogunsheye, the Trade Unionists Addio Moses, and Siaka Stevens, the wide-browed Twum Barima, and an enchanting tall girl, looking exactly like Farleigh's design for G. B. Shaw's *Black Girl in her Search for God*, by name Theodora Morgue, from Cape Coast, but now working at St Monica's Girls School in Northern Ashanti. We heard about night schools, citizenship courses, literacy campaigns, and everyone seemed to be talking to the point, and not for effect. I myself got up, and seemed cogent, being taken up by Fraser himself. But I fear that it was really to impress Theodora, who sat beside me.

18 April. Sunday. I went again to Mary Ward. [...] At lunch in the canteen, I sat with Theodora and her friend Manaam Munir from Baghdad – both girls names mean "gift of god". Theodora's African name is Efua (born on Friday) [Efua Sutherland].* In the afternoon we heard Twum Barima talking about Danish Folk High Schools, and Davidson, highly emotional about "handing on the torch". I fear that my attention was not on higher things, since Efua's shoes, and later her leg, was pressing against mine. The weakness of the blood, the flight from reality.

29 April. John Fig and Vivette Hendricks record in Bush House a splurge of poems, mostly from Jamaica, under the code name "Joy of Living" – quite a good girl called Gloria Escoffery,* quite a good young man called Neville Dawes,* as well as five others. In those marble halls, and folkweave curtains, I feel in a foreign and hostile country, imagining raised eyebrows, where none are present. In the evening with George to see Peter Ustinov in *Frenzy*, a burlesque show of lust.

4 May. An extraordinarily handsome West Indian called Carl Walter,*
with an interesting cold script, "A Matter of Life and Death". An imperial
beard, long, strong face, he comes from Trinidad, but has lived most
of his life in Colombia. He seemed in need of money... Thence to
lunch with Rita at the Piccadilly Lyons, steamed up about Northern
Rhodesia in the *Times*, George Padmore, a "new approach to African
intellectuals". The real trouble is that, after nearly three years of power,
the tenuous alliance between Labour and Colonial Nationalism is almost
over, the "pretence of social reform" almost having been given up by
people like Nkrumah.

11 May. Astonishing effect on Mary Treadgold of belladonna, provided
by her dentist. It gets its name presumably from the enlarged pupil of
the eye. But in her case, it goes much deeper, slowing her up, ironing
out her sharp schoolmistressy approach, making her soft and sleepy,
her voice huskier, her hair less correct. Altogether, a marvel, which I
am tactless enough to comment on. Our relations are certainly curious,
armed neutrality over all these years, broken by the occasional collision,
in which it is always I that come off worst. The Parthians could teach
nothing to our Mary. ... Later, recording Pauline [Henriques], I learned
that she is not married to Heneberry, but is thinking of someone else,
a young actor, much younger than she is, called Neville Crabbe.* She
was reading a sketch by Selvon, "Holidays at Aunt Polly's", whose sad
nostalgia she could not reach at all, with her brisk competence. Perhaps
there was something racial too. Pauline is not East Indian. Only bright
tangerines and mangoes, no dissolving views. At lunch, Milverton, to
a half-empty hall at the RES, attacking the whole "democratic" approach
to Africa. I must say that on the experience of the last three years, I
scarcely differ from him. Interference by ignoramuses in London (like
myself indeed) must be intensely annoying. Yet what "flexibility" has
the exalted administrator? Perhaps the problem is insoluble, and the
relationship will come to an end far sooner than any of us imagine.

12 May. Roy Fuller,* the poet, came to record a talk. I hope that he
will provide a critical verse counterpart to Calder-Marshall on prose.
The reason I asked him was that I liked *Lost Season*, his poems from
East Africa, where he was stationed in the war – the "young warriors
that come down like feathers from the peak". He is a Communist, a
friend of Jack Clark, a lawyer from Lancashire who never went to university.
A pretty, cynocephalic, delicate face, which he makes manly with a
blonde moustache. I think we got on well, although he is withdrawn,
and when he came across for a drink at the Marlborough (Arlott, Craig
and Co.) he embarrassed the company by referring to himself as a "minor

poet". On the phone, a call from Lord Hailey. First, he wants a reference to the obituary of Margaret Wrong, which I gave him four weeks ago. Next, he wants the reference, at the gold medal ceremony, to "Hailey Africanus" cut out. But the real message is the third. I must correct that "unfortunate" reference to the "unreliability" of troops in the Gold Coast...

26 May. Pauline reads a story by Inez Sibley, "Sanders the Sidewalk Seller", and complains of the woes of Coloured actors in London, so full of jealousy, and failure to work together, ending with the fiasco of the hapless *Calypso*, thought up by Edric Connor, but in not enough detail...

27 May. John Fig and Carmen Manley* read some of Michael Smith's long poem,* the best thing so far in two years of *Caribbean Voices*. A tall young RPA called Phillips, who despises 200, was in charge of the recording, but he did not listen to the rehearsal or even read the script. When I asked him what he was doing he replied that he was listening to the Home Service programme *Chapter and Verse*. I felt like shaking him. The stupidity of the orthodox! *Caribbean Voices*, for all its limitations, is really more significant in itself and in its setting, than almost anything going out on the London air. And only a handful of people know it.

1 June. Edgar Mittelholzer comes in to read, "The Toiler" by [R. B. E.] Braithwaite.* The poor dear cannot read to save his life, but in what other way can I help him? I take him endlessly through rehearsal. "Pause before the vital word! In that way, you can build up to it, even more important, you can break the tune that most people give to each sentence, exactly the same". But it is no good. The tune comes out, time and time again, in a rapid, breathless gabble.

6 June. Sunday. I let down Ben [Enwonwu],* who was holding his auction. Instead, I took the children, all three of them, to the Heath, where they played hide-end-seek quite happily. In the evening, in walked Davidson, resplendent in Egba robes of indigo, with an absurd Yoruba hat – his grandfather was an Egba, freed to Sierra Leone. He came, I think, to see Tirzah, rather than me. But he is, I suppose, by now a "friend of the family".

8 June. Arnold Toynbee at Chatham House, rather disappointing as a lecturer, a keen, yet blind look, on his white face. He was content just to summarise some of the points of his great work. [...] I called at the Fabians, to collect copies of *Présence Africaine* and found them coping

with Rita's clanger in her letter to the *Times* which did not indicate that Africans are, in fact, being included in the new Legislative Council. [...] At 200, Calvin Lambert* came in with a script on his experiences in Pakistan, for *Commonwealth and Empire*, rather scrappy. He was much more interesting in discussion, and the final product will be useful, when he records tomorrow.

9 June. Calvin proved hard to record, despite the interview technique, feeding him with leading questions. He is like a river, level on the surface, depths and shallows and unknown depths below. It is hard to tell whether he was a success in Pakistan or not. After all was over, we had lunch in an indifferent Chinese restaurant, and he explained his total absence of racial feeling. But he did not seem happy with the Pakistanis.

17 June. Tirzah still has a temperature of 99 degrees. It is an effort getting breakfast and the children off to school [...] Pauline reads "World's End," an explosive piece by the revolutionary Roger Mais. At lunch, she tells me a little of her family history. Her father came to London to educate their six children, but he lost his business in honey, cloves and pepper (which seems a charming range) and returned to Kingston. [...] After lunch, shopped for John's birthday – boat and crystal set and Tutankhamun's Bat, a weird monster made of black paper and rubber, which flies out of a folded letter card. At tea time, the second Colonial batch, this time smaller and scruffier, bound for Western Nigeria. Two Africans were included, a young man, and a heavy faced older man called Adebo, an Assistant Secretary from Abeokuta. He was pleasant and balanced, but suspicious about the absence of Africans on the staff of *Calling West Africa*.

18 June. Because of the fierce local criticism of John Fig's reading ability, I played back the Michael Smith programme to JGW, Edmett and [Ken] Ablack. They all thought his voice excellent, as did I. I cannot help suspecting that the orchestra of annoyance is organised by the bad poets, whether spontaneously or not, who can tell. Next week, we will have Smith himself in to say whether he considers his poems "murdered". At coffee, S. L. Akintola, the Nigerian economist, returns the book on Nigerian economics. A round face, with the great Yoruba tribal weals. In the evening, the party, the first since our marriage over two years ago. It passed off quite well in the studio, assisted by Ariel Crittall, who arranged the flowers, and also helped Tirzah and Mrs Watkins prepare the sandwiches. The 35 bottles for the 70 odd guests were left to me. We had people from almost all the Continents, and most

of the arts, but there were no lawyers and no politicians or bureaucrats, although I did ask Andrew. Among Tirzah's friends, Gilbert Spencer recently sacked by the Royal College, Barnett Freedman, Percy Horton, the Coxons, John Nash, Helen Binyon, Flavia Snow, Peggy Richards, Helen Wilson. The BBC brigade: Sylvia Hingley, Mary Treadgold, Sheila Stradling, Joy Theobald looking like *primavera*, Willy Edmett, Ken Ablack, Tony McGlone, the Cowans, Harry Craig, but not JGW. Also Elsa and Miss Cloete. From *Caribbean Voices*, John Fig, Pauline, Fernando, Carmen Manley, Mittelholzer, Woolford, Sam Morris, Calvin Lambert, Arthur Calder-Marshall. From Africa, Ogunsheye, Dike, and Davidson Nicol. From *African Affairs*, Heather (the only one in evening dress), the Irvines, the Silvermans, Hughes of the Institute of Education, James Gray. Friends of the past: Arthur Foss, Margret Disher, Ralph Pugh. Friends of the present, the Uhlmans, Miss Gardner, Mrs Abrahams, Bobby, de Wet, Frank, a huge old Etonian actor with ravaged head called Geoffrey Wilmer. Then of course Helen. With them, many wives, mistresses, and friends, the most beautiful a blonde with saucer blue eyes. George [Weidenfeld] arrived at 11.30, when nearly all had gone, to announce that he has bought Nicholson and Watson for £75,000. My cousin Lionel Fleming, Vivette Hendriks, and, alas the Furses, never came.

All these varied people got on very well. Ralph Pugh had been at school with Calder-Marshall, and knew Dike from the Records Office. Miss Cloete and Heather had worked together in Cairo in the war. Helen Binyon got on like a house on fire with Harry Craig. Miss Gardner, who had been a paid-up member of the People's National Party went down well with the Jamaicans. Elsa engaged Sam Morris, the Silvermans, Fernando. The West Indians clustered round Carmen Manley, who looked ravishing. Mittelholzer conquers Bobby, and then Fernando's blonde girl friend. de Wet had served in the RAF with Neville Crabbe, Pauline's friend from the cast of *Anna Lucasta*. "Since 14, I have had a hard fight on the uphill path. Been North, South, and East and West, but still haven't seen the world". Even poor Dorothy Abrahams, who has finally been left by Peter (and whom I visited before the party after receiving a pathetic little note), seemed to forget her troubles a little. The one unpleasant incident was an argument between Elsa, made querulous by a leg hurt in the Grand Central Station, and de Wet, whom she called a Fascist. Nothing daunted, he went out to fetch her a taxi, but when he came back she had gone... An index to his character that he would not ask for his money back from the driver, even after an occupant (John Nash) was found. Tirzah lasted out very well, poor dear, but played no part as hostess. This was shared by Hel and Ariel, the latter put out because she was not asked to mix the drinks...

21 June. One reward for the party effort. With great sincerity Ablack earnestly remarked, "It was the first time that I realised that you could be human". Supper at the Richards. Tirzah is still out of sorts.

23 June. Michael Smith came in with Carmen Manley to hear the playback, a large-headed young Creole, opaque, apparently slow, with rather sullen brown eyes. He is reading Social Anthropology, hopes to study Ibo or Temne next year in the field. On the whole, he seemed to approve the reading. He confirmed what I thought about Rilke, but says he no longer writes poetry... We differed about George Campbell, whom he finds "great and difficult", I not difficult enough.

26 June. Saturday. Frank Singuineau comes in to record a sketch by Egbert Gibbs* on "Country Wakes." He (Frank) is abandoning his optical skills for the stage, for which he has no gift, except his charming face. He is convinced that I am "prejudiced" against him by his West Indian accent. That is what his elocution teacher tells him. How preposterous! The reverse is true.

22 July. Morning at the office: the *Voices* schedule for August, a letter to Mrs Lindo, a script for the specious State Secretary of Mampong, wished on me by JGW. Over lunch, the usual time allotted for Colonial recordings (the arsehole of the Corporation). Edgar Mittelholzer reads a vivid sketch by Selvon, "The Obeah Man".

26 July. Fierce heat, almost African, suitable weather in which to dictate a piece on the women's Bundu society, for Margai to record at Newcastle(!). Calvin Lambert looked in, with an Indian lady from Trinidad, a very intelligent politician, a welfare worker and would-be Legislative Councillor. She is an aunt of Bahadur Singh, friend of the tribune Cola Rienzi, she knows Cameron Tudor. (Her name is Mrs Ramkeesoon). An air letter from [Harold] Telemaque,* who has been approached by Langston Hughes to appear in an anthology he is preparing for Doubleday Doran. How did he hear of Telemaque? I hope, through the article I wrote for *Présence Africaine*, which was never published. This is how the silken cloth of culture is spun around the world. Depression in the evening. Tirzah does not want to go to the Olympic Games.

29 July. To Levy's studio in Wardour Street which we sometimes use, to record Gordon Woolford in a typical story by old Ernest Carr. (One thinks of him as "old" because of his technique, and perhaps he is. How I wish I could see all contributors...). [...] Invited again in the evening, by Helen Binyon, to the finals of a verse reading competition

at the Institut Francais. [...] There were about thirty people there, all women, to hear seven finalists. The winner a dark, intense girl with blue eyes and uneven teeth. The judges were L.A.G. Strong, Cecil Day Lewis (very lined and etiolated), an old man with a magnificent head, Rostrevor Hamilton, a chunky figure, that turned out to be Patric Dickinson, and finally a blonde West Country charmer, very fair, the delightful Laurie Lee. [...] A drink with Helen at the Gargoyle, watching Dylan Thomas, very tight, dance with an embarrassed waiter, and Stephen Potter, cheek to cheek with a tall fair girl, not his wife. I should really be a gossip writer...

4 August. The Gold Coast riots report was released yesterday, but the first I heard of it was from the News Division, as they want a piece for the Reel. Cyril Conner had a copy, but did not tell anybody on the Programmes side. As I mulled over it, he was on the phone: "About the Gold Coast Report, I don't think we need do anything with it, do you? After all, a summary has gone out already. You're doing a talk? Then perhaps you would be good enough to let me see the script. Donald Stephenson told me this morning that I would be responsible... It's a pity that our boundaries are so vague...". JGW knew what he was doing, when he left this man in charge of "the technical side". *Quaere*: if I had been an easier personality, would it have been made so difficult? Oliver Whitley at the CO [Colonial Office] did not even know that I was supposed to be in charge of programme work at all...

6 August. An excellent *Voices* programme, perhaps the most complete half-hour that we have had: Pauline reads a good story by Roger Mais, called "Salome", then discusses it with Arthur Calder-Marshall. This is really what radio is all about.

9 August. At last Arlott returns [my] RAF epic [poem], which he has had for five months, saying that it "dates", to which I replied that true art does not date. *Argal*, it is not true art.

10 August. JGW back from a glittering tour of West Africa, fascinated by the colour and the life, the grandeur and arrogance of Dakar. In Nigeria, he heard the women singing a death song against the Alake. In Accra, he rode to the races with Creasy between lancers. Of the Africans he met, he was most impressed by Clinton, the editor of the *Calabar Post*, and after him Thomas Decker in Freetown. He had virtually nothing to say about broadcasting, a fact on which Mary Treadgold afterwards made some acid comments.

14 August. Saturday morning, spent in recording the second half-yearly summary of *Caribbean Voices*. Again a *catalogue raisonnée*, but anything more ambitious would be unacceptable. I must not tell them how to write, even if I knew. The only thing is to maintain certain critical standards, common to all writing. Rather metaphysical, but defensible. I certainly put on many items that I do not greatly like myself, often to fill up space. Perhaps that is the main use I have: I do not, as I would if I were a West Indian, *compete*.

18 August. In the evening, took Tirzah and John and Dorothy Abrahams to see Katherine Dunham, the Afro-American dancer, at the Prince of Wales. An odd occasion, an audience of bookmakers who clearly expected a girlie show and found to their disgust a tasteful scene set up on the waterside at Bahia; and, in the second part, a long, tangled story of zombies, with dancers who may have had beautiful bodies, but certainly not beautiful faces. Katherine Dunham herself was tall, with a wide mouth, rather beautiful, but a college girl.

26 August. Willy Richardson* records a story by Selvon, "They Also Served", sketches of coastal defence in Trinidad, in a fine voice, not very flexible. At the entrance to 200, I bumped into O. Whitley, who says that there is more chance for Colonial broadcasts, now that the Government want to launch "anti-Communist" propaganda...

30 August. Left very early, suede shoes drenched in mud and dew. No family at Euston – they missed the connection at Crewe. Wrote a piece on the report put out by the Colonial Office, attacking UNO [United Nations Organization], and ran into fire from Elsa, who objected to the line I took – UNO "incompetent and dishonest"? But what has *that* got to do with it! Five years ago, if told that I would support head-hunters and white planters against Communist "liberation forces", I would have gaped open-mouthed. But today it is different, *thy life or my life, who whom...* Even more apposite, *Our evil is not your good.* And yet, it is true; when one looks at *Life*, the *evil* face is the face of the British police captain, watching his men beating Red prisoners with rifle butts... After the argument subsided, I took Elsa, more and more ghostlike, to a drink and a newsreel, with Helen. Even here, brutality. Grey seals in the Hebrides, and their shrill human cries as they are clubbed... It was sweet to see the family again. But not so sweet to read B[ertrand] Russell in *Horizon*, recommended by Arlott. A typical physicists piece, the "six options for humanity": US goes Communist, USSR capitalist, an agreement on spheres of influence, US conquers USSR, USSR conquers US, finally a draw...

1 September. A little more work. Michael Smith comes in to read an appreciation of Claude McKay, the pioneer Jamaican poet, by Clare McFarlane. As he says, it is far more an appreciation of McFarlane. He (Smith) cuts out some of the tautologies, like "most outstanding". Afterwards, I played back the reading by Michael Vowden of part of *Testament*, which Mrs Lindo thinks the best thing that has yet appeared in the *Voices*.

7 September. Willy Richardson reads a humorous sketch by Undine Giuseppe* "Whe-Whe", otherwise A.E.T. Henry. It was an account of London, even of the BBC, with HS delicately using the handle of a knife to stir his tea. I asked for a reference to be made to the lack of spoons in the canteen. In the evening, to Olivier in the film *Hamlet*, hair bleached to make him Nordic. A completely misconceived production, with great empty rooms, and absolutely none of the menace that could have been brought into a film. The performance of a busker outside was better, in many ways: a small man with a scar, blonde and blue eyed, who recited Othello, Shylock, a German Jew from Golders Green. "I am not asking for charity. I am an actor. My stage is the gutter for the moment, but I follow my calling, either inside or outside these buildings".

10 September. A remarkable encounter with a little bouncy friend of Edward Ankrah, the Opobo playwright Prince (sic) N.O.M. MacJajah,* who has a sheaf of grubby manuscripts, from mermaids to missionaries, mostly about the Niger, and the community founded by the trader Mbanefo Jojo, "called by the English Jaja." I turn him over to tough old Sheila Stradling, who immediately categorises him as "barmy". I don't know, there is something about him – he has dramatised a story about the Long Juju of Chuku, used by the Ibo to collect slaves from human sacrifices, who "vanished into a water fall." If only we had a West African literary programme, on the model of *Caribbean Voices*! Tea with D. Nicol at Studio 2. Four cakes, two scones, pot of tea. 6/8... He wants me to write something for the journal of the West African Society...

22 September. At the office, the very last recording, after six years of *Commonwealth and Empire (ci-devant Experiment in Freedom)*. It is not a worthy conclusion, a whimper not a bang. Kenneth Bradley on Africa... I prefer an hour with old Charles Penney, the blind actor, on *Calypsos from 1890 to 1910*, and the wonderful MacJajah, with 27 blotched pages, full of sex, greed, food, a curious wild poetry. I started dictation – editing – the typescript might help him. In the evening, a pleasing tableau.

Four of the new brown pullets roost on the buddleia bush, and have to be coaxed down, with ladder and rake, while Tirzah clips their bright pinions.

23 September. Willy Richardson records a long, brutal and amusing account of a slumyard brothel in Port of Spain, written by Selvon, with the ironic title, "Behind the Humming Bird". A ferocious view of American and British sailors, "pilots" (pimps) and "sagga boys" (thugs) and sports (definition uncompleted). We cut a whole section of abuse, and bowdlerized many too definite expressions and phrases like "rotten when she bends", as well as "live with you", for "sleep with you", "after I knew her better" for "after she got me in bed". We also cut some of the *graffiti*, "I want to sleep with Dorothy", and "Molly thing too big". Even with these cuts, it lasted nearly half an hour, a slice of raw life, which Willy read admirably. I hope it will be received in the spirit in which it was sent, a kind of minor *Playboy of the Western World*. But I shudder to think what Willy Edmett will think of it.

27 September. JGW is not averse to a new West African literary programme, which will at least increase my work, beyond the miserable present commitment: a weekly literary series to the Caribbean, with all scripts laid on, and a monthly Mauritian programme. One must hand it to him that he does not seem unduly disturbed by the furious attack on "Behind the Humming Bird", launched by one Kingsley, an RP assistant, and Overseas Presentation as a whole.

14 October. Two snorters, from Barbados and Trinidad, about the Humming Bird. I drafted a long reply, contrasting literary and social values, but JGW, perhaps rightly, would have none of it. "You can't apply literary values to a programme that can reach into the nursery"… All the same, he is very indulgent. I can imagine what someone like Conner would make of it. Pauline later read a story by Willy Richardson.

15 October. A portmanteau programme of six lesser poets, that turned out remarkably successful, partly because one poem did not fit in, and since John Fig had a cold, we varied him with Vivette Hendriks. We called it "Creole Harvest", the name-poem from Honduras by a man called [Raymond] Barrow,* which starts with a good line, "Slaving October with his brow of tan" and ends equally well "That Autumn on his vast plantation grows". This was followed by a typical [J. R.] Bunting* piece on the dawn, read *minore* in the woman's voice. (3) a poem on women stonebreakers by [R. Carl] Rattray* (JF) (4) a private woman's sorrow by Flora Baker* (VH) (5) a short poem on retreat to a hermit's cave by

Eric Levy* (JF) (6) a Bunting poem on the sunset, read *decrescendo* by VH.(7) perhaps the most radiogenic of all, a comment on memories (by [H. E. C.] Cain* of Honduras) with successive stanzas read alternately by the man and the woman. So it turned out that seven not very good poems, by themselves, produced what I consider the best programme that we have done, at least in impact. (This raises doubts about the merit of radio in conveying the very best?) It was so good that I put it before the Richardson story, so that anyone listening in must hear it. It may soothe some of the sensibilities outraged by the Humming Bird. Ho, hum... Incidentally, JGW showed me a splendid letter from Mrs Lindo, making a spirited rejoinder to violent criticism from Laing, of Barbados Rediffusion (Commercial). What an admirable woman! Or can it be, as is suggested, that the mind that directs this literary enterprise is her husband, Cedric?*

18 October. A morning spent watching JGW fence with Carey, the new editor of *West Africa*. "I know, because I have made a small study of it" etc etc. Also a long talk with A.E.T. Henry, who calls himself "a moderate Socialist" (like me...). Like me also, he is not regarded as serious. When editor of *Public Opinion*, in Kingston, he rejected Padmore's "hate-filled" article, but he thinks him (GP) honest. He told of meeting Padmore and Grantley Adams, the Barbadian, just before Adams' departure for Paris, where he made a strong pro-Western speech against the Soviet. Padmore wanted him to say "A plague on both your houses. Leave us to fight the British by ourselves alone..." A.E.T. at least realises that the Soviet paradise is really the Soviet paradox...So also should Padmore, a member of the Comintern under Kuusinen, with whom he quarrelled over the proposal to make three of the Southern states all-Negro "ghettoes"... Another conversation at tea, this time with Calvin Lambert, whose wife is definitely leaving him, and presented him with proof of adultery one week after he had got it through private detectives... She is quite friendly, explaining that she is only marrying the other man for security, and invited him to the wedding!

19 October. A long directive from Ian Jacob, advocating selection, relevance, very close co-operation with Government departments. In particular, news must be "carefully balanced" presenting the "British way of life". There must be only a "British view", not "British views", and no "BBC attitude". Controversy must only be reported "in proportion to the weight of the backing". He goes further. "Nothing should figure in our output which is not consciously planned as being there for an object"... At the end, he faces the major criticism. "It may be asked whether this implies that we are to conduct political warfare. The answer is that the BBC is

not conducting anything" (!) But, "we must not in any way shrink from giving full expression to the British view, and to assist by all means in our power the national Effort. Only in this way shall we be framing our programmes in the national interest". Where does the "Humming Bird" figure in all this? The problem is the scale and range of our horizons. But I would not like to put this before the General. Perhaps because of this, perhaps for other reasons, I was in a rage all day. Rage at JGW, rage at myself above all: neither artist nor man of action, neither African nor European, neither Communist nor Conservative...

4 November. Two new *Voices*. Neville Crabbe, who has just married Pauline, makes mincemeat of a neat little story by Eileen Ormsby. He is nice and sexy, but I fear, not very gifted intellectually and full of excuses. "If I had more time...if I hadn't had a cold..." On the other hand, Karl Davidson,* a Jamaican economist, very smooth and polished, near-White, with a donnish voice, not unlike R. G. Collingwood. His account of a hitch-hiking holiday, handed me by Willy, is among the best balanced pieces of prose I have seen. "Kent was all rolling hills, orchards and hop-gardens, with cone-shaped oast-houses cluttering beside the farms... Just outside Canterbury, we met a farmer whose wheat had been flattened by the storms. He pointed to sloping fields, which looked as though a giant had trampled on them... At the first glimmer of sun, he had mustered his men, to collect the cube shaped bales of straw that lay scattered like children's bricks..." Like Monsieur Jourdain, the charm of Davidson lay in the fact that he did not realise that he was writing prose.

12 November. Gordon Woolford records a satirical piece, "Three Cheers for Mr Jobber", by "Philipp Fumbles", the pseudonym of one Golding, a Belize journalist, who was jailed for printing an article of 500 words on a budget speech by the Governor. (The word "Blah" repeated 500 times.) Is this also transgressing the "national purpose"?

22 November. A Monday morning row with Mary Treadgold, who has not forgiven me for passing up L.A.G. Strong. Coffee with JGW, describing plans to bring sixty African programme staff for training. I suggest that those giving the training might themselves go to Africa first... Mary says: "John, I think that Sheila Stradling should deal with them. She has lived in Africa, and she is first class in her human relations, unlike Henry and I, who are nowhere." As she has for long disclaimed any interest in working with African individuals, this was no news, so far as she was concerned. I contained my wrath, but she continued to irk me. "By the way, John, has the rumpus died down over Henry's West

Indian brothel programme?" At that I asked her point-blank why she was being so catty? The row went on in my office, when she came to say that her remarks had not been intended to annoy me "consciously". I replied that conscious or unconscious, it did not make much difference. If only she could always have belladonna in her eyes! If I were a saint, which I would like to be... As it is, I am a drudge, a hack.

3 December. My middle tooth is aching badly, almost for the first time since it was hit by a hockey stick fifteen years ago... Perhaps this makes me shorter with poor Mittelholzer than I should have been. I had invited him to record, to help him over Christmas, but as usual our rehearsal time was not long enough, and as usual he was impervious to criticism. When I exploded, he kept his *sang froid* admirably. I think he appreciates that, as I told him, I am one of the few people in London who really want him to succeed. The trouble is he *will* send in potboilers, not wishing hunks out of his novels. From Edgar, to the RAS, and more irritation.

10 December. Back at 200, JGW says that he may have found a billet for Mary in the wider GOS [General Overseas Service] programme, while I take *West African Voices* (so *that* is the reason for her spitefulness the other day). Sam Morris reads an odd claustrophobic story by Stephen Haweis.*

18 December. Saturday. Went to Cambridge to see Efua, more than ever like Farleigh's "black girl" in a white woolly coat. We had tea, and I bought her a Christmas present at Heffer's, *Poetry in the Bible*. The Victorian seducers! At 6 to my room in Hartington Greve, with no one in. We kissed and fondled each other, but did nothing more.

1949

2 January. In the evening, the first of the new Reith Lectures on the Third. Originally conceived as a platform for unknown and vital young thinkers, what do the hierarchs do but invite a series from *Bertrand Russell*? He was not very good, I thought, clear enough, but oddly ignorant of history and literature. No doubt he has not really had enough time to read all this, and mathematics, and philosophy too. But why then does he fix upon affairs?

4 January. An hour at Queen Anne's Gate, then a rush to the School of African Studies, for an inaugural discussion about *West African Voices*. Ida Ward, the good woman, had assembled five of her young men: the

Yoruba Lasebikan,* the Efik Ekanem, the Hausa Mallam Hassan, the Ashanti Boatin, and the Twi [J.H. Kwabena] Nketia.* None of them had heard of the West African Society, or seen a copy of *Africana* (and Ida has never seen *Présence Africaine*). I held forth for an hour, on the stacked piles of material: short stories, political sketches, poems, plays, fables, criticism, music. The acid test: in which language? In vernaculars, with English as lingua franca? This made them *sniff* 'cultural imperialism'. But they saw the possibilities of a "regional mirror", the setting up of a kind of electrical current...

5 January. This morning, an invitation from Oxford to talk on a Colonial Service Course on the missions. [...] I told JGW, as diplomatically as I could. He was quick to point out that *he* had also been asked, but had refused. Work is now piling up, as it has not done at any time since I joined the Corporation. [...] Woolford reads a quite remarkable piece of prose, evidently cut out of a longer work, "Growing Up in the Village", by the young George Lamming, who works in Trinidad, but was born in Barbados. Strange, heavy, solipsistic, saturated with life and the hints of other life, influenced, I should think, most nearly by Herman Melville... By God! I really feel like a Spanish conquistador in sight of El Dorado. Because of all this work, I was unable to see Michael Manley,* the son of the politician, and his difficult English mother, the sculptress lady with literary pretensions. They have sent their journal *Focus*, crammed with bad writing, and pretentious portentous 'statements', although some of the stories, by Victor Reid* and Claude Thompson,* are excellent. Perhaps this judgement is conditioned by the fact that there is no mention of *Caribbean Voices* anywhere to be found.

8 January. Arthur Calder-Marshall criticizes the Lamming poem, with considerably less address than he shows with prose. Instead of close detail, he makes a long and rather useless comparison of modern poetry to *collage*. Indeed, he disagrees with the main theme (elucidated by [H.D.] Carberry*) of the 'sun', creative emotion, at beginning and end, against 'dead money', economics, all through the middle. "'Unheard the seconds of the midnight hour'. I don't get it. What does it mean?" I suggest, low vitality, passion worn out, life run down... We went for a "snifter" at the Marlborough, and he talked about his debts, which are "enormous". The last baby cost £200, and nursery schools are only free to bastards... The Society of Authors are trying to get Cripps to put up £30,000, if only to boost dollar sales...

11 January. *West African Voices* launched with a discussion that took three hours to prepare: E.L. Lasebikan (Tunde), a delicious moustached Yoruba

scholar, like a seal; Joseph Nketia a lively Twi; K. A. B. Jones-Quartey,* the secretary of the West African Society; and Dennis Osadebay,* the Ibo poet from Asaba, the only one to qualify as a literary man, I suppose.

19 January. Relief – 15 guineas arrived from *Contact*, for the migration article, which they do not like... By the same post, the proofs of *Compass Points*, which I contribute *bukshee* to the Fabians, having received the all-clear from Administration. At 200, a pedestrian *Diary* from the amiable Mackenzie, and a brilliant little programme from Osadebay, Lasebikan and Nketia, who contribute a series of poems like Japanese haiku, each in the relevant vernacular, accompanied by a translation. Osadebay talks about love and war, Lasebikan about a *fricasée* (sic) of rabbit, Nketia, reads splendidly some Twi songs, one about a child who mistook drums for the call of the toucan.

27 January. Edgar Mittelholzer records "Sorrow Dam and Mr Millbank", much the best script he has so far brought, about a Tolstoyan, who goes to live among the poor peasants of the Guiana Swamplands, with unhappy results. He says that Alfred Knopf, the publishers, are interested in a novel he has sent them, a comedy called *Morning at the Office*. I am so glad that all this should follow the minor breeze we had in December, and the letter that I was moved to write him.

11 February. In the post, the most exciting discovery so far in the *Voices*: *Twenty Five Poems*, by Derek Walcott,* a young poet from St Lucia, influenced by Dylan Thomas, but on the evidence of things like "A City's Death by Fire" (Castries) as good a poet as anyone of his age writing in English anywhere. I can't wait to send it to Fuller.

17 February. Record the usual summary of "The Last Six Months" for the *Voices*. Mittelholzer's "Sorrow Dam", Lincott's* "El Diablo", Lamming's poem on his mother:

> Tending her orchid of flesh,
> The fragile filament of her fibre,
> With tears of delight.

These among many others, including the appearance of the critics, Calder-Marshall, Fuller, Craig. It is a pity that we have not yet been able to broadcast some of the work of Walcott.

2 March. Am I a prig? I find an advertisement in the Tube intolerable. It is for hats, and says in effect "Unless you are pretty, men will not

offer you their seat." When I told Johnny about it, he could see nothing wrong.

16 March. At 200, Osadebay and [Tim] Aluko* read the first poems in English in *West African Voices*, from cuttings I have made in the three Zik papers in the last four years. They have a flavour all their own, which M. Treadgold recognised. Three by Osadebay, two by Giwa-Osagie,* two by Eweka,* one each by Enitan Brown,* Majekodunmi,* and Akiwowo.* The first two Bini, or Rivers, the second Ibo, the last Yoruba. The one I liked best was the lament for Benin by Giwa-Osagie.

> Tis done – but yesterday
> The palaces of crowned kings,
> And now a chaos of hard clay;
> Sleeping on the abyss:
> Without a surge.

19 March. Ralph Currey* records a talk on three little magazines: *Focus*, *Kykoveral*, and the most important of the three, *Bim*. Afterwards he took me to lunch at the National Liberal Club on the Embankment [...]. In the afternoon, to Jones-Quartey's wedding in a church in Belsize Square [...]. The Best Man was Padmore, and others there were Joseph Mitchell, Noni Jabavu, Twum Barima, Boadu, Davidson Nicol (very upset at a man smoking a cigar with the band still on). JQ looked happy, his little bride from the West Indies rather sweet.

24 March. Keith Stanley reads a short story called "Mint Sticks", by one Ulric Simmonds,* a sentimental account of a poor boy, in which we have to cut "bastard" and a string of "Gods", fearing the unco guid. He (KS) is an amiable person, a failed medical student, whose allowance has been docked by his father. A long discussion with Miss Alexander on West African poets' fees. If they get 10/6 a minute, less 9/- in the £ tax, this means 12/- for three minutes... But in Lagos, they would be paid 1/- a minute, according to a letter from Milner Haigh... Nostalgic lunch at the Olde Englishe Choppe House in Witcombe Street, en route to the RAS. The same sluttish girls shouting down the dumb waiter, "Two pigs' trotters". The same mirrors with rose borders, (it must have been a brothel). But oh the joy of vigorous disorder, so unlike Fortes, the canteen, the MM Club! Back to 200, to arrange a reading of Hausa poetry, with translations I have found in Rattray. Two young assistants, smiling and alert, Mallam Hassan from Abuja, Mallam Tukur from Sokoto.

25 March. For some reason I am out of favour with Haroun-al-Rashid.

No coffee, at 2½d a cup, for the last week. I rack my brains for a reason, and can only think that it must be the frequent budgets from Mrs Lindo, containing rather too many references to my name... [...] At Northumberland Avenue, two sops or rather three, for my vanity: Hailey liked the last "Notes"; Patrick Duncan wrote to James from Basutoland to extol "H.V.L.S."; *Sudan Notes and Records* have been reorganised on the exact lines of *African Affairs*. [...] In the evening, a great turn-out for a gathering on South African racialism at Friends House, addressed by Paul Robeson, Michael Scott et al. [...] In came "Big Paul" Robeson, who delivered an emotional speech. "The West was built up on the work of 100 million torn from Africa... Truman was vacationing in Florida when the Dixiecrats defeated a filibuster against reactionary laws... a special snarl for Forrestal... China has won Freedom (a great wave of cheering). The West Indies could have freedom tomorrow if they united. (Frantic clapping from Joseph Mitchell.) The Basuto were civilised when Malan's ancestors were naked savages... The Yakuts of Siberia, once more backward than any African tribe, now have Universities... All the world could be free (Tremendous applause). American will die to the last West European... Hungary has turned out its bigwigs (sic)... There will be no friendly hands in the next war. Throw down the gauntlet to the Neo-Fascists [...]. He ended with songs: "Starlight", (dedicated to Bill Rust), "Right Here we Stand", "Waterboy", a Yiddish song about the Warsaw Ghetto, "When Working Men Defend Their Rights", and finally "Old Man River", with amended words, "I must keep fighting until I'm dying".

2 April. Saturday. Pauline reads Mais' "The Witch", John Fig some "topographical" poems, *videlicet*, bad ones... This prevented my going to lunch with George [Weidenfeld], who I thought had dropped me. In the afternoon, the garden, where James and Anne light their inaugural bonfire. In the evening, the first full illumination of London since before the war. We went to [see] *Angelina*, another film of Socialist realism from Italy, with the admission "capitalists are human" imposed by outside circumstance, not by conviction. [Anna] Magnani as ever very good, in some ways not unlike Tirzah in appearance.

3 April. Tirzah has an idea for starting a shop to sell only Victoriana brand new, like the old lady milliners in King Henry's Road, one of whom has just died. She really seems *zufrieden,* and this reacts on me. I give her a jingle:

> Atom by Atom,
> And Dust by Dust.

If Stalin can't have you,
Truman must.

12 April. Mercedes Mackay* gets what she wants: a chance to produce a *West African Diary*, *vice*, young Olsen, who really does not make the grade. At least she will attend the various events in the calendar, and she *has* lived there. Beau Milton* came in very nervous to record a story by one Adoki,* on "A New Bicycle". He has little to claim, except that he knows what it is to be an outcast.

14 April. Maundy Thursday. Record programmes for Easter. Willy Richardson reads "A Legend of Iere", pre-Columbian, rather clear, by someone called Street. As a foil, a little impressionist "Street Scene" by John Fig: much talking against background noise, card games, slogans, finally a preacher with the surprising theme that we should love one another. Pauline [Henriques], [Neville] Crabbe, A.E.T. [Henry], [Ernest] Eytle,* as well as John Fig himself. After two rehearsals, they were remarkably good, but oh dear, the balance, the rhythm, ruined by the RPA, with two restarts. The fact is that we are not geared for this sort of thing in 200, and really we should have all day, not a mere two hours. At Queen Anne's Gate, a portent. For the first time, the Journal appears before *Africa*. It is mentioned in the *Colonial Review*; and *Zaire* even has long extracts from Danford's January article.

21 April. Pauline reads a story by that rarity, a middle class writer with a middle class setting, R.L.C. Aarons.* Harry Craig reads some poems by C.L. Herbert,* the Trinidadian, in the bow-wow style of Yeats, most inappropriate.

26 April. Lunch to Ord-Jolly, a lugubrious wireless engineer who runs the Kumasi Rediffusion Station, which has 1100 subscribers, for radio on cables. He says that there are twenty-three such centres in the Gold coast. From him, to record Tim Aluko at Egton House, reading the first part of his own story of traditional life, "The Judgement of Heaven," a kind of Patrick-on-the-hill-of-Tara story, involving Christians and fetishists. When I got back to Adelaide Road through the Park, luminous in the evening, the family were unexpectedly charming and welcoming, and were actually re-digging the hole for the pool...Tirzah wanted to go to a cinema, but we were too late at the Everyman.

8 May. Sunday. Finished the piece for the Extra Mural magazine in Trinidad, with a portentous title: "Prolegomena to a Caribbean Culture." It seems ridiculous that I may know more about the present state of

writing there than anyone, with the possible exception of Mrs (or Mr) Lindo, at least, on a superficial level. Walk to the swings. Eridadi Mulira* to tea again, polite, humourless. He explains, the problem of the lands of the dead, the *Bataka*, and the church dispute. "Mulumba lies: Africans *do not* accept majority decisions." He leaves us for a Miss Olive Siggs, who had seen the article on *West African Voices* in the Journal, and wants to translate similar work from East Africa. So the seed germinates.

9 May. Roy Fuller records a splendid critique of Derek Walcott, critic and poet worthy of each other... Calvin Lambert came to lunch. He told me that he had been on a soap box in Hyde Park last Sunday, speaking against the National Health Service. He is considering going to the Sudan, with an Irish girl (his dispenser?). MacJajah looked in, to say that WASU have protested at a BOAC window display in paper moulding (by a Pole), showing an explorer carried in a palanquin by blubber-lipped savages...

10 May. Edgar Mittelholzer, with another pot-boiler, "Mr Jones' Little Problem." I still think he is worth it however annoying it is.

12 May. Trade follows the flag, even in such a despised field as culture... A Mr Tellermans rings up to enquire about material for "a miscellany of West Indian writing". He works for the 'University of London Press'. This is a small private firm which pinched the name, and refused to give it up when the University asked them. It was pleasant toying with him. [...] At Studio 2, that strange beast, the Great British public, tittered when Prince Philip, with nautical forthrightness, said (at Bangor university): "This generation, although reasonably well schooled, is perhaps the worst educated in history..." Later, when Atlee appeared, there were boos. For the general dowdiness, the groundnut scheme, the withdrawal from India, even China?

13 May. Pauline reads an admirable story by Samuel Selvon: "The Baby". (Creole, Indian). Long live our marvellous little incubator!

17 May. Three West Africans to discuss a programme on the oral literature of SE Nigeria: an Ibibio (Ekanem) and two Efiks (Ikpee and Akpayun). They are very lively. Ekanem says that the programme is beginning to catch on in Calabar, according to letters he has received. At lunch, Tirzah, with whom I go to see the Rudolfine treasures from Vienna, at the Tate. Personalities, Christianities, little or no primitives. A beautiful, enormous chalice and monstrance from South Germany.

18 May. I send in my application to the Home Office, to remain a British subject, rather than opt for Eire, on grounds of service, residence and connections. It seems ridiculous, but no doubt will come in useful in the future. Beau Milton reads "Idowu's Luck," a picture of a murderous lorry driver, by Phebean Itayemi,* whom I have not yet met. He tells me that "Beau" is short for "Beaufoy". Rita came in to give a "Colonial Commentary," and had lunch. "The same old story" – one of her key phrases about Nigeria, Kenya, Central Africa, SW Africa... She says she "cannot read" the "Quarterly Notes", hence her lack of knowledge about the Kenya Land debate. The notes are apparently too long, "too much of an intellectual exercise"...

19 May. A day full of indigestible contacts, but very interesting. Willy Wilson, a band leader from St Vincent, grizzled and smelling of scent. Malcolm MacDonald, now High Commissioner in Malaya, in to record a message for Empire Day. Very human, but did recall our contact when I was Resident Clerk at the C.O. He is still simple and unaffected. [...] The talk was brought to an abrupt end by the lean shadow of J.B. Clark, detaching itself from other shadows. Tellermans, the 'University of London Press' man, sharp and good-looking. Daramola, the Hausa trader (mineral water) working at the BIF, come to hear a playback of the programme. To the Council Chamber at BH [Bush House], with 140 others from the Overseas Service, to hear a lecture by S.J. de Lotbirière and Wynford Vaughan Thomas on Outside Broadcasts. A ridiculous contrast: the huge, pale, bony Anglo-Canadian, the little, red, cynical Welshman. They went on for two hours, and were very stimulating. (A code of conduct for commentators, cross references, associated material.) The one discordant note came from Terry Gompertz, who asked, a little too sharply, about the reaction of the "common listener".

23 May. Tony away with a headache, whose other name, I think, is Phyllis. Grinding work, mainly the "Notes", broken by lunch at Freddy Mills' Chinese restaurant with Calvin, so delightfully uninterested in anything but himself.

26 May. Pauline reads a Jamaican story. "Black Crabs" [Elsie Hutton]. After long consideration, I post my resignation to Chatham House. If Wyndham and Phillips resign from the RAS, why not I from them? In any case, it is expensive, and *International Affairs* as a guide to what is going on, is beneath contempt.

27 May. Gerhard Eisler, the German Communist, not to be extradited

to the US. Are we wise? Emotionally, I think Yes, but a nagging voice says No.

28 May. Saturday. Ernest Eytle, one of the athletic clique who really run West Indian programmes, reads a short story by John Wickham,* a Trinidad policeman, very badly. He is a nice, stupid man, a barrister waiting for briefs, and rather too fond of the bottle.

31 May. A last visit to Chatham House, to sit with Pat Lacey, now with the Westminster Press, and E.R.M. Hussey, who is leaving the British Council. Back at 200, two hours wrestling with Orlando Martins, and a vilely written story from Trinidad by [R. B. E.] Braithwaite,* which brings in Yoruba words.

2 June. Vivette Hendricks records a number of new poems, including one by a promising Jamaican, Andrew Salkey,* who seems mentally disturbed.

7 June. Three recordings at 200. Sam Morris reads a blood and thunder from Trinidad by one [James A.] King, "The Devil's Woodyard." He says that he (Sam) has been asked to go on a lecture tour of Czecho-Slovakia, but will not do it. Then he asks me for a recommendation, as he wants, at 40, to become a lawyer. Is he "respectable", trustworthy? All I know is that he has great charm, and an odd residual Christianity. Mercedes makes the second recording. The third comes from the three young Ibibios, with their pretty rhythmic songs, that mean very little. A long letter from Mrs Lindo, complaining of the "patronizing" tone of R. Fuller, R. Currey, H. Swanzy. As it happens, I see Ralph Currey for tea, when he shows me the proofs of an elegant series of translations from mediaeval French, in a collection he calls *Formal Spring*.

10 June. Telemaque over from Trinidad on an oil scholarship. (He is headmaster of a school on the Apex field). He was very black, and a little pompous, but then he is getting on in years. A letter from Ben [Enwonwu].

13 June. At 200, Orlando Martins reading a Yoruba story, "The Last Priestess," with many side kicks at his rivals, all of whom he despises, but for Glyn Lawson. Pauline reads a horrific story by Ulric Simmonds, "Granny Bell," describing the dying memories of an old lady who, as a young woman on the day before Emancipation, is stripped naked and flogged, by her own husband, at the order of a sadistic white overseer. An interesting theme to broadcast, even with amendments... I think

of writing a short story myself, "The Man Who Lived At Second Hand".

[Swanzy and Tirzah on holiday in Ireland, 22nd June to 8th July]

11 July. Letters from the Indies: [Frank] Collymore* writes from Barbados, Lamming from Trinidad, proposing a trip to England. Pearce sends me a cheque for the *Prolegomena*. As for West Africa, a letter from Aluko, and the British Council lady sends me some scripts from the Gambia, rather a vivid account of graft, a folk tale of a parricide. [...] To the Colonial Exhibition on John Lewis' ruined site. Entrance through a jungle. "This is Old Africa, airless, insanitary...". We learn that "the Masai put up a magnificent fight" and passed from "humble" African carving to Maltese lacework, and the "ancient culture of which Cyprus is rightly proud". Then Tree of Government: and then a whole series of wheezes, films, dioramas, beauties in folders (female beauties) they turn out to be but not, thank God, 'belles'). Gold Coast escort police in their pantomime uniforms, dark green with red belts and golden turbans and lances, look bored – JGW says they too have been approached by Communist agents. Anthony Robinson, who is coming to work in London, told me he had to walk through Communist student pickets... Can one hold up the tide, or the gale, of the world?

12 July. Edgar Mittelholzer reads a better story, "The Trip to Berbice." Kathleen Davis* one of Eula Redhead's little Anancy tales "Czien and the Mermaid." Stephen Grenfell who has owed me 10/- since 1943 stops me in the street, and insists on giving me two large double whiskies at the Feathers. He has just learned that his income last year was £6000. "Listen, old boy, I work for twenty different producers". But his main standby are women. "Listen, old boy. Women provide most readers, and they are concerned with four things: men, babies, the stars, and food. Play them up boy, tell them that women are monogamous and men polygamous, and bob's your uncle". He gets 25 guineas for a monthly article, gives a talk in *Woman's Hour* once a fortnight... He gets a guinea for a telephone call. In the last 24 hours he has written 6000 words, every one commissioned. He rolled on, full of euphoria, looking for new worlds...

14 July. At coffee, P. D. Chookolingo, a Trinidad Indian, who writes under the name of Lincott, he was very 'commercial', but very intelligent. I ask him where he got the word "nictate" for his brilliant study of cockfighting, "El Diablo". He says that the late Huey Long was known as the 'nictator' from his habit of seeing only what he wanted to see, like a bird that veils its eyes (nictates)...In the afternoon, Telemaque

who is here on a literature course reads his own verse, in a deep, tense voice. [...] I devoured *1984*, recognizing many things, like the canteen at 200, and many people, down to Hetta [Empson] (I believe), but not the cutting definition of the BBC, "Hacks knocking up stories for politicians to read."

16 July. Saturday. Gordon reads a story by Frank Collymore. In the afternoon, garden and allotment, trying to help Tirzah grow corn for the hens... In the evening, finish *1984* which fizzles out, I think, in lugubrious scenes of torture. Poor Orwell is really very ill; and it must be bitter for him to touch the bitch goddess by her outer hem.

18 July. Visited Ohly's, to see work by the Gold Coaster Kofi Antubam, and the Guianese Denis Williams. The first rather wooden, the second rather remarkable, deliberate, violent, primitive. On to K.C. Murray's masks at Zwemmers, cheek by jowl with Fred's friend Bilbo. In the evening, from 1730 to 1930, recording Eva Fredericks reading the Gambian scripts, which she did quite well, a young Creole girl from Sierra Leone, whom I met at the abortive Negro Theatre Gathering.

21 July. A call from Arnold in Rhodesia House, to complain of the "Notes": "misrepresentation has *not* occurred, the governor on the Beit Trust is *not* an example of *étatisme*, the new leader of the Liberal Party is *not* an Englishman (at least, the former leader was not, quite, an Afrikaner). We end with an amusing quiz, organized by Ken Ablack, between a team from *We See Britain* (AET, Clark, Willy) and *Caribbean Voices* (Pauline, Gordon, H.S.). The result: *Voices* 21, *WSB* 21½, since they shouted quickest, on the last stroke, that the father of Jessica was Shylock...

22 July. At last! JGW tells me that, on orders from Director of Overseas Services, I am to be sent abroad this autumn. "I am *so* glad for you, Henry. I have been pressing for it for such a long time". Where is it to be? "Well, I am going to the West Indies again at the end of October. Perhaps it would be best to go to Nigeria." What brief will I have? "Oh, I suppose something about *West African Voices*."

23 July. An exciting reading by Pauline of one of the best stories yet received in *Caribbean Voices*, and much the best of the folklore. "The Terror Bull and the Taunt Song." A seven-headed devil bull that roams over Jamaica, until routed by a small boy, who has a 'strong' name. "Shemmilimmo O, Me Know Your Name." It had a primeval swing about it, thanks to the total belief of the author, Inez Sibley.

2 August. Letters to Telemaque and Figueroa, forwarded care of Henry Swansea, BBC. I was present when John Fig opened his envelope. It came from Wycliffe Bennett, and invited him to form a Society of West Indian writers, with copious references to various means of communication, but none to *Caribbean Voices*. I am glad that I am cushioned from such malevolence by five thousand miles of rolling sea. It is on a par with Mrs Manley's derisive "Swanky".

4 August. Today I sign my contract as a member of the Established Staff, with pension rights, as from the 1st October 1947. Playing for safety, as always, no cap over the windmill. A new contributor to *Caribbean Voices* records his own poems on loneliness, and linked sketches, a story of a boy and a kite. This is C.E.L [Cy] Grant,* a handsome young ex-RAF man, who was a prisoner of war, and is now studying for the bar, although much more interested in music (he plays the guitar). He comes from Guiana, with its curious, marked sophistication that the mainland seems to bring as against the islands. Phebean Itayemi also comes to read her own sketch "Soup", an exercise in tension, long soaring sentences, like a fountain of steel. She is really a very talented person.

10 August. Mackenzie, otherwise Andrew MacDonald, with a *Diary*, Beau Milton with a story by Nchami* "Nigeria's Precious Bag" (Groundnuts).

11 August. Three recordings. I have produced 21 programmes in little over a week. But one has to prepare a month in advance. Lunch to Nancy Morrison, a nice middle-aged novelist, who worked for four months in a home for delinquents in Trinidad, where she met Lamming, who told her to get in touch with me. She says that he is a remarkable, brooding young man, hard to fathom. While I was recording, Edric Connor got emotional in an interview, and announced that he alone was carrying the burden of 120 million people...The English Robeson...

13 August. A brush with Eva Fredericks, the little Creole from Freetown, who thinks that 4 guineas for a reading is too little, and that contracts should arrive before recording, I suspect she was put up to it by a boyfriend. I explain that we cannot [pay] Home Service rates. Why? Because West African listeners do not pay anything. "In any case, this is an experimental programme, and the kind of schoolboy essays you are reading would never be included in any normal programme."

15 August. Record my summary of the last six months in *Caribbean Voices*, picking out Derek Walcott, that 19-year old portent, and Inez

Sibley's story of the terror bull Gashanami, killed by the hero Tobias. I end with a suggestion that it might be a good thing to award a literary prize. At tea, MacJajah makes the mistake of threatening me for failing to help him in his demand to join the Programme Staff "which has no Africans..." My nerves soothed at 1700 by Telemaque reading, very beautifully, some poems by E.M. Roach, the schoolmaster in Tobago. "And dreams like moths migrate upon the moon."

1 September. I rehearse Orlando Martins, reading another of the Ibo stories by V.C. Nchami. He (Orlando) recalls a woman who insulted him when he was working in a Chiswick factory in 1922[?]. In return, he says, he saved her from being scalped by the machine, by switching off the power. Lunch with Calvin Lambert, who takes me in a fine new car to WASU. We find Jones-Quartey very put out. Half an hour before, there was an attempt on his cash box; the local post office has refused to accept ten cables, deposited by Gold Coasters. Among the stained glass windows of Proserpine (it is on the Chelsea embankment) a large poster advertising a Youth Rally in Budapest and another announcing a lecture by Peter Blackman, "Robeson in the Soviet Union." Calvin takes a gentleman called Antonio, with the ten cable forms, to another post office... The afternoon is spent with Lasebikan, recording his talk on Yoruba poetry, with sundry remarks about "explosion" and "implosion". It is very sensitive and scholarly, and he delivers it very well, with aid from a squeeze drum. One understands a delicate play on the word ilò, which means "refuse" in one mode, and "stork" in another, and "crooked" in another, depending on the tonal expression. A long drawn out jò-o-o for "rubber," a quick búté-búté for "cotton wool"... I fancy that the Third will be interested, even though the script conveys little of the real interest. He analysed four poems in close detail. If only all one's work were so interesting! I look forward more than ever to the trip to Nigeria.

[From 15 September to 15 October Swanzy travels to Nigeria]

17 October. There is a very persistent little rumour that the Colonial Office were wanting to rearrange my itinerary, to give me longer time in the country. When Tony mentions this to JGW, he replies "Out of the question! I am going away to the Caribbean, and he must be there to fill my place". But now I am back, it is Oliver Whitley, who is "filling his place".

19 October. The office hums with stories of Milner Haigh, his ruthless attitude to Africa, his orgies... Sylvia is particularly horrified. Mary

Hicks describes the piles of lost papers, the taxes taken to Egton House (250 yards away)... Perhaps he is pulling their legs? We are a little bloodless at 200. Lennox de Paiva* reads one of his social protest stories, "A Hunting We Will Go". He is a young Creole with a tiny, rather immature, but not unhandsome face. Lunch at Lyons, now self-service, and inhuman, plastic trays, ribbed aluminum ledges.

21 October. An apologetic note from Oliver Whitley. ACOES (it conceals the cunning face of Conner) has asked that he see all scripts on the Gold Coast constitution...

22 October. Tea with Efua in her hostel in Cartwright Gardens. She is now at the School of African Studies, upset by the death of Ida Ward. She gives me an assignation, which I cannot fulfil: tomorrow evening at the City Temple to hear the Rev. Leslie Weatherhead. When I look in the mirror, I do not like what I see.

25 October. The Coussey report on the Gold Coast Constitution. It comes from an all-African sub-committee of an all-African committee of 38 men. What part was played by the European joint secretary, a thin-faced young man called Dickenson?

27 October. A piece on press reactions to the Gold Coast report for *Calling West Africa*. No mention at all in *Mirror*, *Mail* or *Sketch*. The *Herald* is dismissive. The *Worker* abusive. Only *Times*, *Guardian*, and *Telegraph* serious and informed.

29 October. At 200, another kettle of fish: a tall, serious, modest young man called Errol Hill from Trinidad, studying at RADA, who reads a gripping story by Selvon, "Dry River Murder." I am crushing about the chances of radio drama as an art-form, not concealing our own lack of resources, mainly technical. The PRO at Accra wants a copy of the press summary urgently, I hope not for a reprimand, as last year...

5 November. I found that Pauline does not have enough emotion to carry a nostalgic piece by John Wickham, looking back on his childhood, "Time Out of Mind." So I read it myself. Immediately afterwards, Calder-Marshall to criticize. He was in good form, describing children as "infantile onions"... We adjourned for a drink at the Marlborough, where he was indiscreet about Unilevers, for whom the film company he works with hope to do some films, on cocoa [...]. I have to remember that Arthur is still much in the Russian camp. He has been bear-leading two Soviet visitors for the SCR, and spoke of a meeting last Sunday,

when they described all the nationalities, and we could only talk about the diminished English scene... Yet I have just given him stories by [Cyprian] Ekwensi* and Phebean Itayemi to read.

7 November. Lunch with James Millar,* Whitley's successor at the CO, a neat, fair man, with a small head, and twisted lips. He seems very Left wing, having been concerned with Tito in the war, and angered by propaganda against the Soviets in the Russian Service. He hinted, indeed, that he might well have been removed from the Corporation altogether, but for powerful connections in Scotland (an uncle who was a Scottish law lord). For tea, two Gas, Djabanor and Sowa who are to read the rather limp verse of an Accra poetaster A. L. Milner-Brown,* with Efua.

8 November. In the afternoon recording with Efua and the two Gas: "Fish Season", "Starch Woho", "The Weed" and the "Orange Tree." After the two had gone, I took Efua to a deserted studio, the Brown Continuity Suites, and abandoned myself to the lusts of the flesh, stopping short as ever from the final commitment. It was a foolish thing to do, someone nearly came in, but they went away. At 6, I went round to her room at the hostel, not to continue the encounter, but to collect some of her translations of Fanti folk tales. On her bookcase, I saw that she has the big book by the German sexologist Hersfeld...

10 November. Edgar Mittelholzer records a review of a book on Charles Waterton, the eccentric Victorian biologist (who specialized in eating unknown things, the most unpleasant being the musty heart of Louis XIV). Cy Grant records five poets, including "Seeds of the Pomegranate", by [Barnabas] Ramon Fortune. [...] Later, to a party given by George, back from Israel to launch the firm of Weidenfeld and Nicolson. Pretty, crinkled women, undistinguished men, oceans of champagne, which Nicholson says is cheaper than cocktails.

16 November. The ground-nut scandal – that is the word – breaks in the press. At lunchtime, the usual Colonial hour, Jones-Quartey with a rhetorical statement rather than a report on the West African Society, in the throes of breaking up. A large Jamaican lady called Noel Foster Davis* sings some folk songs very well to her own guitar: "This long time, gal, I never see you, come make me shake yo hand" (some of them are collected by Inez Sibley).

20 November. Four books from *Tribune* for a review; I choose Ingrams' *Seven Across the Sahara*. Why do I do all this work, for nothing? I am

not really a convinced Socialist. On the radio, listen to D. Garnett wishing he were E. Garnett, and Spender wishing he were Goethe. "Poitry ... Centry ... World litrtre..."

21 November. A strange experience with JGW, just back from the West Indies. As I sat with O. Whitley, (perhaps through a trick of the light) I felt that I was looking into his very soul. Gone the bonhomous exterior, the Commonwealth gladhand, the fat cheeks, the thick glasses. In their place, a tiny frightened man, with small eyes, a long, wandering nose, and basilisk lips. The impression faded almost as soon as it registered, but I am convinced that it was objective reality, not subjective judgement. I have never had such an experience before. He does not seem at all upset that the entire scheme for a Caribbean radio "working party" is off, thanks to the opposition of Huggins, the Governor of Jamaica, and Rance, the Governor of Trinidad. One interesting thing: all the literary work of Gladys Lindo, so useful and so well arranged, is done by her husband Cedric.

23 November. Back at 200, JGW says that the *Voices* are restored to Rediffusion in Trinidad and Barbados, after a hundred letters of protest were received.

25 November. JGW passes on a long letter from A. J. Seymour to Guiana writers, "God's Secretaries", with a bitter paragraph about the "schoolmasterly" BBC, and its attempt to organise Caribbean writing into "a certain kind of easily assimilable literature". The programme will never be any good until run by a West Indian, or by someone "carefully advised" by West Indians. There is a grain of truth in this. But then, radio is not an ideal vehicle for things written There can be second and third readings, but only one hearing. In any case, I should have thought that the main danger of a fledgling culture like the Caribbean's, precisely lies in a tight control by motivated people, who want to impose their standards of writing on the others. When I am gone, I am sure they will regret the "catholicity" of the programme choice, precisely because I am not competing with West Indian writers, or indeed, with writers in London.

30 November. George Spence* tries to raise another loan, no longer for "his sister", Gordon [Woolford] wants me to back an application to join the Welfare service at the CO. I help him by getting him to read one of his own stories. (It is some time since he has had one accepted). He also reads an interesting Ekwensi story, "Sharro", about trial by ordeal in Northern Nigeria. (His father was a wandering Ibo elephant

hunter, and so he knows the North). Mercedes Mackay with a *Diary*. Then the hospital round: Efua looks blooming, with Twum Barima in attendance. Tirzah, not so well. I drop my spectacles, through a hole in the overcoat pocket, down the escalator at Swiss Cottage.

2 December. At 200, another protest from an Announcer, this time on "Sharro." "Outrage … bad for BBC prestige … writing like a child of six … sadism…"

10 December. Tirzah is really ill, without resilience, serenity lost for the first time since I have known her.

12 December. More work for Gordon Woolford, reading "The Young Millionaire" by Nchami. He is now working for a tourist agency, as a guide, being given expenses… A man called MacNeill Stewart,* living in the Gold Coast, sends a story about a White man and his African mistress on the Coast, a Black man with his English mistress in Britain…

16 December. Christmas recordings by the Crabbes and John Fig, (two stories and some poetry by the reliable ladies, Albinia Hutton* and Lena Kent*). Immense tidying of files – it is quite impossible for Tony to index the African material. Send Newby a cross-section of the *Voices*, for Third consideration, without much hope.

1950

4 January. [At 200 to] record Mercedes, who now has to provide for her family, since her husband has lost his job as a geologist. She is becoming steadily better as a broadcaster, quite a character. She says that A. M. Jones is getting £180 for his Third talk, with repeats, at £30 a time. The figure is £15 more than his total annual salary as a missionary… A small pass at Phebean Itayemi, whom I took to see Peter Brook's production of *Rigoletto* at the Garden. (We had hoped for a ballet). She was surprised that opera glasses were on hire. In Nigeria, they would all have been stolen.

6 January. Recording by the brash young Trinidad Indian Seunarine, who reads an excellent protest story by Samuel Selvon, "Cane is Bitter". It is amusing to see the emendation he made in the reading. Selvon wrote about the "indifferent" look of the Indian, the apparent faithlessness of their women worn by toil, and then added that such thoughts would never come from a fellow Indian. Seunarine changed this to "fellow citizen".

11 January. Record the twice yearly survey of the *Voices*. The prose includes Selvon, Mittelholzer, and "The Terror Bull" [by Inez Sibley]. But it is the poetry that remains in the head, especially Walcott:

> You in the castle of your skin, I the swineherd

and his celebration of islands where

> The fine arts flourish on irregular Thursdays.

And there is the simple mnemonic of Noel Foster Davis' Jamaican songs.

> This long time gal Ah never see you.
> Come mak me shake your han.

After this, Gordon Woolford reads a story by Eileen Ormsby Cooper, one of the Jamaican muses. He is happy because of a treacly story about a girl called Cherry Melville, sold to one of the London women's magazines.

15 January. Annoyed to learn from John Fig that the Institute of Education, which is starting a writing course for African students, has never heard of *West African Voices*.

16 January. A letter from Ekwensi, in Lagos. The Scribblers Club is dissolved. Oddly enough, Eva Fredericks records a story by one of them, Adoki. At 1800, a white literary lady from Dominica calls. Tall, vague, pathetic, a typist in the Victoria district with a tragic history (I guess) and a great desire for fame. Her poems have got something. She uses "delirium" and "rave" on the same line, without any thought of Yeats. Her name is Emily Lockhart.*

19 January. Lennox de Paiva with a manufactured story of the war in Italy, "Chocolate Soldier" (it is surprising how seldom West Indian writers write about the war, in which some at least of them took part). Gordon Woolford was outgunned by a stark, violent piece by Roger Mais, the stormy petrel of Jamaica, involving a stabbing and a suicide: "See That Sun Go Down". Fortunately Errol Hill appeared, to take it over.

27 January. In the evening, a British Council reception for students. Not very impressive, although the handsome Helen Roberts was there.

I spoke to [Joseph] Ghartey* and Sam of the Gold Coast station ZOY. Ghartey, a heavy faced bureaucrat, Sam a babyish, round headed man, who does children's programmes under the sobriquet Uncle Albert... When I got back to Adelaide Road, I was met by a dark figure clutching a large bottle of liqueur called Llandovery. It was AET [Henry], who sat up till of after one, praising Oxford, and cursing Ken Ablack.

30 January. In the afternoon, a calypso recording, organised by Dennis Preston at the Parlophone studios in the Abbey Road, attended by all the Caribbean service, with Mona Baptiste, a very good-looking crooner, and Cottrell and his wife, both affable. Lord Kitchener wore a "Youth for Peace" badge, and Rudolph Dunbar* was just back from a triumphant tour in Poland.

8 February. At 200, Mercedes with a "Diary", and Errol Hill reading some rather sweet little poems about the Gold Coast from the exiled West Indian, Kenneth MacNeill Stewart. Bending to the grindstone of "the Notes". In a way, it is like working at a jewellers, except that they are not jewels.

9 February. Tirzah rings up again, in a panic, fearing that, after all, after all, it is cancer that is biting at her back.

10 February. Tirzah is to have another X-ray tomorrow, in an area which has not yet been examined, the lower part of her back. [...] I change tomorrow's recording times to get down sooner. It is hard to concentrate on *Caribbean Voices*, on "the Notes", on the ten letters at the RAS. But the routine helps in a way.

14 February. St. Valentines Day, and MacQueen sends a letter. "Dr Fox states: a review of the old films, in search of secondaries, shows probable deposits in the bodies of two of the vertebrae, and in the pelvic bone... The diagnosis is at present entirely dependent on the X-ray. There is nothing to be felt, and no definite clinical symptoms." As I read the letter, Suzanne said, "*My* Mummy won't die". In the bus, I gave Rossdale's telephone number, when asked for the fare. All outside things fade into insignificance, Mercedes and Ogunkeye chatting about radio plays in Ibadan, the matron at BH dressing my carbuncle. [...] Rossdale came round, penitent for his long neglect, and rang in the evening to say that he had received the letter from MacQueen, and was writing for the X-rays. He advised me to tell Tirzah a little, which I did. Her first thought was of course for the children, particularly Anne. Later she came to my room, and I said

all the things I should have said over the last four years, and did occasionally when things were right. It is really true, I love her essence more than that of anyone I have ever known. She said that she loved me too, in her fashion, only her heart was broken by John Aldridge... At the end, one plucked up a little heart. The doctors are so vague, it may not be true.

16 February. Errol Hill records some excellent snapshots of Carnival by Willy Richardson, with some passages on copulation removed. *Mas* with his Kokeeay broom, buljol, zaboca, Gregorio, doctor, lawyer (defending carnal knowledge), Wild Indian, Mavis, Clown, Bats, Moko-Jumbie, Pierrot Grenades, Blue Devil, Red Army, Destination Tokyo... Tirzah was delighted to hear all about them afterwards. The sad fate of the Calypsonians, who blew their thousand dollars in the next half year, taking girls in taxis from one side of Trinidad to the other.

18 February. Tirzah complains of pain in her arms, but I am optimistic again. It <u>cannot</u> be true. Willy Richardson reads a piece on the history of Carnival, by Alfred Mendes,* recalling the evil day in 1881, when it was closed down by "Brave Butler of the Bobbies." Gardening in the afternoon, typing notes in the evening, reading to Tirzah.

22 February. Ash Wednesday. Tirzah was sick all day, a green bile, perhaps from the morphia, perhaps from a sleeping draught. She knows; for Rossdale has come, with a nice quiet house surgeon. The cancer is all over her bones, spine, ribs, but not in her organs. With treatment, "she may last up to two years."

23 February. [Tirzah] was still sick, this time white curds. It was wonderful to see her smile. Perhaps there is something rather vulgar about noting down these details? But I want, if I can, to preserve her.

1 March. The card at the end of Tirzah's bed talks of carcinoma of the breast, a whole paragraph on secondary outbreaks, in ilium, sacrum etc. A kind letter from Ariel Crittall. I run through the crowded little desk at home, unearthing a perfect photograph of Tirz, surprised at the edge of a wood collecting wild flowers, in a shapeless frock, her little straw hat on the back of her head. There is a danger that with my peculiar temperament I am feasting on this grief, ridden with guilt for the anger of former years. Poetry, any poetry, is a solace, and today Errol Hill and Vivette Hendricks read some of the best of the Caribbean poets: Walcott, Roach, Seymour, Vaughan [H.A.]. They have perhaps, what I have not, the single mind.

> For this is the country
> Where the primal gifts are lovingly hoarded.

7 March. A conference on Colonies and International Relations at Cambridge, a Colonial symposium at Bristol, neither of which I know anything about. I spent an hour going through the lists of Colonial students, hoping to find contributors for *West African Voices*. Out of 3500 names, barely any reading the humanities: four on History, none on Philosophy. [...] Then record up to 2030 a kitsch short story by Vic Reid, "No Mourning in the Valley," well read by Errol Hill.

13 March. At 6, a drink (Chablis) at the broken-down Savage club, by the fat editor of *Arena*, John Davenport, a minor Connolly, interested in Sam Selvon's stories. He said that one Lyle, of the sugar family, is running a little magazine, with the help of Roy Campbell. Why couldn't he put up a prize for writers in the Caribbean. Back to find Tirzah with Olive. She was gay, but collapsed immediately after Olive left.

18 March. At 200, Beau Milton and Gloria Vaz* read five poets, including the good new one from St. Vincent, called E McG. Keane.* Beau was looking wild and unshaven, and smelt strongly of liquor, and I wondered what Gloria thought.

23 March. Pandit Seunarine records "Sonya's Luck", a sensitive story of a marriage by a Trinidad journalist, Seepersad Naipaul.* Later Pauline read a much less accomplished story by Ernest Carr, "She Named Him Roderick (!)" We were warned to stand by for the visit of three BBC Governors (Tedder, Clydesmuir and Barbara Wootton) but they went elsewhere. The only result, as Sylvia said, was that there were better cakes for tea in the canteen.

24 March. Ghartey and [Ben] Gadzekpo*, the Talks Assistants from ZOY in Accra, look in to enquire about *West African Voices*. After them, a probation officer from Trinidad, called Felix Ramon Fortune,* who spoke with jealousy about his younger brother Barnabas. He left behind a sheaf of humourless religious verses. Ogunkeye read a good little story about Yorubaland, "Kwale the Jester".

27 March. Lunch in the canteen with Paul Johnstone, Bill Ash, a producer in GOS, from the Southern States, and another young man in the North American service, Tony Wedgwood Benn, nice looking and well groomed, with a reputation for wildness – he recently set fire to a waste paper basket in a Control Room by throwing a cigar into it, and was supremely

unconcerned at the ensuing panic. How isolated I feel among all this *jeunesse dorée*, far up country, beyond the mangrove swamps! At 200, Sydney Hill, a younger brother of Errol, who is training to be a singer. He was small and sharp-faced, with a sheaf of sporting papers, since he backs gee-gees. He read a story by Selvon, "Johnson and the Cascadura".

29 March. Stewart Perowne's script for the Third is merely a historical survey of West Indian culture, with perfunctory remarks about Walcott, and no mention at all of the *Voices*, although he lists three factors for helping Caribbean self-consciousness: Colonial Development and Welfare, the Caribbean Commission, bulk-buying of sugar (!).

31 March. Tirzah went to the Royal Free for an inspection, and returned in double quick time. A good sign? Ben [Enwonwu] left, to go to stay with friends in Surrey. Little Suzanne, who had been friendly earlier, flounced off, when he made to kiss her, saying that she would not be kissed by a black man, "Black is ugly"... Ben merely laughed. He has achieved something, and feels no "inferiority". That is what I am working for. Last night, he joked about the advertisement for 'Nigger' dates, which had stung little Carberry into a violent rage. Even this morning, at breakfast, he joked about the golliwog on the Robertson's marmalade jar...

3 April. Errol Hill reads Easter poems by five poets (including the Ramon Fortune brothers), and another St Vincent poet, Owen Campbell.* Christopher Onwuegbuzia* read an Ekwensi story. Gordon Woolford, now with a travel agency, coped with a story by Michael Browne*, which overran by 6½ minutes, cutting blind, I reduced this on the disc to within 2 seconds of the right length. I find this interesting, since I now find it impossible to estimate the shorter Newsreel length (3 minutes). Routine is a curious thing.

12 April. At work, Mercedes, pleased as punch by a note in *West Africa*, which says that her *Diary* is the most popular thing in the broadcasts to the Coast. In the afternoon, to see the handsome Kay Shirlaw, to plead for a re-grading of Tony MacGlone. At 5, the first meeting of the Working Party on the RAS. "To examine the whole field of African interests in Britain, with a view to determining whether every function is being satisfactorily filled at the moment, and, if not, whether a society like the RAS might be able to take some or any of them". Present: AB Cohen, RE Norton, Canon Bewes, PH Canham, Haig, Oxbury, Mulira, Wraith. Pedler did not turn up, so there is little commercial representation. Andrew immediately jibbed at the terms of reference, and harped on

the African students. Haig was not a very good Chairman, and the conversation was rambling, with Wraith throwing up the idea of industrial training, and Norton restive. I was gauche, with accounts of previous attempts to find "a continuing function", including letters to the press... At least, they agreed on the need for a centre... Mulira is to bring along Ogunsheye, Kobina Taylor and one other African next week. Heather and Haig hurried off to listen to the talk by Hussey, at the "discussion evening" at the Victoria League (at which three Africans turned up. We are playing games with the wind).

14 April. JGW, comes to tell me that Bush House are sending two scriptwriters, Walter Kolarz and Austin Kark, on an extended tour of Africa. Would you believe it, they declare that *African Affairs* or rather "The Quarterly Notes" is their Bible? Such things are sent to try me. [...] At 200, AET Henry records a thriller by de Paiva, "The Spy and the Informers". We discussed the shortcomings of the USA – he has just seen the odious newsreel on the soap box Derby, ruthless adult commercial exploitation of the young... Pauline read a little story by one of the literary ladies, Elsie Hutton,* less well than usual. She is out of practice, and I suspect that living with Neville Crabbe cannot improve the brain.

18 April. Hard work all day: letters and schedules at 200, a dozen post cards and letters at the RAS. Recording MacJajah's "Reincarnation" in the afternoon, the most exhausting of all. Instead of an African girl, he brought along a little coloured person, talking Cockney. Instead of a guitarist, he brought a drummer. Onwuegbuzia, who was taking part, found these things a little odd. After a long argument, I got him to take on his Scotch secretary, Miss Butcher, for second narration. Another half hour of argument over production points. "The first scene opens in the mystic apartment of a big cave palace of rocks, bordered by four volcanos, lit by embroidery of twilight rays of blue, pink, green and red". How could one resist this visual treat? Then I recalled that it was, basically, a rehash of a legend in *Ikolo the Wrestler*, needless to say unacknowledged. As ever, the second rehearsal was better than the recorded performance – we should have recorded it as well. MacJajah was tranced, and very nervous, saying "reetoon" for "routine", and zoo-like in his incantations. "Hoo-hoo-ja-hoo". At the end, one could not help asking oneself whether it was worth all the trouble, Certainly the young RPA, a pleasant boy, was annoyed.

20 April. With JGW and Willy Edmett we went to see the touring version of the Colonial Exhibition (at the Imperial Institute) accompanied by

J. B. Millar and Noakes, a publicity man. An auspicious occasion, perhaps the first time the Colonial Section of the BBC has gone together to anything in the last five years... The show was more tactful than the original version: instead of a noisome jungle at entry, a Hausa court. The "talking kitchen" had been scaled down... In the technical photographs, three show cinema, press and radio.

21 April. In return for my work with MacJajah, I get a rocket from Connley, Recorded Programmes Manager, for an overrun of ten minutes and an unauthorised play-back. There is also a furious telephone call from MacJajah himself, incoherent with rage that he only got 2 guineas for reading, 10 guineas for copyright. He threatens to write to Governments, to declare war. The tirade went on for half an hour. The main event of the day was the arrival of the two young writers, Lamming (23) and Selvon (26), come to try and find fame and fortune in the metropolis. They were very impressive, Lamming with a magnificent large head, strongly marked nose and mouth, deep rumbling voice, and Selvon, lighter, more charming, more sensitive perhaps. I took them to lunch at the Gargoyle. Selvon is a trained journalist, and may find things easier than Lamming, who said that he had not come to write, but to "sharpen his mind". How little I can offer them! A few guineas here and there, a few contacts, very limited. The British Council might be able to help. I found myself getting excited, as I outlined some of the "democratic pleasures" of London, the museums, the art galleries. But I felt inadequate. They will no doubt forge their own path, working through the West Indians already in London, Mittelholzer (although he may be a competitor), Richardson, John Fig, Henry, de Paiva. If only I had a more recognised base myself!

26 April. A West African day. Olowu, the young Nigerian, calls by appointment. He claims to have met me at Ibadan, wants to study engineering, is penniless. I write the name of Buckle in the UAC on a slip of paper, and give him £3. Then to Mercedes and the *Diary*, with such praise of Lugard, in a style best calculated to anger the West African listener, that I have to tone it down.

27 April. My annual increment has gone through, and I now earn the princely salary of £1010. This, with the £200 from the RAS gives £1210. Then there is £60 odd from my small capital. £1270. Then £600 for the children's education grant, and £130 from Tirzah's pension as the widow of Eric. In all, £2000 a year! And we live rent-free. (Perhaps I should include Bobby's rent of £90, but that has not come in since the third quarter of 1949). Where does all this go? £250 in taxes on

the BBC salary, £75 in tax for the RAS, £30 in income tax on the house. £100 in rates, £4 groundrent. £12 water rate. The boys' schools come to about £400, Annie's about £60. All this amounts to £930. Food for three comes to about £6 a week, £1230. Then we pay £100 for a charlady. My own feeding out must take £2 a week, £1430. This leaves about £550 for clothes, journeys, children's holidays, extras, telephone. (What about a housekeeper?) (£150 in cash, £100 in food). This leaves about £180 available. Poorly as we live, we must still go very carefully.

28 April. I have written to Wellesley Cole resigning from the West African Society. Let them encourage culture by all means through organising football matches, but do not let them call upon Europeans to do the organising!

3 May. Just before lunch, another West Indian aspirant, a lively *jolie laide* from Jamaica, called Terry Burke,* whom I find curiously attractive with bright brown cheeks and flashing spectacles, and immoderate ambitions. Lunch to Gavin Ewart, who is involved in Davenport's *Arena*. Mercedes delivers her *Diary*, Carberry reads "My Poetic Life" by the pompous Clare McFarlane: but suffers from not knowing what a *villanelle* is.

5 May. Sam Selvon comes in to record six minutes on the first press reactions to Mittelholzer's *Morning at the Office*, published by Peter Nevill. So far we have seen four reviews, all favourable: *Times, Guardian, Times Literary Supplement, Worker*. The last, of course, gives no account of the book (a comedy I have not yet read), but simply quotes a few anti-British comments. Selvon handles it very well, and reads in a delightful, rapid, slurred voice, a little like Edgar's, but easier to understand. He has just sold something to *Lilliput*, a racy account of the steel bands (dustbin lids).

8 May. A sentimental scene, on the way to work. A poor old gelding was standing, depressed and drooping, between the shafts of a milk-float by the side of the road. In the distance, a rattle of harness, the clip-clop of horses' hooves, as a section of Household Cavalry come up from exercise in the Park. At the sound, the unhappy slave, straightens up and whinnies. But the unfeeling cavalcade swept by without a glance. A symbol, perhaps, of more than horses. At the office, JGW continues pleasant, Oliver Whitley now has the office next to him, and was, I think, in charge of the negotiations over a Nigerian radio service, which the Government wish to control. (He saw Foot at the weekend alone). Ah well, my role in life, simple observation.

10 May. In the small hours before dawn, Tirzah takes hold of me more urgently than I ever remember. She needs comfort, reassurance, warmth, even sex. (The disease presses). In the morning, she is serene again, painting a cruel little scene in the doll's house. I swing in the chair, losing my balance, while she watches from the bed, lips pursed, a chamber pot very visible. At 200, dazed from the draft "Notes" (Central Africa), I lunch with Mittelholzer and Lamming. The former is pleased with Selvon's press summary, gay and well-dressed, savouring the sweet smell of success, if only of esteem. Lamming, on the other hand, is down, and extends a small, limp hand, a contrast to his Godlike head. He criticises the programme, which could, he said, be a "majority" programme. He remarks, rather acidly, that I have many interests. He is disappointed by the calibre of the West Indians he has met in London. He defends Communism against the *élitiste* Mittelholzer, proud of his Swiss ancestor, a plantation overseer in the great slave rising of the 1760s. Roy Fuller and Ralph Currey have seen him, they are trying to do something for him, a clerk's job in the Post Office? He then went on to read some poems by a new name, Jan Carew,* a Guianese specialising in legends... Later at 5 I took Tirzah out, to see Jacques Tati, a French Russian, excruciatingly funny as a rural postman in *Jour de Fête*, long and angular, like a daddy long legs, furiously riding a bicycle.

15 May. Samuel Selvon at 10, reading a story by Seepersad Naipaul, "Gratuity", brilliant and funny. I took him to coffee and cakes at Fortes, and found that he, like Lamming, is finding life in London hard and the English unsympathetic. We discussed Tradition, which he detests – after all, he is barely 26. I asked him how he could work as a writer without a tradition to fall back on, the unspoken but understood communication. He sees that the two things are not exclusive, but he was not conceited enough to claim that he and others like him were *making* a tradition (although that is what I hope they are doing). A coral reef... Later, Onwuegbuzia read a story by Nchami, "The Spirit of Smallpox". "A Mallam" rebukes superstitious Yoruba villagers who think that *itseku* grass will drive away *Shakpona*, the smallpox God. For "Mallam" I mentally substituted "Ibo" and we had to cut some things out that might have been offensive, tribally... We were watched by George Lamming, who had looked in to collect a script he is reading tomorrow. After the recording, I took him and Onwuegbuzia for a drink at the Marlborough, and then went home to supper, taking Lamming, very much at a loose end. He is edgy. As I guessed he has a Mother. (And also a wife, which I had not guessed). He never opens his mouth but to criticize England, the programme, West Africa, the ridiculous Onwuegbuzia, who had tried to slip a packet of cigarettes into my pocket

in the pub. *Caribbean Voices*, he thinks, is too "kind", and many beginners think they have "arrived", and act accordingly, like Telemaque, who puts on airs. Quite good food from Mrs Severs... We talked about seminal books, in his case *Over One's Shoulder*, by Robert Graves. (He had not read Calder-Marshall's *Glory Dead*). Afterwards, I took him round the house, showing the Ravilious *incunabula*, and the recent work of Tirzah. Basketball on the box. When he left for the Balmoral, and [Albert] Gomes,* the Trinidad poet-politician, I hoped he was happier. Read myself to sleep with Mittelholzer's novel. It is almost impossible to believe that it is the same Edgar, the burning, humourless fanatic. This was crisp, colourful, barbed with delightful humour. The life of an office, dissected before one, with brilliant timing – the delayed entry of Mrs Hinckson, beloved of the office boy. The one false note, or so it seemed, the green beret worn by a young queer, symbol of *volupté* for the repressed Mr Reynolds. They say that the *Evening Standard* may serialize it.

16 May. At 200, George Lamming records some poems by the excellent Tobago poet [E. M.] Roach. They are lyrics, which he chants in a tragic voice. When he reads faster, he loses his emotion. It is like playing minuets on a great organ. But the brutal fact is that the main consideration is cash. We are joined by Alfred Mendes, the novelist, over on a six months course connected with his job in Trinidad harbour administration. He is very different in character from the dramatic young Lamming, who may have genius, and certainly acts as though he has. Much older, long head, kind brown eyes, neat, very smooth. We adjourn for coffee and a conversation which I wish I had time to reproduce. It is a great privilege to be connected with this programme. I am really beginning to feel that it has an atmosphere totally different from anything I have ever done in radio; and I venture to think, totally different from anything that is being done in the Overseas Service, even in the rest of the BBC.

23 May. At the office, JGW says that Dunstan de Silva is dead in Lagos, El Ansari at Kafduna sentenced to 33 months in gaol. I suggest that we give a party to the dozen Caribbean writers now in London, possibly in honour of Mittelholzer's novel, which continues to get good notices. This is the first real breakthrough, (when I called at Bumpus, I gathered that they had never even heard of Vic Reid's *New Day*). Aluko to record a little piece on Empire Day – memories of school parades, that meant absolutely nothing to him or any of his friends. In the afternoon, rehearsed a little verse play by Derek Walcott, *Senza Alcun Sospetto*, the story of Francesca da Rimini, taken from Dante. Errol Hill is in overall charge, and had chosen a little Jamaican student at RADA, Valerie Bolton,*

who resented production by an amateur like myself: "Have you ever been to the West Indies?" Very sweetly she informed me that she had never heard of *Caribbean Voices*. Lamming, true to form, chipped in, "Neither has anyone else". Later on, however, he made some animated versions on Edna Manley, and almost came to blows with the little vixen. It was now my turn to cool the atmosphere down. But, by and large, the rehearsal did not go at all badly.

24 May. A tepid leader in the *Times* for Empire Day, abandoned by all but Lord Elton. Bishop Bardsley, Collin Brooks, and F. S. Joelson... In our own small world, Mercedes with the *Diary*. Mrs Elsie Barsoe* looks in, a Jamaican journalist, rather fun, a brown version of Elsa, with wild hair and restless eye. At tea, George Lamming, come to look through old files for "outstanding programmes". I suggest he select 10,000 words for Davenport and *Arena*. He is after all Left Wing, speaks Spanish, knows Pablo Neruda... As he is still unoccupied, I again take him back to supper. He is boorish, but I recognise myself at 21. Needless to say, he shows no inclination to help wash up, or even talk to Anne. He studies my two books of Victorian holographs, while I potter in the garden, preparing for Tirzah. The peony is out at last, but sinks to the earth with the weight of its great head. No bad metaphor for George, with his own splendid head, and small, limp, female hands.

26 May. Drinks, Marlborough and Cock, with the cast of *Senza Alcun Sospetto*, and Roy Fuller, who is to be critic in attendance. Then to Studio 3E at BH, where we had an excellent JPE, who coped admirably with all the effects. On one small production point, Walcott had given the stage direction, "Music unbearably loud" before a door opens and Paolo says "We will die", with music fading to a woman crying. The JPE suggests that the music should peak only after the door has opened. In this way, the music expresses the act of murder, rather than the decision to die, and dramatically, it succeeds much better. One lives and learns. As for the reading, it was not as good as on rehearsal, but still for all that good, with Valerie Bolton and Sydney Hill excellent as the lovers, and Lamming and Errol Hill more than passable, the latter as Dante, the narrator. Roy Fuller, who says his ulcer is mending, was affable to all.

31 May. Tea with Boscoe Holder,* a tall young dancer and singer from Trinidad, and a very pretty wife. There seems to be a real migration this summer from the Caribbean. A playback of the Dante play, which JGW and Oliver W. attended with Errol Hill and Valerie Bolton. Many useful lessons. I did some propaganda for the absent Lamming.

1 June. At 200, Gordon reads "The Sibilant and Lost", a nightmare story from the pen of Mittelholzer, engendered from a strange mixture, his German and Indian origins, the murderer Haig, the BBC ban on broadcasting sibilants... Louise Bennett, the fat and lively Jamaican soubrette, fires off some dialect poems, some by herself.

6 June. An English businessman called Bedford, who works in Trinidad for Caroni, looked in with some animal stories. At lunch time recording Ben Gadzekpo, a pleasant trainee from ZOY in Accra, who reads very well a colourless Ewe legend.

9 June. Then announcements, editing Creech, George Lamming reads poems by Collymore and others, in his magnificent deep voice. Calder-Marshall comments on the story read by Terry, "Crock of Gold". After supper, I take GL to see *The Cocktail Party*, seats quite easily obtainable in the gallery. I found it disappointing, tinny, with no real psychological background. The charming Rex Harrison causes laughter, when he intones "Go in peace. Seek your salvation with diligence". Lamming was a difficult companion, still hating England and full of nostalgia for the Caribbean. But I am too immature myself to be a good guide for the young. Not to speak of the problems of production in the narrow sense in the studio, which George resents.

13 June. Edgar Mittelholzer, came to listen to Gordon's reading of "The Sibilant and Lost" and Calder-Marshall's criticisms, denies that has been influenced in any way by the Haigh trial. He is very serene, I suppose he can brush off this minor comment in the euphoria of a genuine London success. Not so some others. Mrs Lindo reports a savage onslaught from Virtue about Roy Fuller's reservations on Walcott. "He is not a West Indian regional poet, he is an absolute poet. Poetry knows no frontiers". Very true. But only the local is real (Chesterton).

16 June. Albert Gomes, Alfred Mendes, John Fig and Calder, for lunch and then recording; a veritable symposium, spoiled only by three breakdowns of circuit in OS 1. Figueroa was reading a story "Christopher", an extract from a work in progress, by the appalling pretentious Jamaican Basil McFarlane.* It was rent by Mendes; "dissecting a newt" (Gomes). I do not think this was mere inter-island rivalry. No European would dare be so rude, and even then, he had to be toned down. Afterwards, Mendes came to BH, where Doreen Goodwin Grason* was recording five Jamaican poets, including John Fig, B. McFarlane, and Archie Lindo. She professed keen interest in the poor young literati now flooding in

to London. Mendes, whose hand was hovering round her back, tried to get her to come to the Regent Palace Hotel, where there is a nightly assembly of the members of the sugar mission and other West Indians, including "one George Padmore, a most eloquent fellow". He does not succeed.

19 June. At 200, working on programmes – a tart letter to my main correspondent, Mrs (or Mr) Lindo. An exciting discovery from West Africa, a Yoruba called Babalola,* with graphic translations of traditional poetry. *When I First Heard of Forest Farms...* It had definite dactylic quality; and memorable generalisations.

> For by singing a chorus as if
> It were a solo piece, one makes one's death
> Come earlier than God would have it come.

20 June. At the office, an account (from Lamming?) of Sam Selvon deliberately reading the newspaper upside down in the Tube...

23 June. Tirzah has a new symptom: when she bends her head, she feels a pain behind her knees. She had to go today to the Royal Free [...]. At the BBC, George Lamming came to record poetry, including some by the St. Vincent "school" and some from Trinidad. He came half an hour too early, and when challenged by the receptionist, replied "I'm thinking". But he was easier later, having been "conquered" by a day in Cambridge. The charming Shelia Clarke,* Mrs Boscoe Holder, read a story by Sam Selvon, with an assurance that comes from a schooling in Tottenham. Arthur Calder-Marshall followed with a criticism. At home, we watched a television discussion on Colour Bar, which started in such a thunderous atmosphere...

27 June. The headlines blare the news of the fighting erupted in Korea. The jingle seems wonderfully apt:

> The King of Korea is gay and harmonious,
> He has one idea, and that is erroneous

I tackle Mrs Severs, who thinks that she is underpaid and overworked. Bed and board for herself and Charles, and £3 a week, with occasional help from Mrs Andrews to do the heavy work. She says she got £5 at her last job, and more housekeeping money. When I realise my incapacity to obtain loyal service from one little woman, I groan at my temerity in criticizing administrators overseas. At the office, [...] Onwuegbuzia reads a West African story by D. Hearn very well: "Daddy Brown meets an Earnest Young Man."

30 June. At home, Olive came to supper, and was regaled with the ego book. We watched the box, with amusing pictures of West Indians, guitars and zoot suits, frolicking on the sacred enclosure at Lord's. Boscoe Holder was brilliant in *Bal Creole*, with Willy Richardson acting as a guide to an English onlooker, with a very awkward sounding script.

4 July. A pleasant hour and a half with the attractive (to me) Terry Burke, reading a story by Inez Sibley about the Kingston earthquake, *pergielas* aptly named "Presentiment." Terry is well aware that she has an effect on me. Curious, because in the eyes of the world, she has none of the beauty of Gloria Vaz, Carmen Manley, Sheila Clarke, Valerie Bolton, Doreen Grason. […] At home, turn over old copies of *African Affairs*, to see how wrong I have been. On the whole, not really very often.

8 July. Saturday. West Indian writers come in today with Calder, for a symposium in the stuffy studio 0S3. Have we a culture? Haven't we? Should we have one? Mittelholzer, Mendes, Selvon, Carberry, Richardson agree on two and three. The Jamaicans AET and Mrs Barsoe, not in the first flight, bitter about 'cliquism'. John Fig critical about our lack of criticism. Gordon [Woolford], Emily Lockhart, Doreen Grason, Terry Burke, contribute their own points of view. Neither Louise Bennett nor Vivette Hendricks could come, and George Lamming called off at the last minute. Afterwards, eight stayed to lunch. Mary Treadgold was gracious over a bottle of Tokay. "Hugh Sykes Davies recommends it. He buys for St John's, you know". I feel the hand of JGW behind the event.

9 July. Hot and breathless weather, and Tirzah can barely drag herself from bedroom to sitting-room. She has no appetite at all, and the spine is numb, and hot in the painful part. Annie asks again, "Are you going to die?" and she replies, "We are all going to die". [. . .] Tasha came to tea, Anne's friend, a handsome, bold girl. I left them watching the box, and called on Fred Uhlman, finding him with John Berger, the young critic, selected by Mary [Treadgold] to talk about art to West Africa, very far to the left, a surprising choice for her.

10 July. Sam Selvon read an odd story by Seepersad Naipaul, his fellow Indian, with a very odd title, "Shouters Visit China in the Spirit World." I found him (S.S.) rather difficult, breaking a (second) invitation to lunch, and suggesting supper instead, despite my explanation about

Tirzah. One has not done very much for him, I suppose, less than for Lamming, and that was little enough. As he left he said "I should like to work in your office in Kingston". I think the real trouble is that he is homesick. London must be a very frightening city, when you have no money except some savings, and you have to live on your wits, and the favour of literary bosses and newspaper editors. Perhaps I judge him harshly, Tirzah is really very ill, as bad, if not worse, than she was in February.

12 July. Two interesting encounters. The first with twelve Nigerian local authorities, bear-led by Greatbatch, DO Birnin Kebbi, once of Brasenose. They came for lunch and record messages in English, Hausa, Fulani and Kanuri. [...] The other encounter was odder. Jan Carew, a young writer from Guiana, after six years schooling in America, did a sojourn in Prague, with a Communist party official, is now living in Paris, with a banker. One wonders what his relations were with these varied people. He was very tall, with a pale babyish face, with a large brow, pointed chin. The most striking thing about him, apart from his elegant coffee-coloured summer suit, was a green and purple foulard scarf, under a thick green shirt. He spoke with a permanent smile, very slowly and carefully, avoiding my eye, about a novel he is publishing next week in the States. When I mention *Présence Africaine*, Richard Wright and Peter Abrahams, his nose distended slightly. I had a feeling that his life story would prove more interesting than any novel.

13 July. Took Tirzah back to the hospital. [...] Then I go down to the office to record AET [Henry] in an excruciating detective story by Jack J. Gordon* of Georgetown, "The Affair of the Meamu Diamond." "Reynard Lozenge contemplatively stroked his neatly trimmed beard which some people thought rather caprine".

17 July. Lunch with Carew, to learn a little more. He is living in the Faubourg St. Honoré, not with a banker, but with the secretary of the French Steel Federation. It <u>must</u> be a homo network? He seems to have rejected Communism – "the control of writing by bureaucrats is impossible". The main thing is "the liberation of hundreds of millions from Colonial exploitation". Perhaps we may inject the process with a love that Marxism has lost, or never known?

24 July. Read Walcott's chronicle play *Henri Christophe*, clotted, but verbally very exciting.

25 July. I had a most interesting time at 200, recording Babalola reading

his excellent translations of Yoruba poetry. They make me realize how different Africa is. When he "first heard of forest farms", the main attraction was the possibility of shooting down the unsuspecting deer… and he really appreciated his cruel wizard "the lonely son of Abuteri." No doubt, these sentiments would have been shared by the makars of the border ballads? But not for the last four hundred years among our over-sensitive literati.

26 July. Around 17.30, a party for *Caribbean Voices* in LG 7. Three large jugs of cider-cup, twenty beers, snowy cloth, adorned with carnations. Those who took part in the (spiritual) symposium took part [sic], with the critics Calder, Fuller, Gavin, Ralph, a sprinkling of BBC, including Willy, and Boyd from Home Service, and Robert Herring. Pauline was in high spirits, having got a break at last – the young producer Kenneth Tynan has a theory that Iago's wife Bianca was really black, hence his hatred of Othello… The occasion ended with an unexpected presentation by John Fig of an impressionist print, and a book token for 24/-, in lieu of Denis de Rougemont, unobtainable. I think most of the motivation for all this is Tirzah's illness.

28 July. A headache dictating the six month summary on the *Voices*. I singled out in the poetry, Walcott, and the reactions of Lamming and Selvon. The first, with his poem to Marian Anderson:

> Now I venturing from scattered islands
> To rediscover my roots,
> Have found an impersonal city
> Where your tales are incredibly true.

And Selvon, finding release in the beauty of the countryside. I praised, perhaps unduly, Jan Carew.

> Potaro, song of the world,
> River of the world…

If only because he was able to fuse Guianese place names with the wider world. And Roach, with his comparison of the fruit of the poui tree to golden semibreves. For the prose, mainly Seepersad Naipaul, with the Indian road mender, "as though he were all moustache and nothing else", and the Gagat Guru (World Teacher – "but only the elders called him that"). There was also the deft satire, intelletuals arguing with their house on fire ("The Argument", by Willy Richardson), and a *tour de force* by George Phillips*, of a racial encounter in Trinidad, witnessed by a beggar, who is only revealed as blind, in the very last sentence, his stick "tap-tap-tapping". I end by stressing that only the local is universal. "Of course, we do not want to compel you to write up insincere details of local colour, ... simply to flatter what you may think is the bias of the producer". After this, record Gordon and Errol Hill.

31 July. At 200, lunch with Crozier, who built up the *Advocate* in Barbados, founded the little magazine *Bim*, and now works on the Caribbean Commission. He looks and sounds like an American.

4 August. Up at 6.30, preparing the front room for the faithful Tony McGlone, my prop in good times and bad. At 10.15, Philip Gbeho, with two others, Akpabla and Jiagge, to demonstrate the *gong-gong* and rattle, for a talk on Gold Coast music. It was amusing to see how the English rhythms in Gbeho's voice gradually subside, as he goes on talking, until they stand out like patches on a carpet.

14 August. A day in London. [...] Onwuegbuzia reads a story by Nchami about a quack doctor. Ekwensi writes to say that he has won a four year scholarship in pharmacy.

16 August. At 200, recorded three tribal chiefs from Sierra Leone. At BH, Efua, in the lovely green studio B2. She was reading love poetry in Fante and English sent her by Joseph Ghartey, and did it beautifully, touchingly. She had on a pretty blue velvet jumper, a white skirt, printed with the Fante saying, "Life is Broken Glass." The message went home. After tea, we sat on a green knoll by Chester Gate, and she told me that she is sailing back to the Gold Coast in a week or two. If things had been different, she said, she would have married over here... I said, "Tirzah once suggested that I should marry you..." Would I come to the Gold Coast? It would be easier there... For the first time in my selfish, self-centred life, I was conscious of my shocking impact on another. The spoiled boy baby! She said she was still a virgin, although "pestered" in the last few years. Why was she so fond of me? "Because of something more than physical love"... She was amazed that I had married Tirzah after three short months, only 4½ years ago. I have indeed behaved very badly.

26 August. Read [Anthony] West to Tirzah, who is a little more at ease, but for her neck. One learns (a) one should not be a Nazi general (b) one should not fuck around the Riviera (c) one should not devote oneself wholly to art.

30 August. Once more in London, a whirl of work. Record Mercedes in a *Diary*, and the *Voices* summary. Phone Olive and Powe. Much bumf to read. Skidmore of the British Council writes to say that a Dutch journal published in Surinam, *Eldorado*, wants 6000 words on literary work in the British Caribbean.

8 September. At the office, Oliver asks for proposals for the Reith Lecture, (a ritual, since they are never accepted and never will be). A series on the rape of the earth by G. B. Masefield? Bush House propose "A Hundred Years of Marxism," and put up Isaiah Berlin as the speaker. It will probably be someone like Whitehead, if he is still alive. Proofs back from Baylis. Edgar Mittelholzer reads a good story, "In the Beginning." He no longer offers pot boilers, not needing to boil the pot.

15 September. Saturday. In the morning, six West African journalists, shepherded by a blunt-faced man called Lennard A. Aloba, contribute quite a good piece on the tour, better than the Gold Coaster Moses Danquah. They were very much a 2nd XI, with none of the probing Ibo questions, but they were waited on by our brass, McCall, Beechcroft of publicity, and HCS and ARCS. I receive a letter from James Welch, the Lucifer fallen from heaven, now going from the groundnut scheme to Ibadan University. I had talked of extracting the *Deus* from the African *machina*. He says that God is a subject, not an object... Pelting rain to Paddington.

21 September. At 200, John Fig reads some poems by Vidia Naipaul,* a son of Seepersad, Andrew Salkey, the Jamaican screwball, George Lamming... For tea, a keen Indian lady with screwed-up hair, and distant manner: Beryl McBurnie,* the Trinidad drama producer, the mentor of Errol Hill.

25 September. At 200, Beau Milton reads an odd little Victorian story, like something out of a reading book, "Courting a Hind", by Macaulay John, the kindly bewhiskered seal in Ibadan. A visit from Victor Frost, Assistant Personnel Manager in Apex Oil and friend of the Trinidad muses. A kindly Northumbrian, with decided views. Beryl McBurnie? "A third-rate Variety artist". *Morning at the Office*? "Never heard of it". He said that the theatre and music groups he organises have to be divided according to race. In the Company there are two Coloured people out of seventy in the senior posts...

30 September. BBC salary increases announced in the papers. Gordon Woolford, who is going to Paris, in pursuit of a girl who works for

Jacques Fath, read a curious satirical story by the Barbadian W. S. Arthur:* "Voices". At least, I thought it was satirical, although Gordon read it in a treacly, sentimental voice. It was about a Barbadian, who had wet dreams about white pen friends in England, notably a girl called Joan, who finally committed suicide. The contempt for local girls, like the cook Martha, was a trifle crude. It certainly probed a little deeper into one of the underlying reefs of race relations...

4 October. It is perhaps a mark of a well-spent life that a man has no time to keep a diary. These entries have been reconstituted four days late, and may be even more they usually are. Mercedes recorded a "Diary", and as usual was more interesting on what she did not record for publication. Tunde Lasebikan has made a break-through, appearing in costume on *In Town Tonight*. In a few days he will be on Television's *Picture Page*. He has even had an invitation, which he has refused, to go to the Gold Coast to make a film. And finally, he has got his scholarship at the Institute. All perhaps due, in the first place, to *West African Voices*.

9 October. At the office, Ogunkeye reads Babalola's story. The latter exposes one of the problems of dealing with Africa. Here is a bright young man, a Christian, who presents a story, "Wrong Hut", about a teacher who attempts to seduce a girl pupil from her true love, a farmer. The hero, i.e. the teacher, arranges to attack him using a masked gang at the Egungun festival, and if arrested, bribe the court. All this deadpan, with no moral comment, indeed with approval...

24 October. Infuriated in the train by an anthology of West Indian poetry, collected by Clare McFarlane, and published by the "University of London Press". There were, at most, three good gems in the whole collection. But no doubt it will be used as a textbook, at least in Jamaica, where McFarlane is a power in the Civil Service.

28 October. As it happens, today there is rather an elaborate recording: seven people, including the brothers Hill and Sam Selvon, with a sketch by Errol on steelbands, called "The PingPong". After two rehearsals, it fell into place very well.

1 November. At tea, Gloria Escoffery, an artist who works on the Jamaican *Public Opinion*, over here, under her own steam, to attend the Slade, She has a sad, beaky face, with beautiful brown eyes: French, Scots, English, Jewish, perhaps Negro blood. Her attitude to the Jamaican literary Establishment is the same as mine. At home (home is where the heart is) old Mrs Nicholas, now 97, comes up to see Tirzah, whose

leg is better, but neck the same. It is an extraordinary disease: why does it ebb and flow?

2 November. Another dreadful night. My darling in a muck sweat, and sleepless. All one can do is wipe her with a towel. At the office, Gordon reads a story by Edgar Boyce,* "Bajan Henry":
You know what the Bajans call a spree?
A bottle of cola divided in three.
Jamaican Henry (AET) is full of the death of G. B. Shaw, and works a reference into one of his old-world essays. "After Dickens, Henry, he is my favourite author. I must have read every word he ever wrote". Why must Tirzah suffer, while the old rip goes scot-free at the last? The *Standard* says that there are 100,000 new victims of cancer every year.

11 November. At the office, Sylvia looking pretty and excited – she has been told by JGW that she is to go in January to Nairobi and Salisbury... An uproarious Mauritius recording with Wynford Vaughan Thomas, reading, in a curious French accent, from an UNESCO report, by Opper, on the valley of Marbial in Haiti, and its continuous erosion through over-populations since the turn of the century.

22 November. [Tirzah] uses for the first time the word "bedridden", not having recovered from the last attack, as in the past, within five days. In London [...] we had a playback of the successful "PingPong", and tea with Willy Richardson, and Jan Carew, who argued about cricket. I overheard JGW on the telephone to McCall. "Sylvia is to go to East Africa at the end of the year. Edmett to the West Indies in February. (A pause). Oh yes, him. Well, he has his good points, but really there isn't enough work for two. We can reserve him for special projects, like *English by Radio*".

24 November. An exciting recording of five poets, including some from St Vincent, and the New York exile Louis Simpson,* by John Fig and the younger Hill. One excellent image, a fisherman's seine net, a bundle of nerves.

26 November. [Tirzah] says she is "ecstatically happy" – it must be the growth pressing on her organs. But it allows her the release of daydreams. Afterwards, she sits a long time in my dressing gown, trying to get the painting right.

28 November. Lunch with J. Harrison, who says that the British Council

are abolishing the Advisers for Art and Music in the Caribbean. Sydney Hill reads some naive poems from the Gold Coast by the West Indian exile in Koforidua, Kenneth McNeill Stewart. He says that his brother was turned down for the film *Cry, the Beloved Country*.

6 December. At 1, the humourless John Quansah produces a *Diary*, and immediately starts complaining about the fees: 8, guineas for a 10-minute Diary, 3 guineas for reading a story, not enough! Ogunkeye does not complain, reading with enjoyment "A Clash of Values," by one Gbola Aiyedun, about a Southerner's love for a beautiful Hausa girl in Kano. "He was a symbol of Western civilisation, beautifully dressed in sharkskin and a mauve tie. She fingered the pink telegram slip. 'A message from a rival?' she queried".

7 December. My 1000th recording – or thereabouts – since I started working for JGW in 1944. It was Beau Milton, rather appropriately, reading a typical heartless Ekwensi story about a Lagos street-woman, "Just because of Christmas." (Heartless? It may be that he is aware of the cruelty of the world.) Afterwards, over coffee, a long discussion with Beau on Eros and Agape, he is living with, or has even married, a prostitute. Then a set-to by telephone with Stephenson of Overseas Correspondence, about an "illiterate versifier" in Barbados. Edgar Mittelholzer comes in to record another story "A Plague of Kindnesses", a title which conveys his Nietzschean philosophy in a nutshell. We have a long argument on religion, a propos a vote in the Commons, against Sunday entertainment being included in the Festival of Britain.

8 December. Errol Hill reading very well an excellent account of a kite-fight by Barnabas Ramon Fortune, with technical names, *zwill* and *mange* (the powdered glass you stick to the cord, with which to cut your opponent's life line). It is so good that I send the script to *Children's Hour*.

12 December. At 200, Louise Bennett, with her rich chuckle, records an Anancy story. "Hear Anancy... Jack Mandora me no chose one".

13 December. George Lamming records some Christmas poems, collected through the year, partly because I want to help his Christmas. He seems more settled, moves around Bohemia, with his magnificent voice and appearance, not without impact. Disgusted by the goings on that he sees – lesbians in a houseboat off Chelsea Embankment. He is working away at his novel. [...] A call from Peter Pooley, now with the Crown Film Unit. They have a beautiful series of shots of the West Indies,

mangled by a pansy producer called John Hyde, and an ignorant scriptwriter, who does not know the Caribbean. I tell him of the five or six young writers who would give their eyes to be asked to write a narration... Over a cup of tea, he complains of the "wastage" in Government departments. [...] At the next table, Denis Williams,* with the critic John Berger, and Mary Treadgold, who talks of our moving to Bush House, a thing that JGW has not yet told me anything about. Williams is a small man, "high yellow", with a fine brow and exceedingly sensitive eyes. He talks of a genius called Wilson Harris,* a former land surveyor, who writes remarkable poetry.

31 December. Once more our heroine [Tirzah] is rising from her pain, no longer "abject", even writing letters. She recalls her early life in London. In 1930, she was vetoed as designer of the calendar of the Curwen Press, by the insidious Oliver Simon, who objected to her drawing of the Jewish girl Marina in Ivanhoe. Gerald Gould prevented Robert Gibbings from asking her to illustrate *The Private Life of a British Bluejacket.* The trouble is that they were partly right – her forté is realism, not imagination. She recalls Eric [Ravilious] saying, "Oh well, what does it matter". The male egotist... Yet Eric Gill and J. C. Squire were admirers, and her first etchings at the Engraving Society were singled out for praise in the *Times*. She went on to memories of 'Dad' Ravilious, who put his money behind the sink, and forgot that it was there.

[From VOLUME 4: 1st January 1951 – 31st December 1954]

1951
5 January. Record Cy Grant, who is out of work, and with his Irish wife, in deep psychiatric trouble. AET borrows £25. Gordon [Woolford], back from Paris, also without a job, takes £3...

11 January. George Collymore* reads, not very well, a brilliant little story "The Engagement" by Seepersad Naipaul. He says that Graham Hyslop actually flew out to Accra, to stage his East African play, but failed to find a cast. Incredible. He left after six weeks. Mrs Barrett, a friend of Eyo Ita, sounds and indeed looks, like a Communist. Lunch with George Lamming, very amicable, full of A. N. Whitehead. I tried to be tutorial, but found it difficult, with one so much deeper than myself. How can I really help these young wandering scholars find direction, when I have so little direction myself? George presents me with a paperback edition of [Whitehead's] *Adventures in Ideas*, as a New Year present. We walk in Regent's Park, and he tells me that a young

English composer, Graham Whettam, wants to set some of his poems to music.

12 January. In the train, decide to give up reading the life of Disraeli, by Moneypenny and Buckle, so much less interesting than Morley's *Gladstone*. Instead a collection of poems by Wilson Harris "Closets of Sunset," so highly praised by Denis Williams. An extraordinary archetypal talent lurking behind the usual tropical images. Where can his ideas come from? India? They prompted me to write a poem on the world, as I looked at it through the window, stiff and out of practice:

> My mind desires, in thickets trapped for long,
> The equal stress and freedom of a song,
> Whatever skies may cloak, or wide sea shields:
> The strict and lovely discipline of fields.
>
> Too long the lushness of the tropic flower
> Has bred in England in the arms of Power.
> Now comes the Winter that our harvest yields:
> The strict and lovely discipline of fields.
>
> Princes and peoples that in Time are dead,
> I say once more what you have often said,
> The strength that God our Father wields
> The strict and lovely discipline of fields.

17 January. Francis Nwokedi records a professional *Diary*, and comes to lunch with Betty, looking stronger. He is afraid of Nigerian trends: *prende qui peut*, no direction. Pauline [Henriques] looks in, fresh from a five months tour of Othello, where she played Iago's wife, because of Tynan's reading of the line:
 How if she be black and witty?

29 January. Once more at 200, Beau Milton looks in, with a dachshund on a lead. Rudolph Dunbar, full of beans. He has just written music for a film he is producing. "Terrific stuff, Henry".

3 February. Saturday, the one day we can assemble the seven actors, including Edric Connor, to rehearse the first part of the new verse play by Derek Walcott, *Henri Christophe*, the tyrant emperor of Haiti. It was cleverly adapted by Errol Hill, who does most of the production, bells clanging, seas surging, a "French crowd rioting". On the whole I

thought it more successful than the disastrous last poetic drama occasion. Edric, in the title part, was suitably emotional, at one stage almost too emotional, when he had to say, of the murdered Tousaaint "Because he was Black"... If the rival dictator Dessalines had been a little more flexible, and General Petion a little stronger, the whole thing would have been first rate.

8 February. In London, a problem over Edric Connor, who "longs" to read *Henri Christophe*. The problem is finance. We only have £38 for the programme, half of this from the saving on my "Summary". Of this, 15 guineas to Derek Walcott, £5.10 to Errol Hill for the adaptation, £2.10 each for the seven actors... But these things cannot be quantified, and Edric pleaded to be allowed to take the part. But now our own specialists weigh in, one Newman of Variety Bookings literally choking with rage down the line. The repeat performance **must** be given 15 guineas, which is anyway much less than the normal 25 guineas. At this rate, *Caribbean Voices* can never have Edric Connor again.

10 February. The second part of *Christophe* was not so good as the first, due to the emotionalism of Edric Connor, which ruined the level, not to speak of the sobriety of the verse. The whole script inevitably has a bad edge. There is an exceedingly unpleasant Archbishop Brelle (white). G. Collymore read him straight on rehearsal, but on the recording like a canting hypocrite, in such exchanges as this.

Brelle: This is the curse of the nation,
Eating your own stomach where the sickness is.
Your smell of blood offends the nostrils of God.

Christophe: Perhaps the smell of sweat under my arms
Offends that God too, quickening his white crooked nostrils.
Well, tell him after death that it is honest
As the seven wounds of blood broken on his flesh, tell him
The nigger smell, that even kings must wear
Is bread and wine to life.

During a break, Sam Morris came in waving a newspaper. "They are going to let Nkrumah out".

13 February. A play-back of *Christophe*, which sounded dreadful, far worse than imagined at the time. Poor Errol wrote a distraught letter. "The timing was terrible, Edric unspeakable." Quite apart from anything else, a Saturday morning is simply not enough time to realize a verse

play by a very young man, like nearly all poets with no instinctive sense of the theatre, or rather drama.

16 February. The usual *catalogue raisonnée* for the six monthly summary of the *Caribbean Voices*. 50 items, 22 short stories, 13 poetry programmes, 11 prose sketches, 3 critical talks, 2 plays... As an example of the trend, 18 of the 50 were by writers now in London... I dwelt on the "St Vincent school": [Shake] Keane, [Owen] Campbell, [Daniel] Williams.*

"The uncertain seine, a bundle of nerves, molests the sad sand..."

There was also Wilson Harris, and the Jamaican Simpson in New York:

"Far from your crumpled mountains, plains that vultures ponder..."

Or Roach in Tobago:

"Oh that we could carve open the stone skull of the dull time!"

Among the prose, a long extract from Barnabas Ramon Fortune, and his brilliant evocation of a kite fight:

"The two stood close to each other about the same level in the sky. The Dragon made a little rush, but went back to its former position like a boxer feinting at his opponent, but the red had already ducked. Now it was coming up slowly again. It paused for a little while, and made a dart at the Dragon. The Dragon swerved making an enormous loop low in the sky; then it rose, its yellow, snake-like head nodding jerkily from side to side, climbing up the sky. They stood for a long time close to each other, their tails, *zwills* shining, streaming out rigid behind them, almost, it seemed, like living things".

Finally, the victor, the kite belonging to the little boy Philip:

"As it sang to the brave altitudes, he could feel the vibration in the cord".

I was not able to give the pleasant news, just heard today that George Lamming made a successful reading of his poetry at the Institute of Contemporary Arts, where he was taken by Gloria Escoffery. He impressed Spender, who invited him to tea, and wants him to appear in a mid-century anthology...

23 February. Gordon Woolford records a story, "Nachofuchette(!)". He is back once more as a *plongeur* at Lyons. Calder-Marshall comments on it, and the story recorded yesterday by Sam Morris. He was, as usual,

full of "good" things, if you regard a pass made at a young RPA in a Bush House lavatory by Hugh Ross Williamson to be "good". He is writing a book on black magic, and listened to my brief memories of Aleister Crowley, the "wickedest man in the world". The "Loveday" in the book is Victor Newburgh, one of the main acolytes in the scandal at Cefalù in Sicily in the 20s. "Is it true that Crowley summoned the Devil to his pentagon in the Sahara, and turned you into a zebra for two years?" Other callers include MacJajah in a smart bowler, John Fig in search of an anthology, AET obsessional as ever on a BBC job…

1 March. A playback for Edric Connor, who apologizes after three years, for his non-arrival at the Theatre Group. "I was encompassed about by enemies at the time – I had even given myself up at Scotland Yard as a member of a subversive group". Such are the tensions of a simple artist in our time. […] Tonight [Tirzah] reads a comedy from W. W. Jacobs aloud. But the night is terrible as ever, the drugs failing, the ghastly awakening in the small hours, the realization that she is who she is, and where she, and what she has.

5 March. Edgar Mittelholzer's next book, *Children of Kaywana*, is full of sex – a woman "micturates" over the face of a sleeping rival, with a paragraph describing how it smelt etc. Gordon says that he fucked his woman every single night for a year, logging everything… Ogunkeye was simpler, with a story by Tim Aluko, about beggars in Lagos, Yoruba hymns, and *Ayo*, which is the word for Joy. JGW talks about Africa as "a fountain of new blood for Europe," and rejects my idea of its being a "stabiliser"…

7 March. George Lamming rang. Spender was kind, gave him tea, and said he would mention him in an article he is writing for *Picture Post*. The photographers visited him this morning. He says it is a "springboard." Ralph Currey closes the day at Oxford Street with a neat review of *Christophe*, *BIM*, Geoffrey Drayton, E. McG. Keane.

15 March. A disagreeable chore, producing Lewis Hastings, 'special broadcasts' to West Africa on the world political situation, commissioned by JGW, on behalf of Lillie-Costello, the Public Relations Officer in Accra. It seems to me entirely counter-productive, with the governing-class voice of Lewis savagely attacking the "all-powerful" dictator in Moscow. "Gutted with booty, he has again released his hordes… to enslave the rest of Europe"… It seems typical that he fails to mention (a) the Communists' tight control of dissident Negro intellectuals like Padmore; (b) the disappearance since the war of every non-Russian

republic or autonomous area in the line of the German advance. But what is the use? I was not consulted, all I am asked to do is to hold a stop watch... Lewis says that he bored with this kind of work, and seems much more interested in a short story he is contemplating, with a dragon hatched from an egg brought from Africa, eating a barmaid, who is not a virgin... Home to sad sights: Tirzah pale and tortured, Erskine [the cat] a grey neuter, the jolly cook ill from an overdose of aspirin.

18 March. Raining all day. When [Tirzah] was awake she told me that she has completed 41 models and paintings in the last few years (I think there more, over 50). She is sending in the Nicol portrait to the Royal Academy: and, perhaps foolishly, I wrote to Edward Bawden, who is on the hanging committee...asking him to look out for it.

19 March. Monday. A stimulating meeting with Barry Reckord,* who is reading English under Leavis at Cambridge. (Perhaps it was he who invited Lamming?) He is a friend of Gloria Escoffery, a little man, with a large head. Like all Jamaican intellectuals, he has not heard of *Caribbean Voices*, but unlike so many of them, he seems prepared to listen. He is interested in writing plays, and has a brother Lloyd* who wants to be an actor.

22 March. The small hours most pitiful, [Tirzah in] great tides of pain breaking over the Kon Tiki raft, and terrible groans, "What can I do? What can I do?" I feel washed out in the gale of her pain, the day knocked sideways. But life, work, must go on. Bumf, a lunch with Edgar Mittelholzer, to discuss the nature of Love. He has a new novel on the stocks, a sequel to *Kaywana*...

23 March. Good Friday. The District Nurse, a kind woman called Alderton from the North Country, comes to wash her. She says she thinks that she is "toxic" and comments that [Dr] Bradshaw, who comes so seldom can really have no idea of her suffering. She will ring him for new drugs, no doubt morphia, which means the point of no return.

26 March. Agony, to the small hours, when she stops crying, bathed in sweat. She was sick four times, the last green bile. An enema was wonderfully successful. Now she is empty, purified. They say that it is uraemia, that her kidneys have failed. It seems a blessing – the prospect of months more of this torture is not endurable. As Billy says, it is the blessing of Providence that she did not move to a hospital, where the bed was taken by someone else. Then she would have to die among

strangers. But what does it really matter now, to her? All day she lay silent with contorted face, rain beating on the pains. At 5, I went into Colchester for chloral, and a prescription for Mrs Withers. Returned to find Billy shaken, by two hours of groaning and cries. I mumbled useless endearments "Baby, Sweet Beast, Tirzie, Sweetie Pie, Lovie, Good Brute". She smiles, when I say that I would go down into hell for her again. When Billy said goodnight, the eyes, opened in four distinct fluttering movements, did not recognize her.

27 March. Woken around 2 by Sister Alderton, to find Tirzah in convulsions, with wide open wandering eyes, and a twitching face. We put through two calls to the unfortunate Bradshaw, who came at 0240, with his needle. At 0345 he was in the lounge, confirming that it was uraemia. We went back to her room, where she lay with the smell of eau de cologne all round her, the smell she has always disliked. Her eyes were strangely pale and luminous. I thought how beautiful she is, with her long thin face, strong nose, fine brow, beautiful eyes under brows like wings, the soft matted hair. Sister Alderton thought that Erasmus was her father! Her beautiful hands glistening with sweat. By 6, she was grey, face turned to the wall, breathing stertorously, and Sister Alderton thought the end was coming, and went for Billy. But it was a false alarm. When they left, I found myself on my knees, praying for what? A blank. Perhaps, that the picture would be accepted at the Academy. At 8.30, against my advice, Sister Alderton changed pyjamas, which were wringing wet with sweat. From the very depths of her spirit, in a deep, gruff voice, like a medium, she uttered the last words I ever heard from her in life. "Please, please." Her last communication – and it was not obeyed... As the door opened, she opened an eye. That was all. 09.40. A heavy cough. 10.15. Dr Bradshaw gives a new injection. She is making a long fight, on the sill of worlds. I think that it is really like witnessing the retreat of some great army. 11.40. The Vicar of Stanway gives us Communion in Lottie Hartle's room. 12. Christine came to take Anne to Bottengoms. Painful telephone calls, especially to Q, with whom, for so many reasons, and for the first and only time, my voice broke. 12.30. The brave heart falters and rallies. 15.05. Q comes, and I go down to talk to her. Hardly had we done so, when the nurse (not Sister Alderton) comes to say that she is gone. Poor Q! I cursed her under my breath, I have no need of her. But she meant well. We all mean well.

Back in Tirzah's room, we found the sunlight flooding, the first for weeks. She looked like some spring flower, a daffodil. Later, when she lay under the sheet, cotton wool in her nostrils, I thought how small she was – her body scarcely disturbs the smooth sheet. The room seems horribly empty, especially when we speak. Erskine, a ghost, hungry and perplexed. Down below, chores as anodyne: letters to *Times*, *Telegraph*, the undertakers. I write to Olive, Peggy Richards, Davidson, Mrs Hepher, Gray, the little boys. Memories, how she would say, "notabit" (all in one word). Sister Alderton says something that would have pleased her. She "went out more straight than I ever could have expected".

30 March. The day of the funeral. I learn that one does not weep for others, only for oneself. There were flurries of snow in the High Street when we went to pay our last visit behind Shephard's bolted door. After three days, she was marble, no longer wax, beautiful as ever, lying among soft white folds, all lines erased, no ugly blemish showing, a little rouge. I kissed her for the last time on the forehead, still the smell of eau de cologne, and the cotton wool delicately stopping her nostrils. [...] Just before setting out for the church, I went in to old Mrs Withers and pressed her hand – she has gone through the same ritual in the same house, the same church. Procession of ten cars, a slow drive by the catkins of the river. Beside family mourners, Q and Eve, who really loved and admired her. Peggy Richards, Olive and Edwin (who looked very ill), Percy Horton, Davidson, Sibby Morgan, Ariel, Flavia, two Rothensteins, two Rowntrees, two Bawdens, two Aldridges, Susannah, Dorothy, Mrs Garrett-Smith, Mr Geere, Fred Irvine, the dear fellow, and most of the staff, Mrs Prior, Mrs Palmer, Barbara and Elsa. John R. sat bolt upright, eyes fixed ahead. When we reached Copford Plains, the site praised by Matthew Arnold a hundred years ago, the sun broke through the clouds, it was almost vernal, rooks soaring over the trees. The organist played "I know that my Redeemer Liveth". Everyone seemed touched when we sang "Now the Day is Over." While they were lowering the coffin into the deep grave, I saw that they had got her name wrong, Ellen Lucy... The flowers were beautiful, mostly yellow, with some beautiful and rare ones from the Aldridge garden, and wreaths from the president and council of the RAS, the Colonial Service of the BBC. As we walked away, a swan reared on its hind legs, furiously biting at a lop-eared white spaniel, barking outside the sexton's house... Most came to tea, although the London party departed by the 4.18. Then Johnny packed us into the car for Coggeshall, where again we had a kind of wake, without alcohol. Marchant Holliday rang up to say how James had received the news. He was as usual full of praise and advice. I should apply to the RAF Benevolent Fund right away. "But Eric was in the Royal Marines"... Drinks at the Swan with Francis Lamb.

31 March. To break the tension, I went up to London, to lose myself in work (although most of the recordings this week were made by others).

At lunch, JGW, John Fig, AET Henry. [...] Then to Helen Wilson, a little distant, with exchanges over the peace petition, China, the atom bomb, the possibilities of an independent British form of communism.

13 April. At the office, Lamming reads some poems by Roach very well indeed. Cy Grant records a story about vampires, "Apologia de Lucio", by one Malcolm [?]. At lunch, Chris Cilliers says that he has heard from Hetta [Empson], who seems less enthusiastic about the Communists – the pressures after Korea must be enormous.

16 April. At the office, held the stopwatch for two more of Lewis Hastings' anti-Communist broadsides. Perhaps it is as well that they can only be heard in the Gold Coast.

20 April. At 200, a fiasco, the result of under-production, not enough time. Gloria Escoffery, who dislikes the Mittelholzer *Kaywana* novel, was to debate it with Marghanita Laski, who praised it so excessively in the *Observer*. There was a lunch, and three quarters of an hour discussion afterwards: Gloria dried up... On the other hand Errol Hill read an excellent story by George Phillips, "Witches Brew." [...] I told Erroll, and young Michael Manley, who was with him, that I was glad that I had no administrative responsibility. [...] The Academy have turned my darling down. Perhaps the portrait of Davidson <u>was</u> a little wooden...

24 April. Changes in the Caribbean. Ken Ablack is to be BBC representative in Trinidad. Sabine's firm Rediffusion are offering £1000 a year towards the £250,000 required for "sustaining" government programmes in their nine stations. He is now a manager of the Rediffusion board, so he was probably negotiating with them at the time he was supposed to be keeping them out...

Ah well. I turn to Patrick Leigh Fermor's *Travellers Tree*, mannered in the style of the Sitwells, but charming in the evocation of the French Antilles, and very accurate in description – the violent American neck-ties, for instance, like "lanced ulcers". No mention, of course, of any indigenous writing... In the afternoon, John Akar* reads a story by Willy Conton,* "The Orange Seller". He is a tall and handsome young Syrian-African, reeking of scent. Born in Rotifunk in the Sierra Leone Protectorate, he has been studying in Ohio and at Berkeley. He seemed over-anxious to please, "just a poor black boy"; and has ambitions in Films – he was given an audition by Rank, and asked to read *De Profundis*, "a favourite of mine".

25 April. At the office, [...] Jonathan Vincent* looks in, the crazy Sierra Leonean writer, a slight man, with a sweetish smell about him – it

may have been anxiety. He is a fugitive from the Peterborough brickyards, and a white Messalina, who, he said, married him.

6 May. Sunday in Bedford, and work on Africa. [...] The Ersingers came to tea, and Aunt Norah describes the overnight conversion of the residents of "Woodland" after the TV programme on the South Bank... Incredible power of the new medium. [...] In Hel's *Catholic Herald*, an appeal by the Mill Hill Fathers for recruits to go "into the very heart of Satan's Empire, the vast pagan lands of Africa".

7 May. Lloyd Reckord, a brash young Jamaican actor, reads a story by his brother Barry, "Dancer", very well. His ambition is burning and infectious. At tea, a very different person, a charming, diffident Chinese artist from Trinidad, Carlisle Chang,* a friend of Gloria Escoffery.

16 May. Jonathan Vincent reads a piece on "The Life of the Mendi", by Marcus Jones. Beecham, the Town Clerk of Kumasi, to whom I give lunch, contributes a *Diary*. Most of the day is spent on typing the "Notes", seven hours in all, including the evening. A tailor writes to enquire whether it would be safe to give Gordon Woolford £36 credit. Regretfully, I give a truthful answer, in the negative. I must make up for it, by finding him a little more work.

21 May. Work, work, work. "Notes," the schedules, an excellent reading by Seth [Jectson]* of a bloodthirsty little story by one Adamafio, "I Killed My Uncle", a deathbed confession which reads like autobiography. JGW is preparing his talk to Hancock's seminar on "Communism in Africa". He may, or may not, be assisted by a contribution from John Akar, who has no doubt been approached by agents of the Comintern.

22 May. Sam Morris comes in to read "A Brotherly Tear" by Bob Jakes.* After lunch, he is photographed with Pauline, George Lamming, Valerie Bolton, and Lloyd Reckord, for some publicity in Jamaica.

23 May. Denis Williams and Jan Carew came in unexpectedly, and we held a long conversation over coffee. Carew dislikes the Babalola translations sent to him in Holland, and Williams agrees. They "lack the anguish" of some pygmy poems. They agreed not at all with my theory of the artist as "recognizer", not as prophet, coming at the end of a period, not the beginning. How does that tie up with Williams' prophetic pictures, his belief in Wilson Harris? He said emphatically, "We come at the end of nothing". I suggested "Africa", but he said that this does not apply to the modern Caribbean. When I said that we did

not have space in the programme for the discussion, Carew was silent, like a hurt baby.

27 May. Spent the night with the Furses. [...] They had with them the Pagets, a handsome young man who had a nervous breakdown in the war, and his sister Caroline [Lady Caroline Paget], who, it was said, caused the death of Rex Whistler. The two babies seemed happy, thanks to the devoted Swiss girl Rose-Marie. The latter is to be succeeded by a Dutch girl, Henriette Van Eeghen, tall and golden, a kind of Cranach Madonna, very proud of her grandfather, who expelled the ex-Kaiser Wilhelm from his garden at Doorn.

4 June. Louise Bennett reads "The Black Bull" by Edgar Boyce (not as well as she interprets her own). Sam Selvon, a story of his own, "Pandee Pays a Visit." He was charming, and seems happy, life panning out quite well for him, I hope. At lunchtime, I. Idris from Lagos, "interested in literature" – he had not heard of *West African Voices*, or of the West African Society, or of the Cudjoe outfit, or of Ekwensi, much less Fiawoo or Danquah. What had he heard of? [Ruskin's] *Sesame and Lilies*.

5 June. Lunch and a walk round St James Park with Clifford Sealy.* He is not a Communist but inclined that way for rather special reasons. "Whenever I see an English uniform, man, I think of it keeping us Colonials down by force." The Party gives status – and a quick approach to white women...

7 June. George Lamming records a story by the interesting Marjorie Brown,* "When the Clouds in the South are Red." A visit from Akinsemoyin,* a rich, introverted, rather sad Yoruba student, who talked of a beloved sister, who died in France six years ago, of tuberculosis contracted in a concentration camp. He left a novel, based on her story. Another caller, the tall and graceful Sierra Leone schoolmaster, Willy Conton, who said that the programme is making headway in Freetown. He is West Indian on both sides, a Bermudan missionary father, a mother from Antigua. [...] Back at 200, Lewis Hastings concludes his diatribes for the Gold Coast. He says that Kenneth de Courcy put up a scheme some years ago to "squeeze Africa and the Africans dry". In the *Standard*, there is a pen portrait of Guy Burgess, the FO man, thought to have fled to Russia. It reads very like me: highly strung, friend of artists, member of the Gargoyle, dresses informally, has outspoken views on his superiors...

8 June. Calder-Marshall in to criticise two items in the *Voices*, and interesting on the news of the day. He knows Goronwy Rees, the friend of Burgess, a beautiful son of the people, who had a homosexual phase, "but he did his duty by Lizzie Bowen later on". Now he works three hours a day in an engineering firm that also contains Henry Green, and devotes the rest of the time to novel writing. As for his own work, Calder has finished the book about Crowley, and is starting on the tale of a modern Christ, crucified by the BMA, and given shock treatment. [...] More recordings in the afternoon, until 7. Angela Christian with some little Gold Coast sketches, Georges Rozan ("Le saison bat son plein"), Lloyd Reckord hamming "The Bougainvillea Flower", by John Wickham.

13 June. Mercedes with a *Diary*. Jan Carew, ambiguous as ever, with that curious fixed smile. He had an awful story of panic flight from some white youths down a railway siding in the USA.

14 June. 36, and at a low ebb. What have I achieved in the last six years? A tiny dint in my egotism, a growing realization of my own limitations. [...] Work from 18.00 to 21.00 at the house, which is slowly coming back into shape, after the dust sheets. A hot bath at 1.22, and sleep without nightmares. But what a parasite I am.

15 June. At 200, Gordon Woolford reads "This is Home," by Vidia Naipaul, a sharp story by a son of Seepersad, who is coming to England on an island scholarship in English. A journalist called Cary reports the conference given by Nkrumah. In the afternoon, I recovered the last of Tirzah's pictures from West on Rosslyn Hill – he admired the picture of the cat and Annie's brickhouse, and said that his own wife had died of cancer, although she was 70 when she went.

27 June. At the office, Mrs Ronke Dougherty, a formidable black battle-axe, with a *Diary*, and Willy Richardson, with a sexy piece about the beach by Karl Sealy,* "The Cool of the Day." He says that W. J. Locke, of *Beloved Vagabond* fame, came from Trinidad. The garden party, organised by Mercedes and her friend, the handsome Peggy Chalk, was a great success. [...] The dances started with the South – two Bechuana, and two Zulu, Mahu and Ngcobo, almost naked, with white wool at knee and elbow, lithe and beautiful and insolent, as they capered among the tables, watched by Wilhelmina Ness with disapproving eyes. The Gold Coast scene that followed, was painfully slow by comparison: miming of bad-tempered old men among the fishing nets, libations of gin poured on the earth, a ritual dance. It lasted 35 minutes, which

was 15 minutes too long, and there was a crisis with one of the leading ladies, the temperamental Miss Lomotey, who complained that Cudjoe's society had not been properly credited. But it had its charm under the acacia tree, with the public looking over the RGS wall. [...] It was hard to come from all this to Adelaide Road, and very unpleasant, to go through Tirzah's papers, mostly letters to her children, every one stamped with her own peculiar mark. But it makes me feel her near me, and Eric as well, whom I never knew. And who has been such an awkward presence in the background. As I sort his letters, I wonder whether he ought not to have an artistic executor. What about Bawden, his friend, who has plenty of storage space in his Bardfield home?

3 July. At 200, JGW is hot on "regional culture" – he has taken to marking the scripts as they come from Mrs Lindo, for the first time in 5 years... This is apparently an offshoot of C. Y. Carstairs, who is excited by the (mediocre) examples we played back to him. "The most important items that we have heard on this course". After four years in the Caribbean, the good Charles had never even heard of *Caribbean Voices*, which by now must have broadcast nearly 3000 separate items, in 450 separate programmes. A prophet is not without honour... Still, I made three recordings today, in better heart. Pauline reads a story "The Leotta" by one Fitzgerald [Alex], and comes to lunch, where I learn that she is now working for the WEA, with the thirty men in her class all with mother-complexes. [...] Returning by 31 bus through Paddington and Kilburn, I am amazed by the <u>crowds</u> of black people, and the white children jitterbugging, chewing gum.

5 July. Sheila Clarke reads a story by [Barnabas] Ramon Fortune, "A Silver Piece," and Gordon Woolford "The Shakers", a piece of religious folklore by Daniel Williams, one of the St Vincent poets.

6 July. Calder-Marshall criticises the Ramon Fortune and Fitzgerald stories, for the first time a little unfair to the writers, even in my opinion misunderstanding them at certain points. This may come from his own desperate financial straits.

9 July. Sam Selvon came to read a story by Seepersad Naipaul, "Obeah". Great news, he has sold his novel *Never Burned the Sun So Bright* [later published as *A Brighter Sun* (1952)] to Allen and Wingate, who are enthusiastic.

12 July. Went again to say goodbye to Terry, but although her name was on the carriage window, she wasn't inside. Others there, Louise

Bennett, and two I know from West Africa. [...] At the office, an irritating time with Stephen Spender, who arrives a quarter of an hour before the recording, with the announcement that the one copy of the script, written in long-hand, had been sent to "George Lamming, West Indian Section, Bush House". He suggests an interview, and when I modestly say that they were not easy, kindly remarks "I can write the questions for you"... All the time, he was talking to a BBC executive about the Burgess imbroglio and the Italian village where he was staying, when the news broke. "All the village is on my side. I am going back there this week. I find I can write poetry (sic) there". While waiting for the fake interview, he never looked at Caribbean material, to refresh his memory (if indeed he had read it) but only at a new volume of Cavafy. A detestable person. With his broad, flushed, stupid, almost honest, entirely self-righteous face. (But in writing all this, it has to be said that I have in the past made several foolish approaches to him on my own account, a fact that he may possibly have remembered, to justify him.) All the same, I noted that he took the last cigarette from a packet offered him without hesitation. His comments were general in the extreme, but he is a name which will go down well in the Caribbean papers.

13 July. Gordon Woolford reads a story, "Suspicion." I note that the last six monthly summary was not reprinted in any West Indian paper. I wonder why. Perhaps it was bad, perhaps it did not contain any of the big names now appearing.

17 July. At BH, a lunch for West Indian journalists, clumsily conducted by Tom Beachcroft, who writes short stories. A radical from Barbados called Mapp, a sad-eyed man from Guiana called Willock, the three Heads of Service, Willy Richardson (who has got the Ablack job) and myself. Then after a sun-bathe in the park, to produce Seth Jectson, reading by a new Ibo, Kiea Epelle,* on the usual West African theme of the Old Cults versus Christianity, with the balance for the former, "O Mother's God."

20 July. A pleasant tea with Bob Le Page,* a young English Lit. specialist at the University of the West Indies. Inclined to be arrogant, he quickly thawed. He had not heard of Vivian Virtue or Michael Smith, still less of Seymour or Roach.

26 July. Sam Morris reads an account of seine fishing in Tobago (!) by one Vincent Bowles. Lunch at the RES, where I talk to Sally Chilver [Elizabeth Millicent Chilver], whom I knew at Oxford as the epigrammatic Miss Graves, a stringy, charming girl-boy, now involved at a high level

in Colonial sociology. We go on to hear Schapera discourse on "Witchcraft in Bechuanaland." Back to 200, to record Le Page making an analysis of the one West Indian writer he knows, Derek Walcott, in "A Packet for Eros".

14 August. "Notes" again. At coffee, Sidney Carter, a friend of Le Page, a poet aged 36, who resigned from the British council to write a novel, and is now "studying folklore round the world", hoping for a grant from somewhere. We got on very well.

15 August. A tea for African trainees, and JGW at his worst, playing the big man, and losing his temper with Sheila Stradling, who would not play her part as big man's acolyte.

17 August. Hammered out the summary of the last six months in *Caribbean Voices*, starting with Mittelholzer's third novel, *Shadows Move Among Them*, and George Lamming's more esoteric success at the ICA with Spender. Then Selvon's sale of *Never Burns the Sun So Bright*. Then, the first story by Seepersad Naipaul's son Vidia, "This is Home", with a sharp family scene leading to the climactic line of the husband: "He was not ashamed anymore, he was telling himself. And yet he could feel that he was lying". In the poetry, there was Roach:

> Once naked in the wood
> Their hot green rhythms wrote
> A native rhyme and story,
> A saga that was good.

There are also the St. Vincent school, with their islands, "a stark chain of unresolved Calvaries" (Keane). I also quoted from an account of a dying wife by Hugh Blackman "Looking into his wife's brown eyes, he saw a deep well of shimmering brown gems. Beautiful gems, formed two brown orbs, descending lower and lower into the well of her very being"...

21 August. Young Michael Manley recounts some of the details of the Jamaican hurricane, leaving me without words. Record Errol John* on "Five Rivers".

28 August. At 200, Vivian Virtue reads poems by five Jamaican poets, including himself, assembled for the victims of the hurricane. A sensitive, small man, with a touching loyalty to his Gods, Tom Redcam, Langston Hughes.

29 August. Once more a mass recording of 11 Nigerian local authorities, including the inevitable joker. In the afternoon, Macjajah, with the first of his trilogy, which reads like an inventory: "Because he (she, they) went abroad". We made quite a good job of his account of the deserted village maiden, played by Doris Akuro, a little cockney girl of mixed blood, who has been touring for the last two years in a play appropriately enough called "Blood". At first I did not take to her, but she responded to production, and at the end she was kind of enough to say that I had given her more confidence than any producer she has met so far. Pauses for discussions with the Prince on the morals of his hero, who only fails to seduce his pupil at the school "because of the trouble," and who in England, regards the RAF mainly as a place in which to make money. Later in the afternoon, a meeting of the West African Writers and Artists Club at the Imperial Institute. Routine speeches by Cudjoe, Jones-Quartey, Fagg, and the young sculptor Tamakloe, on proverbs, linguists' sticks, etc. The general discussion, as ever, turned to the difference between "primitive" and "tribal", the clash between aesthete and anthropologist.

11 September. At tea, Jan Carew, whose novel has been rejected, of course "for political reasons"! His present Egeria is Rosey Pool, a Dutch woman who runs a travel agency.

18 September. Cyprian Ekwensi to lunch, the Ibo writer, like a mask from Aro Chukwu, long, distinguished, scalloped face, exceedingly tense, reminding me, in attitude only of Mittelholzer. One feels he will succeed in life. He is in England on a pharmacy scholarship, but his only real interest is writing. At tea, another young man of talent, V. S. Naipaul, in revolt against the Oxford School of English. He is small and wiry, with a handsome, sensitive, discontented face. I asked him about his father Seepersad. As I suspected, he is a Brahmin, but not well endowed with this world's goods. At least his son will be getting a far better chance in life. I offer to do what I can to let him escape from the groves of Academe from time to time. This was at 200.

22 September. Supper with Pauline in her new flat off the Bayswater Road. A charming young English actor, who has been with her in the touring *Othello*: nothing nicer than a young actor, nothing nastier than an old one. [...] Pauline has an improving story of half an ox, sent to her husband Neville by an American gentleman who admired his torso in *Anthony and Cleopatra*.

25 September. In the afternoon, I made a careful visit to the South Bank, using the guide. Festival of Britain. What is Britain? I took in most things, apart from the Physics in the Dome, but the image that remains is very limited, clear, material. [...] When the ice cap melts, all land in Europe below a 100 feet, bordering the sea, will be flooded... Far more space is devoted to the Polar regions than the Tropics. They have clearly written off the Empire and the Commonwealth.

26 September. Mercedes on McGill University, for her *Diary*. One wonders whether a white ex-patriate should act as the ears and eyes of West Africa in London, but she does it so much better than anyone else I know, of either race, of either sex. At tea, Neville Dawes, a sensitive Jamaican, who writes stories and poetry, and is thinking of working in the Gold Coast, perhaps in some higher centre if there are any on literature.

27 September. Tea with John Fig, Willy and JGW, Fig just back from Jamaica, where there is a ban on using dollar credits, and general complaints about the shoddy goods provided by the "Mother Country", cars, textiles, everything but whiskey. (It occurs to me that this general atmosphere may also motivate literary attitudes). There is also a general suspicion of *Caribbean Voices*. "What department is this man Swansky attached to?"

2 October. At 200, Denis Williams and Jan Carew discuss art, the foil against the sabre. Jan is to provide another torso for the Olivier company...

12 October. At the RAS, Heather despondent about the future. She showed me a Ponsonby memo to Daryll Forde, who had asked for a list of subscribers to *African Affairs*. The vulture poised over the kill? It would not be so bad, if *Africa* provided anything like the service of the Journal. MacMillans want to see a copy, (they published it before it went to Baylis). Archer Cust, secretary of the RES, had never even heard of the "Notes"...Straws in the wind, Ponsonby refers to "Mr Swanzy finding a more lucrative (sic) post in which to display his undoubted talents".

15 October. JGW on leave. I find four Gold Coast radio trainees next door, and take them down to lunch: an oily little man, [Kobla Emmanuel] Senayah,* the punctilious Amarteifio, little Mrs Florence Prah,* big Marian Smith-Mensah. At 3 some Nigerians, also trainees, incensed because their talks are not being recorded. The usual story, inadequate or non-existent briefing by JGW. After ringing round, the whole thing is cleared up, their talks <u>are</u> to be recorded.

16 October. Pauline records a story "Disillusion" by Rupert Meikle.* She has had a letter from a friend of hers, a doctor in an RAF camp outside Singapore, who regularly listens to *Caribbean Voices*, at 7.30 on Monday mornings! One should tell this to the engineers. She talked about her life with her first husband, Jeff Henneberry, an ardent member of the Party (he worked for Pearl Assurance, whose office in Holborn is on the site of the First International, from which Marx used to launch his thunderbolts).

17 October. Gold Coast recording, with an excellent script (Amarteifio, Senayah, Prah, Smith-Mensah). Nigerians, the reverse (Ladan, Fadayiro, Faneye, Atuona, Alakija). One difference is that ZOY has been functioning much longer than Lagos. I wonder whether Chalmers realises the quality of the people sent here.

20 October. Florence Prah and Ogunkeye record poems by Babalola, Akinsemoyin, and Efua. As it happens, I have to read the best and most sensual of all, a poem by my sweet Gold Coast girl torn between body and spirit, called "The Redeemed." As I read it, I felt remorseful. But there is so much to regret. Lunch with Errol Hill, who is wearing a violent pistachio coloured tie, with domino spots. I feel like asking him why the picture of Louise Bennett adorns to-day's *Daily Worker*. In the afternoon, down to Bedford. The apple tree, barely two years old, has borne at least forty apples, excellent, Cox's Orange pippins.

24 October. Cyprian Ekwensi comes in to make his first contribution *in propria persona*, an odd sketch "From My Porthole", full of bowels and brothels, his idea of England. He says that he has written a story about the leopard men for the editor of *Wide World*, who has a passion for such things.

25 October. I swim with the tide, and vote for Henry Brooke, the Tory candidate in Hampstead; but the Labour man Richardson is a blind worm, and Watson the liberal a joke. One among 26 million, very important. The fact is, I am too egotistic to support any party but my own, and that is rather disorganised at the moment. I prophesy that the Tory majority will be between 40 and 50 (not inaccurately). [...] In the evening, the first of what I hope may be something useful, a *causerie de jeudi* (but I have no female to run my salon). The flat looks very cosy and attractive, with Tirzah's screen shutting off the window, and the front room discreetly appearing through the folding door. Quite a number of writers, West Indian and West African came: Richardson, Mittelholzer, Selvon, Lamming, Figuroa, Denis Williams; Davidson

Nicol, Ekwensi, Babalola, Adisa Williams,* Peter Abrahams. I also brought along Faneye, the Nigerian engineer, who was at a loose end. All they got to set them off were buns, orange pippins, beer, cider, ginger wine, orangeade. It sounds absurd. And in fact, it proved hard to mix the two groups, although Ekwensi looking so like an Ekei head, got on well with Willy Richardson, and Babalola with Denis Williams. The West Indians stayed longer than the others, in an amusing discussion on social morality. Of those invited, Gordon Woolford, Virtue, Drayton and de Paiva could not come.

26 October. In the evening, the Cudjoe Club held a meeting at Hans Crescent, to listen to Rosey Pool on "American Negro Poetry," and I found myself to my embarrassment in the chair. There were 20 people there, 5 of them African (they included Babalola, Ekwensi and Adisa Williams). As Miss (Mrs?) Pool talked, a continuous procession of young Africans tiptoed by, to and from the sports room (ping pong). I suppose one could scarcely blame them. From my strategic position behind a pot of chrysanthemums, I could watch the comedy, as Rosey gallantly puffed and blew, with quotations about lynching and the burden of Afro-American identity. On the whole, her talk was better than I had expected. In the front row beneath her, the beautiful Millington-Drake, and the insignificant Willems. During the discussion, the main voice was that of Jan Carew, until a very smooth, handsome older man, the colour of coffee, revealed himself as Cedric Dover, the friend of Nancy Cunard, and the hero of the salons in the 30s.

1 November. A letter from Efua. She was dining with two District Commissioners in Kumasi, when the poetry programme came over the box. She says that my reading of "The Redeemed" "electrified" them, but I think that she was extending to them her own reaction. Curious ways of love. [...] John Fig reads "Nature Unpredictable", a story about a nature walk, rather well told by a St Vincent writer called [Bob] Jakes. George Lamming reads in a little programme on West Indian poets in the Gold Coast. They are the only two to come to the second Thursday evening. Decidedly I am not St. Beuve.

5 November. Mercedes took me to see the Afro-American dancer Pearl Primus, who had had very poor notices. One found her... energetic.

6 November. George Lamming records a truly admirable reminiscence called "Birthday Weather", which reminds me of *Dubliners*. Otherwise trying to find a frame for Tirzah. In the evening, George Weiden[feld] [...] He also said that should be on the Committee for the Defence of

Cultural Freedom, founded by Koestler and subsidised by the Pentagon. President: Spender. Secretary: Amery. Treasurer: Michael Godwin. Members: Calvocoressi, J. Lehmann, Weidenfeld...

7 November. Cyprian Ekwensi records a bloodcurdling story by Kiea Epelle, "The War is Done." The hero lusts for blood, his dog, which he brought to market to sell for food, is cut in two with a matchet, a Tribal war is brought to an end by an old woman wielding the ceremonial chalk of peace. We follow with a discussion: should the gory, "heroic" past be given expression in this way? It was clear where Cyprian's sympathies lay. I think of Proust, on the superior spiritual energy of the barbarian.

8 November. For the third Thursday evening, only one writer turned up, Cyprian Ekwensi. Fortunately Gavin looks in, with a friend Eunice Frost from Penguin, and they plied him with questions about Nigeria, which he answered with wonderful shrewdness. So the venture is not totally useless.

9 November. At the office, an instructive day, watching Reggie Smith, that large teddy bear from Birmingham produce Walcott's latest verse play *Harry Dernier*, the end of the world. It consists mainly of a soliloquy on lust and death and God, delivered by Errol Hill exceedingly well, with Betty Linton, Reggie's girlfriend, I think, in support. Almost the best thing was the control studio, where Reggie presided like a submarine commander. Two young technicians, who had recorded the effects the day before – crinkly paper for fires etc. [...]. Noel Vaz* also appeared, McAlpine and his wife, Dylan Thomas... The last was loud in praise of Errol's acting, and told us in The Stag later that MacNeice had said to him "They don't come any better". Suitably sybilline praise. Reggie was in his element, enthusiastic on his recipe for getting "vultures" out of "seagulls". "Simply by slowing the speed down, dear boy".

13 November. At the office JGW tries to keep me tied to my adolescent tail, by repeated personal enquiries. Possibly some of them are kindly meant, but the general line is clear, conscious or unconscious. Poor Henry, a cross between Ariel and Caliban, kept in thrall by Prospero. Lunch with Rex Moorfoot, a steely eyed young blonde man, who talks with longing of the New York office, now vacant. "You're putting in for it, of course?" He is genuinely astonished when I say that I will plug away at *African Affairs*. With all its drawbacks, surely it is more significant than anything being done by any single person in Overseas Radio? I think this more than ever after a talk with Mary Treadgold,

who is spending a great deal of time on a book by Angela Thirkell...
At 18.00, record Seth Jectson, reading a Cameroons story by Nchami.

15 November. Errol John reads another item connected with the Jamaica hurricane, "Cloud Burst" by Kenneth Newton.* There is better attendance at the *causerie*, to which I have added a bottle of gin as an inducement... John Fig and George Lamming in animated discussion, with Babalola a silent third. We listened to a compilation by Edwin Muir, including Marvell's beautiful "Nymph on the Death of a Fawn," which I hoped made some impact on the young Nigerian, with his different approach to killing deer. I read to them *The Rite of Spring*, and Babalola, Spender on the express train. When I tried reading Betjeman, I had to desist, because GL 'cannot abide him'... John Fig, for some reason, read aloud the anti-semitic outbursts by T. S. Eliot ("Bleistein with a Cigar"). The discussion that followed was lively. It was joined by Fred Uhlman, with a long monologue recalling a meeting at which Emmanuel Litvinoff had attacked the great man. Fig has a Jewish grandmother, all Fred's family died in the gas chambers. We went on to less debatable themes. Lamming reading Lorca very beautifully in Spanish, and I trying my hand at some of Goethe's lyrics. "Über allen Gipfeln ist Ruh..." [...] They left at 11, after a very stimulating 3½ hours, and I went up to a small party at the Reas, which seemed in the doldrums – a cold young man, whom I diagnosed as a Communist.

16 November. At the office, Arthur Calder-Marshall listens to Gordon read an excruciatingly bad story by Harrison Lloyd,* "The Porter Incident", and then crucifies it in a criticism that made us laugh as much as the story had done, with its naïve snobbism, and really "deplorable values." Is this fair? One has such strange indirect effects, at times.

19 November. At the office, Jonathan Vincent, who has been picketing and waving placards in the Park, writes to ask me to assemble Joad, Huxley, and the "scatterbrains of Oxford and Cambridge" to examine his writings, and certify his genius.

21 November. At the office AET says that the twenty-five West Indians now studying at Cambridge regularly listen to the *Voices*, and were all delighted when Calder tore strips off the unfortunate Harrison Lloyd.

22 November. In the evening, the *causerie*, attended by the faithful three, Ekwensi, John Fig, George Lamming, accompanied by a young lady from the Institute of Education Miss Hoyt, the daughter of medical missionaries in Katanga. They talked mainly of death and cemeteries.

23 November. Rosey Pool's programme on Negro Poetry, with George Lamming, who spoke brusquely, "like a king," as the RPA remarked. It sounded better than one might have expected, with curious traditional songs, like this from the southern Sudan, very cleverly inserted.

> Clear out! Fly off! The stork is King.
> The holy bird of birds, it is the stork.

Later in the afternoon, a different offering: Vivian Virtue, reading poems by Neville Dawes, Owen Campbell and A.N. Forde.* The little man is going back soon to Jamaica, I hope converted to a kinder view of Swansky [sic].

25 November. Sunday. I find by the evening that I must have typed 50,000 words of the memoir on Tirzah. It seems sad that it must not see the light of day, until perhaps all are dead who figure in it. The references to people like Bawden are really too cruel, marked by the sharp childish eye, that concentrates on one or two facets of a character.

26 November. Supper with the Furses, whom I succeeded in cheering up, even for a time reconciling. Drinks at The Antelope, with the nice Dutch girl Tid, a real *coeur simple*, I think. Elisabeth is full of the theory that the missing dipomats, Burgess and Maclean, have been bumped off by the *Deuxieme Bureau*.

3 December. More and more, the work at the African Society, obscure and ill-paid though it is, is still immeasurably more significant than the treadmill at the BBC, where both *Caribbean Voices* and *West African Voices*, not to speak of *Calling Mauritius*, are falling into uninspired routine. In the case of the Caribbean, this is a good sign. The promising writers are concentrating on the only real literary labour, that which ends in the achievement of a published book.

5 December. A letter from Harrison Lloyd, to complain that he did not know that Calder's vivisection of his story was going out. Just as well. The two poems he encloses are as bad as the prose. [...] The West African Arts Club organised a concert for Beryl McBurnie's Little Carib Theatre at the Chelsea Town Hall. A sweet little dancer Cecile Maurice, Louise Bennett, splendid and bulging in a close purple gown, Carlisle Chang, very graceful and supple, with the charm of Walter Crisham, a Calypsonian from Grenada called Peter Ricardo. Alas, Miss McBurnie, rather ungainly and angular, an East Indian school marm, took up nearly an hour of the time with a lecture demonstration, reminding

me a little of a female Mittelholzer. In the audience, [...] Featherstone, the Nigerian High Commissioner, who stiffened at la McBurnie's bitter comments on Anglo-Saxon philistinism.

6 December. Visits from Gordon Woolford, and Lloyd Reckord, who had danced rather clumsily at Chelsea, and cursed the lack of co-ordination between West Indians. It was a Thursday, and Gavin Ewart came to supper. After a long interval, George Lamming arrived with John Fig, bringing two friends, a sharp young white teacher from Jamaica, and a painter who never opened his mouth. John was in good form, having just addressed the Newman Society on the *Voices*. An East Indian woman teacher in Wales, reciting "La Belle Dame Sans Merci." The discussion developed very well, with John urging regional claims and George the internal proletariat, and personality.

19 December. Someone with a monocle from Admin, and an inspector from the CID, looked in during the morning to enquire about Jonathan Vincent, who is to appear at the West Kensington Court on Saturday on various "serious charges", using two food ration cards, concealing BBC earnings from Public Assistance (who give him the princely dole of £2.8d a week). The inspector said that deportation is impossible from Britain, only from Sierra Leone. Later the suspected criminal arrived, without an overcoat, clothes grubby, and held forth on his father, Churchill, and Jesus Christ. "I am the Way"... I gave him a miserable 10/-, reflecting that he had come to collect his fees for script and reading, which should tide him over. There is something intensely pathetic about the guinea he spent on the book on physics, the half guinea for the loose-leaved notebook.

20 December. At the office, Gloria Vaz, rather hoity-toity about a sentimental Christmas poem, by Barnabas Ramon-Fortune. (Partly, no doubt, it is the rivalry of Jamaica and Trinidad.) Edgar Mittelholzer gives me lunch at Cathay, another Chinese restaurant, more authentic perhaps than Freddy Mills. He is riding high, the nice gaunt fanatic. 24,000 copies of *Shadows* have been sold in the USA, mainly through a Book Club. It is being translated into French. Moss Hart has offered a huge sum for the dramatic rights.

1952
1 January. Started the New Year by sewing a button on my overcoat, with fawn thread, which I inked over. Then to produce Adisa Williams, reading a poem on New Years Eve by Chijioke, held over since 1950.

[...] Errol Hill brings in a dozen friends to hear the play-back of *Harry Dernier*, ultimately indigestible but he is very good in it.

4 January. Louise Bennett reads a lively Anancy story, to the edification of Calder-Marshall, who records a comment on it, and the story read yesterday by Errol Hill. Sometimes, as the bottom of the barrel appears, one feels that the only purpose of the programme is to provide money for needy literati...

7 January. At the office, JGW has received a letter from Vincent, demanding £225,000 for his manuscripts, which were sent to me on spec... I had to collect them and send them back. They included "The Tramp and the Girl who Made *Signs* to Sailors", and "His Fingernails were Useful", a murder story laid in Northampton... John Akar, who was calling, described a speech Jonathan made before Sierra Leone students. "If madmen are increasing, then the sane must be sent to the asylums". When asked about his lack of a winter overcoat, "It is the failure of mind over matter". There is something heroic about the poor young man.

8 January. Mercedes, indignant that "her" Zulus have been booked by the Frankie Howerd show for a cannibal turn, in which much play is made with pepper and salt. She is getting Africans to monitor the show...

11 January. JGW has persuaded Cecil Madden, Head of Variety, to cut the Zulu sequence from the Frankie Howerd show, sprinkling pepper and salt on a missionary.

16 January. A morning at the West London Court, where Jonathan Vincent elected to go for trial at the Assizes, despite warnings from the bench that penalties can go up to 15 years, instead of a maximum of one, the poor young man had everyone against him, "in his best interests": bench, police, even witnesses. The officials from the Assistance Board spoke quite venomously, the man from the Ministry of Food. (All for two ration books!!). Little Miss Lowman from Accounts was shaken when he asked her, in cross-examination, whether she were Negrophobe, and whether the BBC had "planted" the last cheque he received for *West African Voices*.

21 January. John Fig comes to tell me the details about Babalola, who broke down in November, and is now confined. What are we doing to them? What we have done to ourselves, perhaps. Senayah, the Gold Coaster, records a little piece, "Childish Games and Plays." There

are few break-downs in African village communities? They are coming, with the uprooted population of Accra, far from the extended family, and the protection of 'unmarried' aunts...

24 January. JGW very cockahoop about Sam Selvon's novel, *A Brighter Sun*, which he almost seems to think he has written himself. He is going to try to get him into *In Town Tonight*, with a paragraph in the *Radio Times*. [...] It was a Thursday, and two writers turned up, Ekwensi and Dawes. The former amusing about his visits to sleazy night-clubs, in search of material for his new novel *Darkie*, the latter very quiet as usual. I think these visits do him good. He is still determined against school-mastering.

25 January. Gordon [Woolford] turns up with his little French rose – to record a story "Toast of the Caribs," by Rose Auguste,* a legend from St Lucia, where the *patois* is French. Shortly afterward George Lamming, very unkempt, to read some poems by the policeman Byron Fraser.* The main event of the day was the production of *Henri Christophe* by Errol Hill at the Hans Crescent hotel, a beautiful setting, with high Regency ceiling, for the drama of Haiti in the early 1800s. [...] The decor and costumes were by Carlisle Chang, extremely effective, the officers in Napoleonic uniforms, the guerrillas in straw hats and bast shoes. Hill made a wonderful job of cutting and editing, reducing the overlong speeches, clarifying the crowd scenes, adding a death of Dessalines which made the story line much simpler to follow. Errol John was a magnificently rhetorical Christophe, Errol Hill a sly Vastey, Frank Pilgrim the mulatto general Pétion, Vic Patterson marvellously disguised as Dessalines. After it was all over, I rushed round to the green room, incoherent in praise. When one reflects that Sam Selvon and George Lamming were behind the scenes, it was a real climacteric. The only trouble, the appalling audience, guffawing at the slightest opportunity.

30 January. Sam Selvon, whose novel appears today, to read a story "Day of the School." I have not seen very much of him, not half so much as of George Lamming, his fellow Argonaut, but I like him very much, so open and modest. An hour later, a call from Edgar Mittelholzer, to say that he finds the book "amateurish, the style jagged". He has only read one chapter, so I suggest he persevere. The main motivation, jealousy, or at least rivalry?

1 February. George Lamming reads an extract from his novel *Farewell to the Land*, which is so good it suggests that he will have an even greater success than Sam Selvon when he is finally published.

3 February. Lionel Hale, Sam Selvon's publisher, does not command the publicity of Mittelholzer's firm, but there is a warm little paragraph in the *Observer*. Typical of them to treat it as "exotic", when it really is linked to the main stream of what is left of the British position in the world.

6 February. Later that afternoon, I recorded my summary of the last half-year in *Caribbean Voices*. The centre-piece was, of course, the production of *Henri Christophe*. Vivian Virtue, and in prose Norman Ray's "Egg", George Lamming's "Birthday Weather", V. S. Naipaul's tart "Mourners". On the whole, the year, marked by a development beyond the scope of a weekly half-hour programme.

7 February. It is possible that I took the first oath, in a law court, under the new reign, since I was the first witness heard, at 10.35. Jonathan defended himself with some silliness, and a great deal of shrewdness. He looked quite brisk and well after three weeks in Brixton, and pleaded Not Guilty to all four charges: using someone else's ration book, failing to declare "earnings" while drawing relief. The case lasted 4½ hours, and Jonathan was on his feet a good part of the time, attempting to link "full unemployment" and "need", querying the implication of the phrase "failed to return", defending his alleged misstatements, "I gave the answers according to their questions". He had several sharp exchanges with Strutt, the prosecuting counsel, shouting "Prejudice", whenever they came near an awkward point. At one point, amidst laughter, he asked Strutt if he were "a typical grocer", and cited the recent case of "a typical grocer" enticing another man's wife. At the end, he was congratulated by his opponent, but was found guilty on all four charges, and the deputy Chairman Cockburn bound him over, to the annoyance of the food officials. He broke down a little when the verdict was announced, but it was certainly his hour of glory. Poor Jonathan! What he really needs is someone to take care of him.

14 February. As it is Thursday, I leave for a "practical" with George Lamming and John Fig arguing about Bentham and Nietzsche. I say that *Caribbean Voices* will make West Indian writers self-conscious, and therefore unhappy. I AM BECAUSE I AM NOT. They advance the solvent, Nationalism. After this, listen to the funeral of George VI, very moving.

25 February. JGW tells me that it has been decided to send me to Jamaica for a fortnight before the end of the financial year (the end of March), to make a programme about the new University College at Mona. £238 return air fare, and £100 in expenses... This is the way it is done [...].

But it should prove interesting, and add some flesh to the bones of six years on paper. The only drawback is that it will not include a visit to the South Caribbean, where nearly all the significant work in *Caribbean Voices* has emerged. However, one must not look a gift horse in the mouth, and I gratefully accept. Record Adisa Williams, reading "The Barking Bushman," by Peter Agbonkonkon.* Peter Abrahams calls, and I give him scripts by Nchami, hoping they may attract his publisher. [...] At tea time, poor Jonathan, as usual for money, and perhaps reassurance. He brought an impossible story full of violence and terror, about a Temne python-man, which I agreed to edit for him, and send to the monthly *West African Review*, run by David Williams. I gave him a little something to buy a meal or two. But by the lift, he had the horrors, and skipped into Marmorstein's office. The motherly secretary was there, and took him by the hand, to the entrance, I walking before him.

26 February. A very long letter from Derek Walcott, answering the one I sent him three years ago... A good omen.

28 February. Carlisle Chang records an excellent account of Carnival, Gloria Vaz a horribly snobbish piece by Mrs O. M. Howard,* "Rice and Peas." She was relieved to hear that it is reserved for the scalpel of Calder-Marshall. [...] It was Thursday, and for once there were quite a lot of people for the *causerie*: Gilkey, Lamming, Dawes, Ekwensi, Adisa Williams, Phebean Itayemi. Gin lent wings to the talk, with George Lamming eloquent. Cyprian was silent, after his enquiries for *Darkie*, looking very debauched, bags under his eyes.

29 February. Calder records a critique of the last Selvon, and of Mrs Howard. I give him eight BIM numbers and the names of twenty books, for an article in the *Times Literary Supplement*.

5 March. A briefing from Warren MacAlpine, kind and stumbling in a sunlit room, his diary virgin of entries. He has been to Jamaica recently, felt at home with the Lindos. Una Marson* may be sending his wife a servant girl.

10 March. The air terminal, and the bus to Heathrow. The 56 people in the Stratoliner *Caribou* (Flight BA 457) are not very interestng: to judge from conversations, business executives, and technicians, surveyors going to work for the millionaire Christie, on projects in Nassau, construction men for Jamaica bauxite, a research consultant going to examine the medical faculty at the Mona University College, "which lost nearly everything in the hurricanes."

11 March. Because of [a] delay [to the flight], we did not go inland over the United States, but directly down the coast to Kindley Field in Bermuda. Here again, the plane develops another fault. I left this narrow world, and walked out into magic, through hibiscus and an atmosphere fragrant with flowers, past sea-grasses, down to a white beach piled with coral-like breakfast cereal, the lights of Hamilton glimmering in the South. Then rain began falling heavily.

12 March. We landed at Nassau, to the peppery smell of the tropics, and a grave old Negro hands us a free mint julep, from glasses marked MAKE MINE MYERS. As we sit under the palms, with calypsos blaring from the public address system, a silent little black boy in a red shirt cleans our shoes. I feel embarrassed to see all the workers Coloured, all the passengers White. In Nigeria, at least, some of them would have been Black. The plane takes off again, past endless shoals and islands, and over the long brown spine of Cuba. [...] Montego Bay. Entrancing little girls of many colours, awful capitalist crustaceans. [...] Soon a Viking takes us through mist along the coast, then over the ridges of Jamaica, hundreds and hundreds of crumpled folds, rising to the splendid Blue Mountains, with their forest fleece. Then down to Kingston, which sprawls immense. At the Palisadoes airport by the sea [...]. At the barrier Henry Straker, with his twitching eyes, and the Lindos, much as I expected, she warm and loose and coffee-coloured (a female JGW), and he thin and nervous, with rimless pince-nez and a slight stutter. The car runs past a cement factory on Long Mountain, belching fumes. They live in a comfortable villa, Dunravon, at Half Way Tree, overlooking the town, with a garden stuffed with bougainvillea and hibiscus and the blue plumbago. At supper, mutton and guava jelly, Cedric says grace before and after, with Gladys holding his hand tightly... The conversation is mainly biographical, and Gladys treats me with apparent awe. As I thought, Cedric is the author of all our correspondence over the last six years (her guide is *John O'London's Weekly*.) As they bill and coo, Philip Sherlock* comes for a drink, the Vice-Principal of the College, who has to leave for the South in the morning. He is a handsome, quiet Creole, with a gentle face, and a long record of interest in the arts – he sings the praises of Edna Manley, the patron of Albert Huie, the founder of *Focus*. I am so tired, I find it hard to take it all in, and there is a terrible moment, when I try to record Sherlock without any result. The midget recorder has been shaken up in the flight, a lead perhaps has been wrenched out... All night, dreams broken by dogs barking furiously in the gardens.

13 March. I tinker hopelessly with the BMI machine, changing the

batteries, without avail. It must be a lead. Thank Heaven for the Jamaica Broadcasting Company. I present the Lindos with some of Eric's printed wartime lithographs. Gladys goes off to her welfare work among the victims of consumption, and Cedric takes me to the King's House, where I sign Hugh Foot's visitor's book. Then to Mona, and the University College, in a valley behind long mountain, looking up to the Blue Mountains. A beautiful site, fine white buildings, well designed and built, among masses of flowers and trees. On the way, little donkey carts that would have rejoiced the heart of Tirzah. The people look very poor, much poorer, even, than in the outskirts of Lagos or Ibadan. At the Principal's House, Tom Taylor, a little, spare man, very Oxford, with whom I get on well from the start, answering unspoken questions, put by him and his wife, a younger Ella Garwood, an expert on birds. There are good pictures Cotman, Brangwyn, Dunlop, Ardizzone. I am handed over to the Registrar, a black, bullet-headed Barbadian called Springer, who takes me round the campus. White plaster, pastel colours, beautiful mahogany tables and chairs, a splendid library, laboratories, teaching hospital... There is nothing that I know like it in England. But at the end of the morning, when Springer has gone, a chat with the chauffeur reveals another side: burning indignation, burning poverty. He says that I should visit August Town, the shanty town below the campus in the valley... All this, because I sat in the seat beside him, rather than lord it at the back... Lunch with the Taylors, given for the biologist J. Z. Young, the authority on octopuses, over to advise on research programmes. Should one study general problems or concentrate on things of economic interest to Jamaica, fish and marine biology? An application has to be made soon for a grant from the Nuffield Foundation. [...] In the afternoon, the bitter little chauffeur drives me down the long campus avenue to meet the President of the Students Guild, a man called Charles from St. Lucia, a medical student. He takes me to Irvine Hall, for the secretary Daphne Pilgrim, a cousin of Billy's. It is a small world. Polite young men playing jazz. They then take me to see Derek Walcott the poet, now editor of the University journal, *The Pelican*. He is an edition of Roy Fuller in a different colour: sensitive, wide brown long chin, hazel eyes, rather epicene, if the truth be told. We find it hard to talk, mainly about the great occasion of *Henri Christophe*. But we will meet later. Tea with the Taylors, and a drive to Spanish Town on the other side of Kingston, to show J. Z. Young something of the life. Streets teeming, pullulating, with people, and the houses more sordid than Nigeria with none of the plaster fantasies. No coloured elephants, at best the Union Jack. The people are not beautiful either, perhaps because they are so mixed in origin, with the basic stock from the Gold Coast. Spanish Town is extraordinary: a central square, built in the eighteenth century, to celebrate "England's Salamis," Rodney's victory in 1781, at the Saints on the "Glorious First of June." A square of rich Georgian houses in cream and ochre, dominated by cupola and a huge mass of statuary, part natural, part symbolic. One side was burned down in 1925 and not restored. Another is the library and the archives. Another the offices of the *Custos Rotulorum*. Round the pretty central garden, the swirling crowds. We go to the little cathedral, smells of bats. Monuments to Beckford, Lewis, and Lyttelton. [...] Passing through an industrial estate, [Taylor] explodes against the machinations of Captain Morgan's rum.

14 March. J. Z. Young leaves early for London. I tour the campus. Holdsworth, the salty New Zealand librarian, talks about microfilms and air conditioning, Sandmann, the French Professor, a refugee from Central Europe with a thin, sensitive face, Parry, the tough, authoritative Professor of history, an expert on Spanish colonization. Elsa Goveia,* a little Guianese lecturer, very nationalist, very concerned for the West Indies. At lunch with the Taylors we touch on "culture," and I hold forth on the proper functions of the British Council, and put in a word for John Fig and Fernando Henriques. Taylor is harsh about both of them. John, who has "applied several times for a post" has "pathetically weak qualifications", and besides, he made a bad impression. As for Fernando, he was sacked from a post on the Caribbean Commission because of his penchant for weekends with lovely married ladies... I also put in a word for George Lamming, but he is beyond the pale – no higher qualifications at all (only a touch of genius, which does not count?). In the afternoon, Springer takes me to the hospital, a really splendid block under the eroded hills, where the pathology department opened yesterday. He is very dry, but a good guide. Tea with Walcott, again awkward on both sides. He seems resigned to returning to St. Lucia under his scholarship "bond", showed no interest in Vivian Virtue, was very modest about his reading. What can I give him? I gave him my paperback of Denton Welch. The students here are nothing like as on-coming and exhibitionist as in England. But then, I am really rather a feeble "intellectual."

Supper in hall with some younger Dons: Parry, Coulthard, the Lecturer in Spanish, Mailer, a French lecturer, Bob Le Page, Mrs Robertson, a tall lecturer in Botany. We sat at the meagre high table, the students in their scarlet gowns at tables below. The proceedings were a little edgy.

Early to bed, but not to sleep. I was in my truss when the gaunt maid Gladys announces the arrival of two gentlemen who want to see me. They turn out to be Coulthard [Gabriel] and Mailer, who very kindly offer to show me some of the "dens" of Kingston. The streets were lovely in the darkness, full of the open air *corso*. We first went to Doris, bare white walls, a string curtain in the door, full of whores with sailors from the cruiser *Sheffield*. The girls were all ugly and battered, quite unlike the fresh and beautiful young things in Lagos. We went to the Captain's Cabin, which was empty, with three forlorn hostesses, one sleeping with her head on a table. We discussed literary topics – they are both members of PEN – then sex. Clearly they know a great deal, but I do not suggest a practical follow-up. In any case, we had at the table a middle-aged Polish countess and the conversation was not too free. It turned on the University, which was, they said, "resented", as it must inevitably be, high and dry in Mona. Perhaps I thought it well. If it "linked up", under the present auspices, it would be with the deadened culture of the "whisky line", the houses on Stony Hill, where whisky is served instead of local rum. They criticized the "total lack of interest", shown by the English Department in original local writing.

15 March. A rewarding morning with Lowe the resident architect for the contractors Higgs and Hill, a son of A. M. Lowe, the scientist. He took me round the work in progress with the tough director Jennings. They criticize the Jamaican pattern of "line-employment", and the way the workers support three or four "parasites". On the other hand, they were enthusiastic about the excellence of the work, plasterers and carpenters better in many ways than counterparts in Britain. Lowe wants to start technical classes, an apprenticeship system. A wonderful sight of a line of workers, rhythmically breaking up the hard soil with their picks, to "Brown Skin Gal", very well sung. [...] At 5, the Lindos arrived to take me to the last night of the Drama Festival at the Garrison Theatre. This was a huge bare structure with a cement floor, with one side open to the peanut vendors and their carts with piercing steam-whistles. Children presented various plays before an adjudicator, Thomas from the British Council: an adaptation of Browning's *Grammarian's Funeral*, one of Housman's *Little Plays of St Francis*, *Hiawatha*, even, incredibly, an excerpt from *The importance of Being Earnest*. Some of this was beautiful to look at, if not to hear.

16 March. I said goodbye to the Taylors with real regret. At the Lindos, once more [...]. I found Gladys' continuous non-stop flattery a little irksome, even suspicious. She calls me "Henry Beauclerk". I can see why she was appointed by JGW the BBC representative in the island. Deep calls to deep. But is there anything in the fact that the stray dog she has adopted, is also called "Henry"?

17 March. Straker busy on the phone, arranging his "sustaining" programmes, for public time on the commercial air. I go round to the

JBC in their mansion on the Lyndhurst Road, escorted by Micky Hendricks,* tall, small-headed, coffee-coloured, with very cold eyes. He is Circulation Manager, and I do not think he forgets, or forgives, my remarks about his poetic efforts. A handsome man, rather Spanish, with smouldering black eyes and heavy black eyebrows, turns out to be the execrable "poet" Archie Lindo,* the Programme Manager. To do him justice, Hendricks never mentions the literary scenes, but Lindo immediately complains about his infrequent appearances in *Caribbean Voices*. The building shelters 120 staff, under Bill McLurg, once of the BBC, and a little rubicund Canadian, John Phillips. They broadcast for 16½ hours every day, divided into A, B, C tariffs, with the peak listening period, from 1800 to 2200, charging £6 for a quarter of an hour. They pay £300 for BBC Transcriptions, mostly Variety. In this week of 114 hours, Straker gets 11½ for public broadcasting, mainly to schools. One may not like the arrangement, but at least it provides the wherewithal for the elegant green rooms, the excellent studios, the technical staff. [...] Elsie [Barsoe] drives me back to 20 Hope Road, but the Lindos do not invite her in to drinks. More suitable guests are bespoken: Vivian Virtue, the Clinton Blacks, and a young couple who were involved in an elopement drama a few months ago.

18 March. Down to Harbour Street to see [Theodore] Sealy, the editor of *The Gleaner*. Outside a "madman" addresses a fruitseller: "Once the Black Man was King, and he will be King again". Sealy is large and fat, and talks economics. Bauxite, although it involves £20 million, will only bring in £500,000 in taxes. Fortunately the three companies involved, including the Reynolds Corporation, "have social consciences". Even so, they are not at all labour-intensive. The government have plans to set up two Corporations, one for Industry, one for Agriculture. He does not have much opinion of Foot, compared to MacGillivray, who went to Hong Kong... [...] I went to the Institute where Bob Verity works under the American biologist, Bernard Lewis, a Rhodes Scholar. It was the one organisation founded to help develop the island, and was completely refurbished in 1939, the *annus mirabilis*, after the riots that startled the somnolent British lion. It now has 3000 members, and the lists are closed. [...] The last visit of the morning, to the formidable Esther Chapman in the offices of the *West Indian Review*, a blonde Jewess, said to have been adviser to Bustamante, and a well-known controversialist. [...] After supper, a meeting of the Jamaica branch of the PEN club. Middle-aged, middle-brow, middle-class. Neither Andrew Salkey nor Roger Mais nor even Una Marson, but Mrs Ormsby-Marshall,* and Clare McFarlane OBE. My pep talk, or speech for the defence, went quite well. [...] Afterwards, I talked to the people who have really helped

the programme: Vic Reid, the author of *New Day*, Inez Sibley, a woman with a big nose, the self-possessed black girl Marjorie Brown, Byron Fraser, the policeman from St. Thomas. About 10pm Terry Burke took me away with Elsie Benjamin in Vic Reid's car, up to the Mansfield Club in the mountains above the Hope River. [...] We left at one in the morning, to find the Lindos still up, and annoyed that my window was not locked. "We wouldn't like you to be cut with a matchet, Henry Beauclerk."

19 March. Work from 7 – this diary, a talk on Africa for Straker. The maid Margaret has a beautiful, secret face. According to Gladys, she is "disturbed" by my "few" demands. Life in London must be "dreadful", if I can put up with "so little"… Up to Mona to 9.30 to show Taylor the draft proposed for recording. All would be well if it could be recorded. But again, no result, when I tried to [record] Grace Sherlock. An engineer comes, but the morning is almost over. I had used the play-back knob! I am ham-fisted: but also, I was not given nearly enough practice at 200 [Oxford Street], not more than ten minutes. After this shock, I did better, with Springer at the maps of the campus, with Cruickshank on the hospital, with Derek Walcott reading his poem on "The City's Death by Fire" (although he has just had three teeth out), with Millot the suave zoologist, with a student Val Rogers, singing about a mango raid that coincided with some visiting firemen and ended in the Black Maria, with Holdsworth the librarian, and finally with the patient Grace, who consented to put up with me again, just before supper. I even had the chance of recording Busta, who had come to address the construction workers, striking for higher wages, just beyond the Sherlocks' hibiscus hedge. The target of his wrath was the Black Registrar Swabey. "I am the powerful Bustamante Trade Union. I am the leadah. Mr Swabey better go look. Dr Taylor is a man I have respect for, but he must be an uneasy man tonight to think I impelled to come. For that he could thank Mr Swabey. The bleeack Jimaican [sic] is the worst of all oppressors." Supper with Springer in Hall [...] Waiting for the Lindos to fetch me back to Half Way Tree, a talk with the nightwatchman under the stars. A tall man with a patient face, a Corporal in the war, now with the United Christian Church. "It is not too bad sir. The people have good powers here. They do not knock me hup too much." He had been to England in the war. "Me loving wife, she want to go to England, but I say, Your beloved husband is not going, its too cold. Oh lard, the English wind and the rain! If they send me on a gospel mission at a hot time, I might go". He was against politics. "Look at this hafternoon. Nothing but hatridge, hatridge, hatridge. You come back in ten years, hall politics will be gone. The Church will rule. It will bring peace."

20 March. Supper with the Lindos, and Una Marson at last appears, to take me to her flat up the road, in a car driven by Ettlinger, the Librarian at the Institute. It was a charming old frame house, with a dark stair and Una's flat furnished with African *lappa* cloths, white shells, and coral from Port Antonio, some bad pictures, an American equivalent of *If* on the walls. Looking at her, I realize that she is handsome, handsomer than I remember. Perhaps she has gained through suffering, the poor creature. She is only now "coming back to life", as editor of poetry and other books for the Pioneer Press, which they hope to sell to schools. Talk, half love, half hate, of the BBC. I entertain her with war time memories. In the middle, she shoes away very violently an enchanting Haitian girl with a Jamaican husband, a one-armed man in a flowered shirt. We descend to the first floor to find Ettlinger reading Ovid to an extra-mural class. Culture round here is like the midget recorder: the power is supplied, not from the mains, but from imported batteries.

21 March. Gladys takes me up to Higgs and Hill (Cedric, who chain smokes, is coughing badly). We find Lowe and Jennings sitting among the white stones, and the English foreman Lyttleton organizes the singing of "Brown Skin Gal," which I record. He is a good man with a conscience about past colonial attitudes, that are still with us, "settler mentality, idle wives". One of his staff from England has had 26 servants since he came. As for himself, his wife has had two, and that only because of a pregnancy. [...] At Grace Sherlock's, I record the wizened little gardener Ivan Walters. "The land is *stony* and dry..." Later the Librarian Holdsworth... Walters offers to show me August Town, and we take the Assistant Librarian, Ken Ingrams, who has been here a year and never visited it... Walters, no doubt, is regarded *as* "safe" – he "took Religion" last December, after the hurricane. Certainly the experience is an unnerving one, compared to the paradisal campus, where no money or effort has been spared, at the expense of the British taxpayer, a return for the money squeezed from the island over the centuries. August Town lies below the Mona platform, at the entrance to the gorge, where the dry river leads down to the sea, on this side of Long Mountain. The slopes are arid, with clumps of dead brushwood, which the villagers collect for kindling – it seems almost the only product. From the road, it looks fair enough, among feathery tamarinths, with their long pods littered on the ground. Stockades of the cactus called Jerusalem candlesticks, pink coralita, yellow cassia trees, an occasional silk cotton tree, mangoes and the ackee tree, from which they get the sharp-tasting fruit used to stimulate the taste for rum. There are five cabins where they sell groceries, mineral waters, white rum, loaves that look crumby

and enticing. A donkey cart goes by with blocks of ice. Children play beside a water standpipe. As we walk down the path, behind the clumps of banana leaves, the scene becomes more and more desolate. In the path of the hurricane shanties blown sideways, the gleaming iron roof of the Anglican church level with the ground. A stone structure stands like a skeleton without windows or roof, the church built in 1894 (and again in 1906) by the prophet Alexander Bedward. Walters takes us to the village leader, Ivanhoe Burke, a coachbuilder, a tall man in a filthy hat, who stands over a fire in a crazy lean-to hut. He is the Preacher, and lives in the Prophet's house. Two donkeys stand before his shop with panniers loaded with grey brushwood from the mountain, and beside them two constables, in the brilliant Jamaican uniform, red, white and blue. Ivanhoe Burke tells us that the only hurricane relief so far are sixty tents, put up for homeless families. He denies the legend, used in the *Ballets Negres,* of the attempted Ascension. I give him a miserable ten shillings towards the restoration fund, which they hope to organize among Bedwardites in the surrounding villages, and even in Panama. Ivan Walters then leads us down a sunken path to the Hope River, where, at a bend, the prophet used to baptise adherents. It is now dry sand and gleaming stones, relieved by a few beds of water cress, and a trickle oozing down a tiny channel. All the rest of the water is impounded by the Mona Dam, where, says Walters, it drains away into the soil. Today, there is just enough water for a mother to wash her six children. Such is August Town, a village of 2000 souls. So far, the University has done nothing to help, beyond providing occasional employment: but Huggins hopes to organise some kind of voluntary relief.

22 March. Saturday, and Cedric took me into town. He works in the Banana Producers Corporation, and has a remarkably attractive secretary, with smoky blue eyes and a lovely body, rather disdainful – she has a fiancé "who plays Bridge twenty four hours a day". [...] I took a turn in Water Street, and bought a *Gleaner,* which had a report of the PEN reception, with an appalling photograph, which made us all fat and middle-aged. An old lady sold me two painted *chac-chacs,* calabashes painted with crude faces, seeds rattling inside. Back in the hotel, Joyce Newbill Martin, who is on the point of flying to Aruba, is "tickled to death with Jamaica", as the result of her taxi tour. "Just imagine, my chauffeur was all used up... I gave him a grain of adrenaline, to be exact a grain and a half". Michael Manley arrived, and we talked for an hour over drinks at the swimming-pool, mainly about writing, but also about politics, and the University. The PNP is split, after the chance discovery (from a typewriter flimsy) that Ken Hill and his brother were

paid-up members of the Communist Party: but he seems confident that his father Norman will carry the day, except in Western Kingston, in the slum called the Dungle, with its bearded Ras Tafari men, zealots who have adopted the Emperor of Ethiopia as their leader into a better world. He was critical of Tom Taylor, and described an unfortunate Inaugural, when the band of local pioneers (Verity, Sherlock etc) had expected rhetoric, but were given a stare, and five words. "After tea, we'll start work"... I liked his direct approach, and found myself agreeing to write an article for *Public Opinion* on the London production of *Henri Chistophe*.

In the afternoon, the Lindos took me up to the Blue Mountains, to Hardware Gap, 4380 feet above sea level, it can be reached in less than an hour. [...] Gladys talked about her sons in Europe, one in Dublin, one in Oxford (Keble). They seem pretty rakish. Nothing, in fact, is more interesting than her indulgent attitude to sex, although a Presbyterian. "Elvira is going to have a baby. Lord, C, I wonder about Mr Mack. He seduced her practically in the dentist chair". (Elvira is their pretty junior maid.) I asked what they would do when the baby arrived. "For shame, Henry Beauclerk! Of course we will keep her. She loves us, and she knows that we love her". We were stopped by a strawberry seller. "They're good people. I had to make that old man take a little more money". Cedric gave a snort. "You buy them for scarcely anything". I had not realised that his career has been so chequered. He resigned from accountancy in 1941 to do work for the BBC, then tried teaching, then went to his present job as assistant accountant with the Banana Producers. He is probably an academic, who would have made a much better member of the English Department at UCWI than some of the present incumbents. When the history of the West Indian literary renaissance written, he should get a large share. Around 23.00, Una Marson comes an hour late, to take me to a night club, the Buccaneer, on Springfield Point. The car is driven by a cousin called Wesley, who owns the Excelsior School, and he brings along a white sister-in-law. The evening was not a success. Una was morose, the cousin, just back after five years in Canada health services, full of complexes. These came violently to the surface, when Una made some disparaging remarks about Paul Robeson... We were not made much happier by the atmosphere at the Club, very young people, US Naval officers with local tarts, a university party including the neurotic Mrs Robinson. Terry [Burke] was there, dancing cheek to cheek with a man in a ribbed jersey. The cabaret at midnight was embarrassing, an ugly man in drag, two singers who sang suggestive songs, and wriggled their sterns. For the final scene, a huge, handsome woman, three-quarters naked, sat on a beribboned chair, vibrating breasts and naval, while *pas seuls* went on around her, all indecent. When they stopped, and looked around for the applause that did not come, I felt sorry for them. Poor things, they did their best. It is not surprising to learn that the club is closing in a few weeks time. We left at 01.30, and outside, in the beautiful night, Una showed me the Southern Cross. Four stars like a kite. At Dunravon, in the small hours, I am sure there was a prowler. Rattling steps, the dog beside himself.

23 March. In the morning, I paid some cultural calls. Corder, at the British Council, is enthusiastic about the work of a young painter called Leonard Morris, still in his teens, but producing powerful figure studies in grey and black. [...] The rest of the day was spent in a taxi drive with Una to the North Coast. (£8.5 in all, or £9 with tip). As I found later, this was something of a ploy on her part... For the first twenty miles, the scenery was disappointing [...], but after half an hour, we ran up a lush valley, beside the Waters River, full of fields and plantations and trim homesteads. Beyond Port Maria, we hit the North coast, with Noel Coward's house perched on the hills, above a coast as beautiful as the Italian Riviera, almost more beautiful, from the breakers that rolled in under the mountains. (Even the homes made of packing cases bore the imprint Harrods.) We stopped for lunch at a huge tourist hotel, built by Issa three years ago, for half a million pounds, opposite a little island, Tower Island, with a Gothick folly from which flew a bleached Union Jack, approached by a line of scarlet floats bobbing in the glitttering water. Inside the hotel, palms growing through porthole windows, tesselated pavements, patios and cabanas, and an immense buffet groaning with good things (lunch for 5 dollars), besieged by American tourists in rainbow colours. The young manager John Brimo, a friend of Figueroa's, was not exactly overjoyed to see us, and I soon saw why. Una is probably the first person of Colour ever to partake of his hospitality among the 150 white Americans in their atomic shirts and flowering panties. For her part, she went about her business, which was to interest the bookstall in her books on local customs and history, produced by Pioneer Press... We did not stay too long among the lobsters and champagne, but drove on to a smaller caravanserai towards Oracabessa, the Silver Seas. [...] Una was by now very friendly, and told me that she has been made a JP for Kingston. At Bog Walk, we came on modern development, a sugar factory. [...]. Finally, the Kingston Plain. To my enquiries about the Dungle, Una said that the Rastas had been 'broken up', following an outrage committed by Whopper-boy Jolly last summer... We parted at Half Way Tree, full of a shared experience, full of affection. If it had not been for Una's initiative in setting up the base of *Caribbean Voices*, all this world would have been denied me.

In the evening, the Governor [Hugh Foot] gave me an hour, to "listen to my impressions". As in Lagos, he was remarkably optimistic. We are living in a period which is ending the "fragmentation" of the slave society. The island is homogenous, the country folk are good people, the hurricane was the best thing that could have happened "since it has jolted them up." Banana production has doubled to 12 million stems, he is giving nearly 200,000 to the admirable Brotherhood of Port Royal, a voluntary welfare organisation, to help them build 100 houses, designed by Lowe for Higgs and Hill. In addition, there is bauxite, producing £25 million. Among other projects, there is the development in controlled farming at Yallahs (the Spanish De Ayala), and there are two new government corporations. Then there is tourism, although he thinks the Syrian tycoon Issa is "over-capitalized"... Tonight, he is seeing American industrial consultants from the Massachusetts Institute of Technology. The only real problem, he thinks, is political: the shortage of trained officials, the weakening of the PNP, the only real party beside the demagogue Bustamante. All the contrary facts he brushed aside: the population explosion (forty thousand new mouths to feed every year), the growth of feeling against white and creole, the psychological isolation. I found it odd that he has not yet visited August Town. But then, I am a congenital pessimist, and have never been concerned with action. On leaving, his two little boys came to say goodnight, and one offered to kiss me (Paul). When I got back to Half Way Tree, I repeated some of these judgements and Cedric snapped that the banana figures were "wildly over-optimistic".

24 March. Last full day in Jamaica, with the morning given up to the JBC. In the foyer, the radio begins a Brandenburg Concerto (sustaining time), and the pretty receptionist immediately turns it off. I record an interview with Corder on my impressions, and had an hour with Bill McLurg, the aggressive General Manager, who was irked by remarks I had made at PEN on the failure of commerce to help local writers. He went on to call Arthur Calder-Marshall a "cheapjack" for his "travel" book *Glory Dead*, the account which first turned my interest to the Caribbean. He works his work, I mine. [...] Straker brought me to the Taylors for a farewell lunch. Talk on the local *obeah* men in August Town who bombarded the Natural History Society, come to inspect an Arawak midden. Christians from the campus work in a youth centre created by Edna Manley in Papine. The Lindos were also there; and I selfishly hurried them away, because I had promised John Fig to visit his family on Third Avenue. [...] It was an airy house, with Catholic oleos on the walls. [...] Gladys elected to stay outside in the car, and I had to refuse another lunch, thinking of her frying in the sun, protected only by *The Listener*. She then took me down to *The Gleaner* on Harbour Street, where I made a hurried farewell to Sealy, noticing Abrahams' *Path of Thunder* on his desk. Una works in a bare upper room, for The

Pioneer Press is run by *The Gleaner*, but I had to leave without seeing her in order to catch the last half hour of the shops: pretty fabrics, raffia dolls, beautifully made ash trays from mahoe wood. A last visit, by taxi this time, to beard Edna Manley, the dragon who has loomed over Swansky, ever since that ill-tempered letter. I found her in a large square house behind the King's House, with horses in a paddock stretching down the hill. She was much nicer than I had expected, perhaps because I have shown that I am a complement, not a rival, with the article on *Henri Christophe* in *Public Opinion* as a gauge of peace. A tall, fair figure, with white hair parted in the middle, and widely-spaced teeth. We talk about significant form, regionalism, the psychological defects of Communism... I noticed that she quoted Alec Lowe a great deal... After an hour Michael Manley came to take me back to Hope Road. The atmosphere had been so thoroughly Chelsea that it came as a slight shock to hear him hail a passing labourer as 'Comrade'.

25 March. A lovely cool morning, and Una and Vic Reid turn up to say farewell, a charming gesture. I offended Gladys by singing, but at the airport I felt sad. Everyone has been so kind, and although I was not attached at the deepest level, there are many that I will remember. Even the Lindos, the ambiguous Gladys, whom I cannot really fathom. Why is the stray dog called Henry? Straker or Swanzy, or both? Cedric, in many ways an elective affinity. The regulation exchange of letters should from [here] on have a deeper resonance. It was typical of their thoughtfulness that they got me an AA map, with which to study the landscape to Montego Bay. *Me no sen you no come* (otherwise *Look Behind*). The Blue Mountains, lost in the sun rising. The Rio Cobre, lost in its own mists. Falmouth, and boats making patterns in the Azure water. At Montego Bay, I found Mrs Howard waiting with her lovely daughter and burly Jamaican husband. She had heard her story read, but, thank heaven, *not* Calder's critique. [...] Now I am on a stratocruiser, beside a little black girl, reading *Pilgrim's Progress*, a nurse who is going to Amersham. We are at the back, and the plane seems roomier, with a rack for the unfortunate midget. [...] We circle Bermuda, and the plane is again held up for a few hours, allowing me to collect a little coral. [...] We wait three hours, and leave just after midnight, for the long haul across the Atlantic.

27 March. This is the first anniversary of Tirzah's death. I read in Montaigne: "Life is full of combustion, and death full of love and courtesy". Outside, the first Hebridean Island appears through a rift in the clouds, then another and another, then whole flotillas [...] Back in Adelaide Road, I come back to earth with a bump: damp beds, electric blanket not working.

28 March. Once more on the production line: Pauline with a story by G. M. Hope, "Christmas Holiday", Errol John with a story he wrote himself, "Happy New Year" [...] Delightful news at the Marlborough: George Lamming's book, *In the Castle of My Skin* (a quotation taken from Walcott) has been accepted by Michael Joseph, the reader curiously comparing it to Hemingway, when the style is so completely different. Send out invitations for Tirzah's exhibition in the Towner Gallery.

1 April. All afternoon packing for our move to the Langham, opposite BH, true poor relations.

2 April. Move at last to the Langham, after very nearly ten years at Oxford Street. The Langham only provides memories of the novels of Ouida, and the ghost of the pre-war Prussian officer, who threw himself out of a bedroom window. Moreover, there are no studios, library, canteen, although it is close to the BBC club, and the Bolivar. The office itself is very small, overlooking an inner garden, and it was secured only at the last minute, against Sheila Stradling. JGW made not the slightest attempt to organize the move, or represent absent interests, like HS in Jamaica... Ah well... Mercedes with a *Diary*, to maintain continuity. Then a painful four hours in Portland Place, trying to produce a master tape, with the help of Muriel Howlett, and in the presence of Walter Adams, invited to hear the material. The students, Sandmann, Parry, Goveia, are all useless, despite the reassurances of the JBC technicians... Fortunately Walcott and the calypso are not too bad. Much was my fault (the level too high) but much was the fault of the batteries, not to speak of the leads, upset by the journey. [...] As ever, *no one* interested in Jamaica.

4 April. A letter from McLurg to JGW, accusing "your Mr Swanzy" of "attacking the commercial system" in his talk to the PEN club... The whole thing seemed garbled by the poetasters A. Lindo and M. Hendricks. [...] Elisabeth came to tea with her babies, and urged me to pay court to Tid, her nice Dutch helper. Certainly, she is a sweet girl, one difficult to forget. Henriette Van Eeghen, of a patrician Amsterdam family. [...] The only objection is her size – she is taller than me, and makes me realize, what perhaps I should never forget, my essential littleness.

5 April. In the train, the new Mittelholzer, an *olla podrida* of rape, incest and sadism *Children of Kaywana*. Little historical sense, but very gripping partly because my mind runs on Henriette and Anglo-Dutch colonial encounters...

10 April. It was Thursday, and John Fig, Neville Dawes, and Cyprian Ekwensi looked in, each leaving with a book: Fig *Mr Norris Changes Trains*, Dawes, *The Real Life of Sebastian Knight*, Ekwensi, *Children of Kaywana*.

15 April. In the train, finish examining the 31 essays on music, elicited by Mercedes. The best seems by Gadzekpo, heavily influenced, I think, by Gbeho...

17 April. It is Thursday, and the faithful George rolls up, with the two Jamaicans, Neville Dawes and Andrew Salkey. The latter was brash and amusing about the flotsam of Kingston like Harry Milner. He (Salkey) was expelled from the Catholic Church at 14, and from Government Service at 22.

18 April. Noel Vaz looks in, his tour in ruins, and I lend him £20. An odd letter from one Golden Adewale in Lagos, who wants my photograph. Tea to young V.S. Naipaul, at Quality Inn. He is back from Spain after his break-down at Oxford, and I advised him to try again with his novel, and also to try and get his father published.

21 April. Calder rings up to report that Gordon Woolford is in Horton, a mental home near Epsom [...], refusing to undergo convulsive treatment. At lunchtime, drinks to Ralph Currey at the club, and afterwards at the Bolivar. Roger Cary comes up in one of the Langham corridors. "I've just been having lunch with Evelyn Wrench. Beside yourself, he is the only person I have met who still has a philosophy of Empire". Pauline at 5, to record a sad little piece by Kunle Akinsemoyin, "Bitter Sweet," about a prejudiced London landlady.

23 April. Mercedes and Philip Gbeho on a Catholic conference at Strawberry Hill, "The Pope and Africa". Poor Jonathan Vincent writes from Wormwood Scrubs, a mixture of pleas and threats, and demands for bail. Why do they not have him medically examined? A story from Nigeria, about a boy, "no rogue, but a sincere lad." Later, someone "implants a carefully rolled lump of sputum on the boy's beautiful face."

24 April. It was Thursday, and John Fig comes, with a Virginian professor called Rohrer, just back from the Coast – he says the Gold Coast is more primitive outside the two main towns than he had imagined. Salkey also came, and Ekwensi, immersed in *The Palm Wine Drinkard*. This is an astonishing "tall story", by one Amos Tutuola, a Yoruba,

with an inadequate command of English, but a marvellous feeling for sentence and even paragraph rhythms, a richer and more elaborate version of "Sir Gallant Austere". The talk was on the usual lines. [...] Salkey remained after the others had gone, and I talked to him like a foster father. His centres in London seem largely nightclubs.

25 April. Sheila Clarke not too happy in a sharp satire by Vidia Naipaul, about a little Indian woman who tries to break caste by selling potatoes. [...] Calder rings up about *The Palm Wine Drinkard*, which he has to review. Is it a folk-tale retold? I do not think it is, although really without information.

27 April. In Tim Aluko's manuscript novel I find three references to episodes in the *Drinkard* in fifty pages. Clearly, I am wrong, and the Tutuola book *is* based on Yoruba folklore, or possibly on inventions by the Yoruba novelist, Fagunwa.

5 May. George Lamming's pretty little librarian wife looks in to borrow £10, to pay for the typing of his novel, *In the Castle of my Skin*.

6 May. Lamming and Andrew Salkey record poems by eight different poets, from north and south Caribbean, none of them very good. GL is very affable indeed, perhaps because of the loan. The euphoria of hope! Salkey twitched and vibrated, but he was quick on the uptake – there is no doubt but that he had a good mind.

7 May. At the Langham, Calder returns the West African material, with news of the mysterious Tutuola. He occupies a lowly position in some Government Department in Lagos, I think Public Works. He was adopted at 7 by an Ibo, who made him work. Later his father paid for a limited education. The *Drinkard* uses a good deal of the plots and imagery of the popular Yoruba novelist Fagunwa. It was begun at the insistence of a grandmother, and started in pencil, scribbled three hours a day. Fabers say another book is coming, *My Life in the Bush of Ghosts*. Needless to say, it is anathema to all the educated West Africans I meet, who say that it is a White plot to denigrate Negroes. Perhaps it is hard on them, who have tried so hard to master English grammar.

12 May. George Lamming reads an obscure poem by Walcott, "The Hermit at the Circus," no doubt exploring inner and outer worlds. Sam Selvon reads a racy story by himself, "Gussy and the Boss". He is one I should like to see more of, but he never comes to the Thursdays. He does not have enough money for the passage home, but *A Brighter*

Sun has sold over 2000 copies, not bad for a first novel, and it has been accepted by the New York Viking Press. At tea, Yorke Crompton tells me that Kathleen Raine has been recommending that a promising poet from the West Indies should be given a chance to broadcast on the Third, by name George Lamming. Evening with Fred Uhlman, nostalgic for the black forest. [...] He was asked to design a jacket for Mittelholzer's *Kaywana*, but it was not sexy enough. "Hedy Lamarr we want". The design they finally chose was awful: a piece of woman's flesh in silk in the foreground, a longhaired white man in the background, flogging a slave.

13 May. Arthur Calder-Marshall says what should be said about *Kaywana*. He does not say that you will find it mainly in the Charing Cross Road, but not among the shops selling books...

22 May. Draft notes most of the day. A quaint lunch with Edgar Mittelholzer and Louis Kriel, in which Edgar outlines his blood-curdling *Weltanschauung* to Louis, who sits listening like a startled hare.

27 May. A busy day in the studio. First George Lamming reading a teenage story by Edgar Boyce, "The Hookstick." Then the final revision of the "Notes". A tea party for West African editors, shepherded by dear old Thorne, with many memories of the birds of Ibadan. Finally, from 16.30 to 22.15, the recording of the University programme, aided by a stroke of luck – George Lamming had told me casually that Elsa Goveia was in London, so we were able to re-record her vital little interview, while George himself re-read the Walcott. Muriel Howlett, at first inclined to resent my arriving for the preliminary disc session, when she found I did not want to interfere, became quite charming. She is a good and painstaking producer. But even she could not relieve the programme from its jinx. The machine broke down, and we had to repeat a good half.

4 June. Cyprian Ekwensi records "The Village Schoolboy" by P. Agbonkonkon. His own novel has been rejected by Gollancz. The Mackays record a *Diary* about his discovery of uranium in the Nigerian plateau. Neville Dawes records a piece of general criticism, with covert attacks on Michael Smith, who has trodden on his toes.

5 June. At the Langham, Vic Paterson to record a piece on "Walking in Jamaica", by Claude Thompson.* George Lamming looks in, with the £10 I had lent his wife for the typing of the fair copy of the novel, it has had an enthusiastic report from the publisher's reader, Walter Allen.

A call from Sean Graham, inviting me to a preview of *The Boy Kumasenu*, the film he made for the Gold Coast Cocoa Board. [...] It was Thursday, and there was a better turn out: Gordon, Dawes, Salkey, a Brahmin from Guiana called Ramjass Tuvari, Cyprian, Phebean, and last but not least, Victor Sassoon.

12 June. At the Langham, a swansong from Errol Hill, who returns to Trinidad, and reads a sentimental story "Olga" by [Barnabas] Ramon Fortune. He gives me a photograph of the cast of *Henri Christophe*, and promises me another, his production of *The Antigone* in kente cloth. He may well do wonders in his islands, with designers like Carlisle Chang, and a good business manager. I wonder how long his Red affiliation will endure. [...] Thursday evening, half flat, half garden, with George, John Fig, Pauline, Gordon, Neville Dawes, Phebean. George is getting more and more stuck into the London literary scene, damning MacDiarmid, poking fun at the two Errols, with their talk of the 'people'.

20 June. Listening to Denis Williams read the world-shaking poems of Wilson Harris, whose very titles contain their power. "Troy," "Behring Strait," "Amazon".

25 June. JGW tells me that there is a proposal to stop the literary programmes, which are "not understood" by Ian Jacob and J. B. Clark, but that he has defended them. They are rather thin, after the brief hour when they met the needs of the emerging Caribbean... I read a critique of *Kaywana* by "Eric Coddling", otherwise Collymore; and Chijioke a sketch of Eastern Nigeria by Epelle.

26 June. Gordon reads his story about a disintegrated European, quite brilliantly. The RPA in the control room, when I asked him, thought there would be no cause for any offence even among the most racialist listener.

2 July. At the Langham, George reads a splendid minor epic from St. Vincent by Owen Campbell, "Hurricane Passage". As I explain to the doubters, who are many, included myself, one must always be there trawling with the net, for the occasional exciting catch, among so much that is routine, even worthless.

6 July. [Henriette and I] stay in bed until lunchtime, discussing a marriage date.

9 July. The day overcast by the ordeal of meeting Henriette's father.

[...] In the evening, I go to the Marlborough for Dutch courage, and a long talk with George Lamming on the individual in society (a theme at which I am beginning to think I am not very good). The place of meeting is the Dutch club; and Mijnheer Van Eeeghen proves less alarming than I had expected.

10 July. Mijnheer Van Eeeghen called at the Langham in the morning, and had a half hour talk with JGW. Apparently, JGW was very kind, defended my morals and general character, and said that he would not mind me as his own son-in-law. [...] Considering my general grudging attitude, I consider this handsome of him. [...] I keep an even keel, recording an overwritten account of the Jamaican hurricane, by Andrew Salkey. [...] It was Thursday, and George Lamming alone turned up, for a chat with Gordon. In fact, it turned out to be a very interesting discussion that lasted nearly three hours. George was full of the praises of Frank Collymore, the editor of *Bim*.

12 July. A visit to see Tirzah's grave. By the Roman River, the spring still bubbles at the entrance to the park. The grave was covered with leaves and acorns, the ground lumpy. The Horton stone is streaked by rain, the letters are not cut deep enough, nor dark enough.

18 July. At the Langham, a rigmarole by John Akar, "Reunion in Court", which suggests just how bad the two literary programmes might get if not controlled. It is a pot-boiler, on which I sent a two page letter full of suggestions, to correct a hotch-potch of impossible romantic coincidences, between a young lawyer (JA was a law student) and a beautiful girl (JA is a heart throb). Back it came, still impossible but a long rehearsal disengages a storyline, even then spoiled by moral assumptions. A big man who steels ginger, is obviously admired. A daughter disappears, only to return years later, ready to throw over her lover for a Crown Counsel, but changes her mind when the latter prosecutes her father. Perhaps this is life in Freetown. On the whole, I prefer Jonathan Vincent. In the evening, quite a successful party at the studio, with sixty guests. [...] I made the fruit cup, from a recipe given by Miselle. Henriette produced the most delicious sandwiches and cheeses. She looked most beautiful, tall and golden, and Tony was amazed that she is really ready to marry me. Distant worlds hit it off: George Lamming with Faith Mackenzie, her husband with Phebean, Bob Mackay with Mrs Lamming, Miselle with Phebean, whom she invited to tea.

22 July. Our wedding day, so rushed we had to use a curtain-ring, since

her fingers are so big. We travelled up Rosslyn Hill in a bus, to meet the witnesses. The same room where I married Tirzah.

25 July. Geoffrey Drayton* reads his own short story, "Mr Dombey the Zombie". I read minor poems by minor figures.

19 August. Pauline Henriques, handsome in black, with a black moiré handbag, reads a story by Edgar Boyce, "On the Hill". Will we ever get something with real quality again? She has gone back to Neville Crabbe, who was "very mis" without her. David Delaney, a pleasant cockatoo, with ideas for Commonwealth poetry programmes, turns his nose up at the West Indians, and does not even consider Africans...

29 August. Saturday. Errol John reads a story, I produce my six month summary. The barrel is so scraped, there is little to report, apart from the doings of the exiles in London. Errol, in pistachio shirt, smiling all over – he marries tomorrow.

1 September. Today, George Lamming reads an "Ode to Stool Worship" by the West Indian MacNeill Stewart, who has gone native in Odumase Krobo, a tribe where the girls have *carte blanche* to choose their lovers. John Fig reads an essay on Jamaica by Claude Thompson. Kunle Akinsemoyin, a piece by himself, *The Contenders*.

10 September. Recordings: Angela Christian, overly nervous with a *Diary*, George Lamming reading West African poets, including love poetry from Efua, with a gifted actress from the Old Vic school, Ruth Wyne.

11 September. Tea with Jan Carew. He had his airfare paid down to Guiana from New York, where he was staying with a financier, by a French friend. He is returning to London to share a house with a "General in the Army", a Brigadier from Burma...There is only one inference of the sort of life he leads. At the same time, his imagination, costive on paper, and confined to folklore, takes wing and soars. Wilson Harris is no mere clerk in Surveys, but "virtually Governor of the Southern districts of the Canje". They are writing a book together about Harris' cook who worked for Mrs Roosevelt. He (Carew) has fallen out with Denis Williams. "That fellow...success has turned his head". At 18.30, a visit from Olumide and Sani, Nigerian broadcasters. I am given an African supper by Seth Jectson, smiling all over his charming gap teeth. Delicious cakes – he was once a confectioner. Groundnut soup, a delicate flavour, almost like paprika. Miss Columbia Jones and an ample lady

baker from Kumasi sighing for the African sun. We end with *Kan-you-go*, a simple spelling game with cards.

16 September. More West African recordings: Cyprian with a brilliant little account of shoplifting in Lagos, "Clearance Sale"; and Adisa Williams reading "A Farmer's Dilemma" by Agbonkonkon. [...] A strange caller, the politician Tony Enahoro, the young man whose gaol for libel caused me such difficulty with Bourdillon. He was large, round-headed, extremely crooked, and rather amusing. At one moment, I had a strong inclination to boot him out of the office. This seems an African day, for Accounts ring up to say that they have had a demand for performing rights on a (non-existent) play from Jonathan Vincent. The letter came from the *S.S. Apapa*. So the poor fellow has been repatriated, really the best thing for him.

17 September. Seth Jectson reads an account of an *Nganga* fortune teller by one Umolu. The RPA, a semi-Mongolian, who watches birds, was disturbed at the obstetrical detail. Calder performs an operation on the Barbadian story read by Lloyd Reckord some days ago. Sani and Olumide produce a tepid *Diary*. Really, the quality of Nigerian broadcasting! No doubt, this is sour grapes.

18 September. At tea, a literary pilgrim from the Caribbean. E. Mc G. Keane, a tall young man from St. Vincent, with a lazy voice and elaborate manner, not uncharming, although his written work is rather portentous and humourless, "Berceuse for a Still Born Son", signed and dated... He is a fervent admirer of Carew. The little St. Vincent "group", whose fame has spread to the *Evening Standard*, has now dispersed: Keane to London or Hull to try and live by his trumpet, Owen Campbell to Trinidad, Daniel Williams, American born, back to the States.

19 September. At the Langham, Denis Williams arrives by bicycle, in brown corduroys and bicycle clips. He read a poem by Wilson Harris, "The Fabulous Well", a cloudy excursion, on the life force, that binds Eternity and Time through Man, and, (in our period of the "recreation of the senses"), in particular the Negro... I read the last section, Agamemnon, myself, to get variety, and because Williams did not have enough time to consider it. A long argument about the affinities of artists – he denies the identification of painter and writer, with the musician apart. Piero, and Brahms, and Dostoievsky, came into this typical Langham debate. He was restrained about Carew, who makes vicious attacks on him; although he did say the novel was "terrible", a thing I do not find difficult to believe.

22 September. Chijioke reads poems by Efua (with Ruth Wyne, who found them "interesting", much better than she had expected, meaningful, where she thought they would be meaningless).

23 September. Four recordings: Cyprian, with a story by Nchami; John Stockbridge, a young actor, reading "The Ninth Night", by a Jamaican, Evan Jones,* rather good, if heavily influenced by America; George Lamming, reading work by six poets, including Richard Murphy, who gets in because his father is Governor of the Bahamas. George introduces me to Andrew Pearce, the editor of *Caribbean Quarterly*, for whom I wrote "Prolegomena", a tall, sharp faced, white haired young man, with marks of suffering on his face. He is, George says, boycotted in Trinidad. Finally, Roy Fuller, to criticize Wilson Harris, whose quality he praises against the "deadness" of so much English production.

24 September. A letter from Dorothy Brooks reassuring me. The "Swanzy" put down to speak to her club on "The Gold Coast 1874-1901" is not me, but Kwaw...[...] No less than three batches have come from the Lindos, mostly, it seemed, concerned with wishful sex, the rape of white women. "The naked full-blown bust..." etc etc. What can have provoked this? In the summaries, the switch from slices of life and topography? [...] It was a relief to be called away to meet Roger Mais, the stormy petrel from Jamaica, the bohemian whose links are with the Rasta men. He was a little man, with a large bearded head, perpetually stroking thinning black hair. He has sold a novel to Jonathan Cape.

[From 26 September to 26 October Swanzy travels to Europe on honeymoon with his wife Henriette]

30 October. For supper, to the Figueroas in Fulham, where John has taken up the Thursday meeting, with George Lamming, and Shakes Kean[e], now playing trumpet at the Calypso Club. It is marvellous how the Figueroas create such atmosphere with so little money.

5 November. Disastrous American election. What in earth will Eisenhower do as President, with MacCarthy on the rampage, God alone knows? [...] Lloyd Reckord looks in, with a cheering account of Errol Hill in Jamaica – he has now been sent to develop the drama in Honduras.

10 November. JGW tells me that the little formal garden below my window in the heart of the Langham is the "BBC Garden", on which reports are made on the Home Service every week. How far I am from being 100% Corporation – or even 75%, 40% would be nearer the mark.

[...] A recording by Errol John of a forgettable piece by John E. Grimes, "Eyewash and Molasses," no bad description of what is coming into *Caribbean Voices* nowadays.

12 November. Mercedes with a *Diary*. She enjoyed last night's party. Her great art is enjoyment, and this is why her programmes are so good. Bumf all day.

13 November. Six hours of work on the "Notes", under the disapproving eye of young Miss Lindsay. After all, I am paid by the BBC. But is not the one journal that tries to make out what is really going on in Africa of some national importance? And should the man who makes it be paid a little more than £200 a year. Sometimes I really feel like screaming with rage. There is such ineffable hypocrisy among the English Establishment, pretending to maintain the withered ghost of the British presence in the world. Most of them I am sure would enjoy a deplorable short story by Eileen Ormsby Cooper, the PEN President in Jamaica, about old Hobson the gardener's love for the gracious life of "Windlands", that great house. In the afternoon, as luck would have it, a note comes from Admin. Is the Journal taking up BBC time? If it does not, they will allow it, subject to six-monthly reviews... JGW tells me to ignore the note. To give a statistical example: the cuttings for East Africa alone fell out of their folder today, I counted them, and they came to 343 separate items for the quarter.

14 November. "Notes" all day. JGW again counsels me to sit tight and say nuffin. I think poor little Miss Lindsay is really Not Guilty. Who can it be? One will never know.

20 November. George Lamming reads a poem by Edgar Rose,* a schoolmaster in Grenada, on "Fedon's Camp." Fedon was a French commander, and the poem was more than a little anti-British. We solved the problem by cutting for time, which I think, improved the poem as poem, but perhaps at the expense of its integrity. All afternoon, typing the "Notes".

21 November. Lloyd Reckord reading a story by his Cambridge brother, Barry, brilliant and sick: "Back o' Wall Boy". Then Notes until my head splits. The attempt to outline Mau Mau is really very interesting – all from local documents, not one taken up in England.

23 November. In the afternoon, a visit to the Empsons, back from China after five years, sitting on packing cases in Studio House, and serving

bitter tea. Hetta is thin, still lovely, with her fair hair darker. William is like a Mogul Emperor, with an eruption of hair below the chin, of the type known in Yorkshire as the "hangman's noose". Neither have a job in view. Why have they returned? Presumably because the British Council is shut down in Peking.

24 November. I spent all day polishing the "Notes". Lunch for Roger Mais, silly and sweet and violent, the dedicated artist. He is troubled by the problem of earning his bread, and has a pile of women's magazines to help him find the right formulae.

1 December. In the Langham, I find JGW is soon off to the Gold Coast to make a radio report concerned with a Home Office form. He would find a South African passport rather awkward. Curious battening down of the Imperial hatches? Can it be that some people are concerned with the immigration of the "external proletariat" into the centre of the decaying Empire. If only I had a clearer view, a firmer base, a wider field!

2 December. A parcel from Edgar Mittelholzer in Canada, containing *The Weather at Middenshot*, an interesting attempt to capture life in a London suburb, with admirable images – the large thermometer on the wall outside Smith's but with characters that seem West Indian, especially a sexy little maid. His play has been taken off, after only twelve days. Later, George Lamming, with a proof of *In the Castle of My Skin*. A dip into this as well: very talented, a little hard to read, dense, a touch of Herman Melville? [...] In the afternoon, Frank Pilgrim records one of Eula Redhead's agreeable, childish fantasies, and Chijioke reads Babalola's latest translations from Yoruba poetry.

4 December. A morning wasted in chit-chat with Chazal, now boss of Mauritian radio. Shopping at lunchtime with Henriette at Harrods. I finish George's novel. "A great man is born from mud". But really is it so surprising that someone can grow in a small village, in an island, far from the pressures of the *massemensch*.

5 December. In the afternoon, Mais records his story "Something for a Wedding," a blood and thunder account of a Cuban girl who takes a wrong turning. "Young, uptilted breasts". The juiciest bit is where she is slapped down on a couch by a brother. Supper at Adelaide Road for Shake Keane, who has great ease of manner, thanks perhaps to his skill with the wind instrument. Henriette likes him, despite an understandable but alarming interest in blood, revolution, dictatorship. The night is vile, full of fog, and I cough almost continuously.

6 December. A call from James Millar, whom we had invited to supper with the Lammings. He is ill in bed with TAB injections. Where is he going? "Oh, don't you know? With John to the Gold Coast". I have passed the stage of feeling angry, but Henriette has not – the lack of candour is "contemptible". At supper, she makes a great impression on George, who says that it is agreed on all sides that my temper is much improved since the marriage. He describes someone, whose name he will not give, extravagantly stroking the back of his head. "I am imitating a man called Swanzy". By now, I am struggling for breath and can scarcely laugh.

15 December. Snow began falling in the small hours. At the Langham, depression in the drab little office with nothing to read but manuscripts from African schoolboys, assembled by a British Council lady. The Guggenheim Fellowship Board wants "a candid opinion" on "Jay Rynveld" Carew, who has applied for a scholarship in the States. [...] AET Henry records a rather typical essay, "The Ramparts We Watch", on the theme of dodging charitable appeals. Empson on the radio, reading his own poems. Very strange. A shout, a bed-voice, a flick of an intellectual whip. One really wonders if he is not, after all, crackers.

18 December. The BBC Administration officially give me permission to pursue my work for the Royal African Society, in any time I like, "provided that my broadcasting commitments are carried out properly." How kind. [...] Sam Selvon, looking a little uneasy, came with a pretty little woman, not his wife, to record a potboiler, "The Mouth Organ," and went away much friendlier. Neville Dawes looks in, to take his leave – he returns to Jamaica on Tuesday, still hoping to avoid school teaching. In the post, an excellent talk from Cambridge in the Leavis tradition, by young Edward [Kamau] Brathwaite,* a Barbadian disciple of the great man.

20 December. To a party given by Jan Carew in the Fulham Road. He has a lady he calls his "wife", tall, handsome, lank-haired, humourless, very upper-class English. What a man! He must be ambivalent. Jarrett, the pleasant editor of *Phylon*, the impressive Cedric Dover, companion of Nancy Cunard, George Lamming, Shake Keane, who played his trumpet.

30 December. Cyprian Ekwensi reads "The Curse of Ma Mayo," by V.C. Nchami, perhaps the most consistent of all West African writers.

1953

7 January. Cyprian Ekwensi, to read "The Old Hen Protects Her Chickens" by Epelle. He has good news of Collins, who show interest in *People of the City*, provided modifications are made, on which he asks my help. I doubt whether they will in fact take it, they are far too 'fashionable'.

11 January. Henrietta far from well, and so I do the chores, later reading Emory Ross, and another American, Merlyn Severn, on the Congo. All these metropolitan writers, like Graham Greene, come to Africa with their own subjective excitement, write very well for twenty pages, then tail off, as the initial impressions fade, and they have nothing to add about the inwardness of what they see.

15 January. George Lamming, to read "The Stranger," by [Kenneth] Newton. He was rather under the weather, no word from America, and the review copies out in England. How I hope it will be a financial success – there is no question about its being a *succès d'estime*. He suggests our making a birthday programme for Frank Collymore, who is celebrating his sixtieth birthday. [...] At the office, Willy Edmett, having invited me to talk about Mau Mau, now wants me to chair a discussion group on books in the West Indian service – on Saturday afternoons. No thanks. But no doubt the offer was kindly meant. When the cat's away the mice will play...

16 January. A sweet, silly little actress called Molly Lawson, called in. "Of course, most of my friends wouldn't be seen dead broadcasting Overseas, but *I* don't mind"... She told me that the young Pole Andrzejewski, has made translation of Somali poetry, in the course of his labours to build up a Somali alphabet. "Do you translate the West Indian programmes too?" Such, no doubt, is the general extent of the British knowledge of our work. Tea with AET Henry and Cliff Sealy at Quality Inn. Roger Mais was to have come, and bring a young writer friend called John Hearne,* but he failed to turn up, for the good reason that he has at last found a job. We emerged to find the young man waiting, intelligent, white, with African features. He was modest and rather cagey –Jamaicans have little or nothing of the engaging extrovert quality of the Southern Caribbean. Because the latter are 1000 miles nearer the Equator? Or drawn from Ibo and Nigerian stock instead of the Gold Coast? Or simply through accident? He showed no great anxiety to take part in the programme, in any capacity. I gather from him that Mais has failed to distil the magic elixir for women readers.

19 January. In the afternoon, I went down to Cambridge, to read my

paper on the "Caribbean Imagination," to the West Indian Club. The secretary met me at the station, a Jamaican chemist called Irvine. He gave me supper at the Red Lion, with my real patron the Chairman, Eddie Brathwaite, a thin-faced young Barbadian, who is reading English under Leavis. Afterwards to the British Council room, where about twenty people listened politely for an hour, then spent an hour and a half in discussion. It was sad to hear young Brathwaite damning excellent poets like Roach... But he is filled to the eyes with the appalling cerebral ideas of misleaders like I.A, Richards, failed chemists. A white Barbadian in spectacles, whose name I did not catch, was remarkably silly about Derek Walcott, "the most easily understood of the West Indian writers". Why? "He writes in a language which anyone can understand". Barry Reckord, Lloyd's brother, a sharp, gnome-like figure, was sharp and sensible. At the end, Brathwaite tried, unsuccessfully, to sell some copies of the latest *BIM*. It was a stimulating evening, a compliment which I did not find when I visited the University College.

31 January. Saturday. All morning, John Fig, recording Stanley Sharps' treatment of Derek Walcott, *Writing in the Windward Isles*. He complains of the plots of the Leavisites in the Institute. In the afternoon, a fruitless journey to Highgate, to find the grave of Karl Marx.

2 February. At the office, Beau Milton reads a West African item, "The Leopard is in You and Me", a canter by Davidson [Nicol] through Cary, Greene, etc, English writers who know the Coast. He now calls himself H.M. Beaufoy Milton.

5 February. Sam Morris reads a little story by Eula Redhead, "The Undertaker". He is full of an invitation to Nigeria, and the defence of Jomo Kenyatta, but he will not tell me who it is who has put up £2800 to the League of Coloured People... He talks one day of returning to Grenada, to oust his rival Papa Gary.

12 February. Back at the Langham, Sam Selvon, an infrequent visitant, reads a story, "Calypsonian", adorned with his delicious slurring dialect. It is so long, and he so tired (nearly 6pm) that I go for whiskey from the hospitality room.

13 February. George Lamming came in to show me his novel, new minted from the press, with an elegant cover by Denis Williams. Glory! But I am a little downcast to see that the blurb contains no reference to the BBC (unlike the blurb for *A Brighter Sun*). And yet I have done so much more for George than for Sam... No doubt, such thoughts

are petty. The main thing is that the book is launched.

16 February. I had to rush back for my own recording – Lamming, Keane and Nadia Cattouse,* with poems from the South Caribbean, by Keane, Roach, Telemaque. George was rather pale, with pimples, worried about what reviewers may say, and the strain of living on very little money, except advances from his publisher Joseph. Even so, his sense of timing, the richness of his voice, has never been better, and I am lost in admiration.

18 February. Mercedes with a *Diary*, the metronome of my days. I took the collection of [my] essays and articles and reviews to Fabers, without much hope of acceptance. But an original book, in this episodic life, is beyond my powers. At the office, chat with George, who says that Andrew Salkey is seducing girls, claiming to be a member of the BBC staff. One may even be in the family way. Then there is John Hearne, the protege of Roger Mais, who has translated some of the Minnesingers, including the exquisite *Tandaradei*, the lady with the secret lover, watched by a nightingale, "Place my finger, you know where"... Ho-hum. Clifford Sealy, whom I scarcely know, rings up to ask if I will provide a reference for the bank.

24 February. Cyprian Ekwensi reads a folk tale, and tells me that he had seen Bailey, the owner of the South African monthly *Drum*, to protest at sex incidents *inserted* into a story he had written.

26 February. George and Sam send birthday greetings to Frank Collymore on his 60th anniversary. George's novel has come from the publishers, and I find a reference to the BBC in the blurb at the back. I tax him with failing to acknowledge the source of the title, in Walcott...

27 February. At the office, preparing the summary for the last six months of *Caribbean Voices*. Not much beyond Sam Selvon's Calypsonian, Razor Blade. "It had a time when things was really brown in Trinidad, and he couldn't make a note nohow, no matter what he do, everywhere he turn, people tellin him they aint have work". The equally easy rhythms of Cyril Charles* from St Vincent, with the "saved soul man" in the launch, and the fat lady ending "Well, well, well Cyril Charles, what they will do with you, eh? You must really write that down and get it published". Barry Reckord, with Fosco, the waif who attacks the old man out of revenge for life's cruelties ("Back o' Wall Boy"). Newton in "Mermaids are Chanting", with the madman, who finally drowns himself. "A green smiling giantess rose and struck". One had no time

to give the quality of Wilson Harris in "The Fabulous Well", only the St Vincentian Owen Campbell:

> And the birds come with yelling and blood song;
> Daylong they smite, knifing with blood-stained beaks.

3 March. The death of Stalin, paralysed, speechless. "O eloquent, just and mighty death... whom none could advise, thou hast persuaded." (When Nicholas I died, that was the caption in the *Punch* cartoon... How much more appropriate today.) At the office, as part of his drive to become the one and only African "expert", JGW dangles various posts in front of me. Why not Head of the Western Region in Ibadan? Why not Head of Programmes in the Gold Coast? My inclination, if anywhere, would be Uganda, under Andrew Cohen.

4 March. A grey, dismal day. This year, March comes in like a sea-lion. Mercedes, in her *Diary,* mentions a job going at Entebbe [Uganda]. Not a convenient juncture, with Henriette in the family way. But I *must* get out sooner or later, with JGW taking everything that is going, the literary programmes are at the bottom of the barrel, the African Society tottering along with a hundred generals and one private.

6 March. Keane comes in to read some of Roach's beautiful poems, one magnificent one, on Seven cedars, a celebration of the peasantry, full of clarity and deep emotion. He seems to be really the best poet in the Caribbean known to me, better than Walcott, who is however brilliant, cerebral. Keane reads the poems in a manner worthy of them. He is sleepy unshaven, after working all night on a telephone exchange. He drily says that he was given a spelling-test.

9 March. Frank Pilgrim* reads a story by Barnabas Ramon Fortune, "The Jilting of Richard." He is a delightfully gay young man, and was very funny indeed about the ambitions of Alma La Badie and her interracial magazine, *You and I.* The first publisher (when the title was *Tan*) was imprisoned for pornography, since an American journal with the same name specialized in smut about Hollywood. Then she found support from Lords Milverton and Vansittart but ran into trouble, since the new title *You and I* was already carried by a Christian magazine published by the OUP. Now she is suing her lawyer.

11 March. In the corridor [of the Langham], they have put up a chart showing the relative decline of the BBC as a broadcasting power. In 1946, its programmes outnumbered the rest of the world put together.

In 1950, the Soviet Union outnumbered the BBC and the Voice of America combined. In 1951, the Voice of America jumped in front of the Soviet broadcasts, and the BBC shrank still further.

18 March. Arthur Calder-Marshall came to present *In the Castle of My Skin*, with readings by Gordon. Despite the hospitality cabinet, it was not very successful. It comes through only too clearly that George Lamming is not really Arthur's cup of tea: far too clotted and romantic and private.

20 March. A red letter day for *Caribbean Voices*, a half-hour spot in GOS [General Overseas Service] for the poetry of the last seven years, well recorded by our 'ace' readers, Keane, Lamming and Gloria Vaz. [...] George was looking wan again. There was praise for the book by D. Paul in *The Observer* and from Leigh-Fermor in *The Sunday Times*. But Simon Raven, the Cambridge homosexual, is damning in *Time and Tide*, no doubt offended, among other things, by the hetero sex observed by the old lady. [...] We had to re-record Walcott's "City's Death by Fire", spoiled because the RPE caught his sleeve in the recording machine. George was not best pleased by Arthur's tepid praise.

27 March. Carew and [Ken] Maxwell,* to record a number of poets of the second order. The former arrives a quarter of an hour early with a sharp faced lady, who wants to watch proceedings. "I am his agent". I am afraid that I showed her the door. Carew could be very awkward with his basic dishonesty. He is "currently in negotiation" with a film company to write twenty Caribbean travelogues. At the moment, he has a script which should gross £7000 in American Television rights. He thawed after rehearsal. Ken Maxwell, on the other hand, was simple and modest. Do I sound like a tin-pot Hitler? At home, I start on the life and letters of Douglas Newbold, the Sudan adminstrator-intellectual, who resembles (or resembled, since he is dead) a King from Ur of the Chaldees. A long, portentous introduction by the She-Ancient [Marjorie] Perham. What would my correspondence consist of? Eva, Eyo, Ita, Phyllis, Lindo, Collymore, Alec Dickson, Tom Marealla, Davidson, Ben, Nchami, Epelle, Malcolm de Chazal, Elspeth, Basil Davidson...

30 March. The essays and reviews come back from Fabers, with a polite note from Miss Ashe. One hardly expected anything different. I must accept what Destiny has reserved for me, to be a channel for others. George Lamming comes in to record with Keane Easter poems, by Walcott. He says that 2500 copies have been sold in the first week, a very good start for a first novel. He was annoyed by the people on *In Town Tonight*,

who asked silly questions. "Have you ever been in danger?" "Every day".

2 April. Reading the debates on Central Africa. Some by men who care more for the maintenance of Empire than for the principles on which it is supposed to rest.

7 April. Adisa Williams reads an Ukeni story, "Triumph over Death," which was a classical store of culture borrowing. We had "orisons," "alone in a wide, wide world," a "beatific vision," "the sin is upon his head," a "thousand different sharps and flats," "owleyed women." The Nigerianisms were even more striking: "apparels," "shut your fangs," "cowed down," a "few thousand quids," "skulked back..." One sentence read "The killers led the Biakpan man away, and therafter he soothsayed no more"... Again, "The sun shone in dazzling, but non-exasperating glory". Of the teeth of snakes, "they were pearl white briers". In all this, I am a snapper-up of unconsidered trifles.

8 April. John Morris is reported to like the GOS programme on West Indian poetry very well, and to want it put on the Third.

9 April. In the lift, at the Langham, a maid with a sexy laugh, rather pretty, with sheer silk stockings. "Richard Dimbleby would be just my weight". The one-armed liftman with the golden hair: "He'd squash you". From this to Roger Mais and John Hearne, the latest arrivals from the Golden West. The young man, who has had a poem and a story accepted by the *New Statesman*, reads poems by himself and one Roy Taylor, and goes on to discuss industrialism. Roger Mais, a toad-like, powerful, piratical figure, reads some choruses from his own work "Atalanta at Calydon" (not to be confused with Swinburne). His novel, *The Hills were Joyful Together*, is coming out next week from Cape, with a Book Society Recommendation.

10 April. Mais and Hearne have given me a cold. A long talk with JGW and Willy Richardson on Federation and the Destiny of Mankind, involving a hot defence from me of limited Democracy. As JGW says, we are really a kind of University of the Air, for West Indians. AET [Henry] went down to Sandhurst the other day, to interview cadet officers from the Caribbean. (He found they were West African). He was seen by the GOC, who took him round in his car, with polite salutes all over the ground, from lordlings and commoners alike. They thought he was the Oni of Ife at least. From this, to record Lloyd Reckord reading an analysis of an Indian by his brother Barry, "High Brown".

15 April. John Fig records an Ormsby Marshall effort, "V for Victory." He has had a holiday in Spain, which "casts light on Jamaica." Literary gossip: Carew and his mistress have both had nervous breakdowns, Salkey is in a state of shock from the goings-on at Sugar Hill, which seems a co-operative brothel run by the waiters. The doorman comes from a distinguished Jamaican family, which thinks he is learning to be a dentist, when he has just served six months for living on immoral earnings. Perhaps this is an effort to give a spiritual value to work?

16 April. Bryan Chen,* the first to write about the Chinese in the Caribbean. He was nice-looking, and came with a curious story, Hollywood style, about an American airman talking about the wartime "Hump", and a quiet Trinidadian talking about the clash of colours: the quiet wife, the unworthy husband whoring with Coloured girls. (The story was called "A Girl from China"). In short, it had no literary value whatsoever, but as Chen was interesting, I gave him lunch. His grandfather, who had been a secretary of Sun Yat-Sen, returned to China in 1927, his father in 1938. Now they run a firm of lawyers, and represented the People's Republic in the lawsuit over the grounded planes of General Chenault, a real *cause célèbre*. Is he perhaps drawing the long bow, another Carew? He was very anti-American, declaring among other things that a boat belonging to Jardine Matheson had been sunk by a Nationalist commander on orders from the US consulate. Clearly, he would like to join the Reds, but cannot, since he is a class enemy. [...] At tea, Jan Carew, angered by his omission from the GOS programme, at one moment threatening, at another cajoling. I suggest a discussion with Lamming, Selvon, Mais, Keane: but he is going to Italy for the summer...

17 April. A letter from Cedric Lindo, with a photograph, showing the Crowning of Clare McFarlane as Poet Laureate of Jamaica, in robes, with a wreath of lignum vitae. I reply by quoting Housman:

> The wood of life was never quiet,
> Then twas the Roman, now tis I.

[...] At the office, gloom. The Overseas Service is to be investigated. Lunch with James Millar to whom I put the question point-blank. "How much work did JGW do in the Gold Coast?" "A surprising amount" for "one expected to be lazy."

21 April. An excellent review by [V. S.] Pritchett in the [*New Statesman*], on George's book, the most intelligent and sensitive notice it has evoked. At the office, two more literary men looked in for the first time. D.O.

Fagunwa,* the Yoruba novelist, the source of Tutuola, small and modest, despite publishing eleven books, mostly for schools, with an average sale of between 60,000 and 70,000. He was much nicer than Isaac Delano,* another Yoruba, but writing in English, burly and surly. Perhaps he is offended since he has been some time in England, at least a year. But it was surely up to him to seek us out?

24 April. At the Langham poor young Naipaul up from Oxford, sensitive, given to terrors, with Final Schools looming seven weeks away. He read one of his own sharp stories, "Old Man", very well, I shared his traumas over a cup of tea, wanting afterwards to have him back to supper. But a fresh-faced English friend took him away in his car.

27 April. Kathleen Davis, Auntie Kay, reads a rather good story by Enid Loewenthal,* "At the Big House." What am I now really but a petulant semi-official, at the head of B grade, with £1330 a year, and not much chance of anything else, so far as I can see, approaching my 38th year, and with so very little done?

28 April. Kunle Akinsemoyin, the sad Nigerian, more British than Nigerian, as he says, read a sad script by Agbonkonkon, "The Third Task", in which one finds the haunting sentence, "There are no echoes in dreamland". I find him sympathetic as ever, and gave him lunch, afterwards he accompanied me down to Trafalgar Square, on the stroll to the RAS. There is something very noble about his head, he talks of Jesus and the full life. He tries to understand "everybody, even Malan".

29 April. Later young Brathwaite and Gloria Vaz read six poets, including his own work, very well indeed on rehearsal, less well, as ever, on the final recording. The difference between professional and amateur; the professional can take production, the latter cannot. At the Marlborough, JGW was entertaining a delegate to the Coronation from Honduras, with a very pretty wife, like an exotic poppy. Willy Richardson was there, with a blonde South African girl, and Ernest Eytle, full of the elections in Guiana, won by the "Communist Cheddi Jagan," an Indian dentist, who secured 18 seats out of 24.

30 April. Cyprian reading a savage little story by Epelle, "The Tortoise has devoured the Snail." As usual, the formal victory with White Civilisation, the actual victory lies with Dark Africa.

1 May. Back at the BBC, Willy Richardson brings in an interesting man, a huge politician from Trinidad called Albert Gomes, who is interested

in writing. (He was a writer once himself, in the generation of C.L.R. James and Alfred Mendes). He is here for talks on Caribbean Federation, the fashionable hope of the declining Empire. He was good enough to say that *Caribbean Voices* had played its small part to create a general climate of opinion. That may be true, in some ways, but I wonder. Jamaica is not exactly enthused by the success of people like Lamming and Selvon.

7 May. Local elections, but I do not vote, torn between Labour heart and Tory mind. In any case, the Adelaide Ward is solidly Conservative, and overall, Labour will win, as the sovereign people will always vote *against* anyone in power. The first drafts for the "Notes". Over lunch, Andrew Salkey comes to record a "Letter from London," very neurotic. "The skeleton of a lamp-post pierces the death-aura spreading downwards into the fog"...

12 May. Bad news of Sam Selvon, who has got TB. Probably he has not been having enough to eat. I have done so little for him. And yet, perhaps because of this, I like him very much. Poverty and riches.

14 May. In the midst of typing the "Notes", a visit from Rudolph Dunbar, newly arrived from Haiti, by way of Jamaica. He looked very strange indeed, eyes yellow and swimming with moisture. Could this be due to drugs? He talked of gossip about his drinking habits. Poor dear Rudolph, a victim of propaganda. I thought of the pert girl who had asked him whether he conducted a bus or a tram.

20 May. Cyprian, reading a story by Nchami, "The Family Triangle," the morals of a palm wine drinkard, which provokes from me a half-hour pi-jaw. I am afflicted with a new temporary secretary, who does not try very hard. Jan Carew looks in with an effusion about the Mexican art exhibition, cast in dialogue form, and full of ill-concealed hatreds. "As for the decadence of the Christian tradition, I must say that I fully agree with you". Young Eddie Brathwaite also pays a call, at teatime. "My friend Boris Borzov, a naturalised Russian says that we must live as a natural part of the entire solar system". Altogether, a very spiritual day.

22 May. At tea the enigmatic Bryan Chen, who is in contact with Hetta Empson, and talks about using the *China Pilot* as a bedtime book.

27 May. Supper for Bryan Chen, and his pretty little wife from Chefoo, mainly so that Henriette might hear about Louis Van Eeghen, whom

Chen met in Hong Kong. It was unfortunate that I asked them to stay on to meet old Mr Van Eeghen, who came around 10. Chen was deliberately shocking. "Ludy told me all about his private life. Hot stuff. He took a girl to Paris before he came. Hahaha". After he had gone, I did not improve matters by telling the poor old man that he (Chen) was probably a Communist agent.

29 May. Dennis Selvon* reads a bitter story by his brother Sam, "Foster and the Coronation," and Vivette Hendricks a "Coronation Verse," by E.M. Roach, which contains a stanza on the famous Hawkins, whose coat-of-arms contained a demi-Moor, bound. It is awkward that anti-Imperialism is so much more sincerely felt than Imperialism. The slight alterations that had to be made were improvements, technically, and so admitted by the readers.

3 June. Drinks at the Marlborough with JGW, S.G. Williams, Pelletier, James Millar. They say that the crowds at Oxford Street [for the Coronation] were so small that the police did not have to use the crush barriers. I read a "Hymn to the Coronation" [of Queen Elizabeth II], by the distant loyalist, Kenneth MacNeill Stewart at his farm in Oterkpolu [Ghana]. Henriette came with Annie [daughter of Eric Ravilious and Tirzah Garwood] to hear an elaborate programme for West Africa, with Mercedes and Ellis Kommey on the processions, and a musical extravaganza with traditional Ashanti songs, and *Asafo* drums, played by Koti Tay, and seven Ewe from the arts club, deafening in the small studio. Jokes with little Annie, whom I call Tagalong, only to be dubbed Podge. Q [Swanzy's mother] has sent her a broach, in the form of a crown.

5 June. Ken Ablack looks in, full of complaints about the difficulties of providing 21 hours of sustaining time a week on Trinidad Radio, which is commercial. They will not even lend him a rehearsal studio. His position is so awkward, he confided, that he did not dare "arrive in time" for the Coronation. Willy Richardson was bitter about the absence of Colonials in the procession, apart, of course, from Queen Salote. At 1700, Vic Reid turned up with a colourless *rechauffé* of the Abbey ceremony, slightly the worse for wear, after a lunch given by Robert Herring. We went on to a BBC party for Colonial journalists, very few of whom turned up. I talked to a hostile Ashanti on the *Sentinel*, an alert Muganda on *Matalisi*, an agreeable Guiana editor (English) and to Hewitt and Vic Reid, who said that the way I had survived the drinking party at Gordonstown on my visit was still a folk memory in Kingston circles.

6 June. More West Indian reaction on the Coronation. Vic Reid turned up with his second script, highly critical. Why was he here? "We were not needed. We were left out." Why could there not be a Colonial maid of honour? A Fijian sword-bearer? A South Sea choir? This, from a good Commonwealther, a Queen's man... I tried excuses – the Queen in London was the queen of Great Britain and Northern Ireland etc but it did not convince. George Lamming was more emotional and more favourable, perhaps because he had been watching in the Whitechapel Road, and was touched by the East End crowds waiting in the rain. He was intrigued by the peeresses on the TV. "What is wrong with them, Man? The peers are all red and jolly, their wives are all pale and angular." [...] I started reading the Mais novel, *The Hills were Joyful Together*, a series of savage conversations, mainly about Jamaican poverty. Vic Reid looked in for a drink, leaving for a party with Halcro Ferguson, the *Observer* correspondent, who is marrying a Jamaican girl.

10 June. Seth Jectson reads a little sketch, "In Future," by Jonathan Vincent, about being overcharged for oranges by a Temne woman in Freetown. It has a piercing candour, which comes from poor Jonathan's derangement. If there had been any "art" in it, it would have been absurd. And yet, how artful in his artlessness. He used a perfect phrase for the woman falling back on her last resources in the altercation: *sheep's eyes*. In the Park, under the trees, I finish Mais' novel, which I fear I do not like, unlike Cape and the London critics: a mixture of sadism and fine thoughts, a disgusting detailed account of a knife murder, a woman chopped up with a matchet, several floggings and fights, described with relish, and interspersed by almost equally disgusting "fine writing"... Perhaps this is the Jamaican reality, perhaps I am reverting to type, scuttling for cover among the faded upper-middle-class, to which I think I belong, the colonial gentleman. (CMG = Colonial Made Gent)...

15 June. The nice little Yoruba writer, D. O. Fagunwa, contributes an excellent professional talk, "My Life as a Writer." He is wonderfully un-angry about the fame achieved by his plagiarist Tutuola.

18 June. JGW informs me that I am to be sent for six weeks in November to East And Central Africa, at a cost of £480 air fares, with no brief, except possibly "a few talks..." I feel that I have earned it, through the years of slogging, at the Journal. But it is a very awkward time, so soon after the birth of the baby, and I ask for a postponement. [...] Later, I read a play sent in by Michael Kittermaster, the Broadcasting Officer in Lusaka, the best and most professional mind at work in the entire African field. It assembles types: Marsden, a kind and liberal DO of the older

school; Tyndal, an insensitive newcomer; Jill, a Leftist sympathizer; her father, Merrill, a settler leader. Against them: Kunwele, the educated and rejected Moderate; Temba, a clerk who is also a leader of the African underground. At the climax, Kunwele is shot dead by Merrill, who thinks he has murdered Jill and her mother, when actually he has defended them. The tone is sad. "What do they hate? Everyone – themselves perhaps". And the end is defeated. "The best days in Africa are over… All the best people are going" (sc. the Whites). It is an excellent little play, but I have to return it, not knowing a proper source in the Home Service. I returned to find Henriette, understanding about the trip to Africa.

19 June. Gordon Woolford reads "The Hairpin," by Euton Jarvis.* Will the run of mediocrity ever come to an end? I really feel that I have "exhausted the Mandate of Heaven," so far as the literary programmes are concerned, certainly in the Caribbean, although there is the next generation to try and foster, the Brathwaites and Naipauls.

22 June. Fagunwa kicks off the week with a talk on orthography. It transpires that the young RPA studied Sanskrit for a year. What an extraordinary place Auntie BBC is: As JGW says, we are really a substitute university.

23 June. John Fig, a stranger nowadays, reads "Home is the Hunter," a sharp, sex-obsessed story by Hugh Morrison,* about an exile returned to Jamaica. John did not read well, and took production badly, but otherwise he is the same old amiable badger. […] A painful evening with Hugh Springer, who was teased by George Lamming, somewhat the worse for liquor. "Can anyone be stupid enough to be a nationalist?" A Jamaican girlfriend of Ellis Kommey leaves an extraordinary poem in manuscript:

> That I might list for aye to his guitar.
> Be silent, brat. You are me! Me!
> His acts conform not to th'accepted standard.

With this, some weird orthography:

> For he who, she sees not he…

Yet oddly there is also emotion:

> Yet where are you, that left without adieu?

It is really the kind of standard which, for my sins and in my ignorance, I expected in 1946.

24 June. Spike Hennessy calls, thin after an appendix "blew up" in

Funtua. He is caustic about Nchami, "bloody little twirp", and Ben [Enwonwu], "bone-idle, womanising bastard". Mercedes with a *Diary* and much gossip. Putnams are enthusiastic about the novel *Black Argosy*, which she has written about a Yoruba good boy, and a Yoruba bad boy, based on the material she amassed during the trial of the Gambian drug-addict who murdered his "pusher"; and from her visits to the Methodists, and the Franciscan Mission in Cable Street. She describes the sad end of the Wellcome Collection of Africana, two roomfuls left, after the museums have had their pick. "Real Citizen Kane stuff, from Xanadu".

25 June. In the afternoon, a visit from young Brathwaite. He has got a 2.1 in English, and I suggest he take a teachers' diploma. He thinks of working, for a time, in Africa. With him he had a sheet of what I thought rather bad poems by one Thom Gunn, a protégé of John Lehmann.

27 June. Saturday. Painting a bookcase, sorting the pictures, burning a hideous portrait of a hideous Mallam by Ben, and two ugly little East African tourist statuettes. The stranger kicking vigorously. We decide to call him Martin, if, as Henriette is more and more convinced, it is a boy.

29 June. At last something for *Caribbean Voices* with real quality. Lloyd Reckord reads a "Ballad of the Banana Man," by Evan Jones, a Jamaican script writer.

> Yes, by God and this right hand,
> I'll live and die a banana man.

A "white man tourist" bids him "Go, get some education, be of some service to your nation...", but he still returns the defiant answer. I have not seen so strong a statement of the peasant culture since the first offerings from Roach, the distant poem by Telemaque. At tea time, Sam Morris to read a story by Forde, "The Stick." Sam is riding high, with Dunbar's old job as London correspondent for the Negro Press Association in the States, the "only man of colour to attend the reception at the US Embassy for the Coronation."

30 June. Re-record the poetry anthology for the Third Programme, with the single directive from Newby, "read it rather flatly and colourlessly". What he was really doing was to use the extracts as an illustrated talk, rather than a performance with notes. As a consequence, I thought all the thrilling reading of M. G. Smith's "Madonna and Child" was lost. Ah well, it is a point of view (or hearing). Gloria Vaz, far

gone with child, Keane and Lamming, privately agreed with me, but followed the direction faithfully. George, incidentally, says that the novel [*In the Castle of My Skin*] is being translated into Swedish.

1 July. In the afternoon, Vidia Naipaul read his father's story "Ramdas and the Cow," a beautiful example of his gentle, humorous art, bringing Hinduism into the burning lens of West Indian life. After his inhibitions had been overcome, Naipaul read it very well. I took him home to supper. It is curious what "breeding" is. Seepersad is a struggling journalist, one generation out of the canefields, but he is a Brahmin, and his whole approach is aristocratic. So is his son's. For example, Vidia will not eat the meat that Henriette offers him, and she provides an omelette. He seems confident about his Schools, especially the Early English paper. At the moment, his admiration is reserved for Saki. A sister, whom he evidently respects and loves, is going home, after four years at Benares.

2 July. Noel Vaz, who now affects the diaeresis, like Noel Coward, comes in to read a story "The Door of Darkness," by one Sylvester [Small].* He is very prickly and read the sketch, in his fine baritone, without any real skill. [...] I leave him for another sojourn among the really awful poets whom Kommey pushes. One of them is called Beckford:

> Only the dark retains its It-ness.
> However,
> Delegate to me my duty, O destiny…

27 July. Gordon reading a charming little piece, "Fishing on the Rupununi", by a girl called Edwina Melville*. It comes directly in the post, with a delightful letter and a photograph of the author and her two little children, mounted on a buffalo. A marvellous life, if terribly remote on the savannahs, on a vast ranch with BBC radio almost the one cultural consolation. This was followed by Lloyd Reckord reading "Maroon Defence of Cockpit Country," by the ever-graphic Inez Sibley. Someone has written to George Lamming, asking for "the anthology, from which the programme on the Third was made."

28 July. At tea-time, in the Langham, Willy Richardson brings C.L.R. James, the author of *The Black Jacobins*. He had a charming boyish face, framed in grey hair, and talked endlessly and often amusingly. "*Intolerance* is great. I don't say I like its racist attitude, but it's great. The trouble is, D.W. Griffith could make it like that in 1916. Today he couldn't. He'd have a script conference. Cut that line – the Legion wouldn't like it. Cut that – it would get under the hair of the National Association

for the Advancement of the Negro"... Admirable objectivity.

29 July. Listener Research issue a report on the poetry program put out on the Third. It was heard by 0.1% (which could be 40,000), with an Audience Index of 61% against an average of 66% for poetry readings, and 63% for a programme of Caribbean songs. The panel (clerk, foundry worker, retired schoolteachers) liked the introduction and the reading, but objected to the dialect at the beginning, and the "lugubrious" nature of most of the extracts...

6. August. A letter from Edgar Mittelholzer in Canada, about nudism, and his admiration for Mais' novel. [...] Wynford Vaughan Thomas, just back from ten days in Nigeria holds forth in Sheriffs, consuming half a dozen glasses of the South African white wine, Blankenberghe. [...] He discovered Amos Tutuola after much enquiry, at the Ministry of Labour, where he is a Messenger (Second Class). The white executive had never heard of him, but summoned him to his office. He sidled in, expecting a reprimand. "Oh, you're Tutuola, are you? Well, for some reason, this white Massa wants to talk to you". They went to a local palm-wine drinkery. "It is a great privilege to meet you, Mr Tutuola. I have read your book with great interest and admiration". "You read ma book?" "Yes, indeed." "You *buy* ma book?" "Yes, certainly. And my friends, the poets Thomas and MacNeice." "I get very little money here". "Ah well, the ways of authorship are difficult. Now tell me, Mr T., how did you come to write the book?" "Ah bought a pencil". "Yes, but where did it come from? Inspiration?" "Ma old Mother buy an exercise book, and she say, You write. You do no good otherwise". I left this scene for George Lamming, who read Roach's "In Mango Shade."

11 August. As a comment on West Indian standards, Cedric Lindo writes to say that the consensus in Jamaica is that George Lamming's book is "tedious".

13 August. The "Notes" come more easily than usual, perhaps because there are fewer cuttings to deal with, and this perhaps because Africa is falling into a more definite pattern... Listening to Bornemann on the Third on African music. One most beautiful, ethereal melody from a French African Griot, playing some stringed instrument, music that wavers across the air. There is also a harp, and some lovely Baoule choruses. The commentary is didactic, and full of mispronunciation: *A*ccra, Lahgos, Grenahda (the island). He also says that, "of course", African music is "quite different" today from what is was 400 years ago. How on earth does he know?

28 August. Dictating the six month's summary. The best things seem peasant – the "Song of the Banana Man," by Evan Jones, the "Maroon Defence" by Inez Sibley. "Moon plenty, young, beautiful as wild rose over mountain pass, erect of stature, wide lofty bearing, come of age daughters, and parents gather fe feast time... An' young men, Maroons all, muscle a'plenty, bodies stained with red dirt of Cockpit County, eyes quick, wild and fiery, feet agile and swift, an' hunter blood in dem, nu' have gun an' cutlass fe nutten". The Maroons were runaway slaves who maintained themselves in wild mountain country in North-Central Jamaica. Another tradition, the Hindu culture of the gentle Seepersad Naipaul, "Ramdas and the Cow". The cow is Chitkabari, red and white, barren, and therefore intended by his wife for the butcher, but spared by Ramdas, terrified of Hell and his venomous neighbour Sookhram. A wonderful series of lamps hung on this simple story line, the "cowmothers, Diwali night (in honour of Lakshmi), the red flag of Hanuman the monkey god, the white flag of the sun god, Narayan..." "Careful...don use dem words. Is ah sin. *Gowhatia* Cow murder. Tousan and tousan year for dat"... As a contrast, the returned student Jeffrey Hornsey, in the story "Home is the Hunter" by Hugh Morrison. A Jamaican student whose mind keeps repeating "My people, my people", only to fall foul at the airport of a "short, coal-black pot-bellied official", and, later, a sexual rival Fat Neck, at the Rio Rita Bar.

2 September. Mercedes with a *Diary*, Akinsemoyin with a sharp little story about a gold-digger, "Patience and her Kojo," so sharp that Angela Christian originally refused to read it. At the Finance Committee [of the Royal African Society], Ponsonby suggests I go down to see Groves, Brodie. They joke about Basil Davidson, "deported by the Union, and recommended by Swanzy".

4 September. John Fig comes in to record his last reading, "The Betrayal" by Edgar Boyce. So the heroic period of the Voices comes to an end... He is returning to Jamaica in a fortnight, and describes an interview at the Colonial Office, a 'medical'. It was only at the end that he realised that they were testing his *psychology*. "They write memos home"...

8 September. Isaac Delano, the Yoruba writer, with whom I got on so badly at our first meeting, reads an excellent talk on "My Life as an Author," full of innocent vanity. Failing in English, he is now turning to Yoruba, composing a 12,000 word dictionary, *Yoruba-Yoruba* (like the French Larousse).

18 September. I get up very early to see John Fig off on the boat-train from Waterloo, with his wife and numerous progeny. Four other friends are there, including George Lamming, who could not come back with me for breakfast. [...] In the morning, to the Training School on Marylebone Road, conducted by Ted Livesey, a little sharp man, to hear a play by Frances Quarshie-Idun,* a pretty, sophisticated creature, the daughter of a Gold Coast judge, very much influenced, I think, by [Louis] MacNiece's [radio play] *The Dark Tower*.

21 September. At the office, I sat in, all day, on Lloyd Reckord's production of the verse play by A.N. Forde, "The Plot in the Garden". Lamming, Keane, Salkey, [Norman] Rae, Frank Pilgrim, Gloria Vaz, [Ken] Rudette. The final result was successful, helped by a competent young team in the control room. Henriette brought James to watch the final recording. In the evening to the new colonial hostel Queens Gardens, once the home of Herbert Spencer, bring Nchami to supper. (He is flying this week to a two year course in journalism at the Iowa State University). I found him elaborately decked out in traditional robes, beautifully embroidered, with high stock, and a curious kind of *uhlan* cap, in red, black and white.

22 September. Half an hour with MacDona, who summoned me to his palatial office in Barclay's International Branch in Lombard Street. I find these encounters infinitely exasperating. How dare these tycoons make plans above our heads, on the strength of the £100 odd their organisation, in its vast generosity, doles out to the poor little undercapitalized RAS?

28 September. Akinsemoyin reads a story by Agbonkonkon, "Birds of a Feather." An artist meets a poetess by the side of the lordly Niger. Although she acts like a tart, she will have none of him. The style seems modelled on *Tom Brown's Schooldays*, down to the historical present.

29 September. An unfortunate racial occasion. I had invited Noel Clark, a middle-aged Jamaican white woman, in to read some poems by various hands, including Figueroa and Barbara Ferland, a friend of hers. As luck would have it, Vivian Hazell,* a very sensitive (and very black) Jamaican looked in at the same time, with some poems of his own. Why not combine the two? The trouble was that Miss Clark refused to speak to him, confining all her remarks to me. "Noel Vaz, a dear friend of mine, so talented". The trouble is made worse by the fact that Hazell's "Ballad of the White Wife," is ambiguous. It may be Death, it may be Racial Prejudice. I realize I would not last a week on Radio Jamaica.

1 October. George Lamming reads from his new novel, *The Emigrants*, a long conversation on a steamer, with himself appearing rather portentously as Collis. It is all on the same emotional level. "It was something that moved Collis very deeply". He himself is acquiring the tricks of the booksy world, the exaggerated start, the over-emphatic *"Henry"*. Over tea, he became human again, expressing his love for Whitehead. I think he is really too good for fiction. If he had had the chance of higher education, he would have been a poet or a philosopher. We talk about Selvon, for whom neither of us has done anything, about Gordon Woolford, who is on sick leave and is talking of starting a small dress shop (Luce?). Willy Richardson has heard from Abrahams, who dislikes the Gold Coast; "xenophobic, provincial, tribal. One unlucky man got up to ask PA [Peter Abrahams] what he did. "I am a writer". "Yes, but what do you really do for a living?"

6 October. George Lamming borrows £8, AET [Henry] £5. But I am working on an article on Caribbean writing, for which the University of Oklahoma will pay me $100. Who lives on whom? In any case, George at least is bound to pay it back. Ken Rudette, the singer training at the Garden, reads a story about "Czien and La Diablesse," by Eula Redhead. What do they get?

14 October. Vidia Naipaul reads a sharp little satire, "Epicurean Service", aimed at a pompous Hindu journalist, who tried to patronise him on a plane to Paris. He is distressed, because his father Seepersad died last Saturday, aged only 47. Poor boy, he wants to make money quickly, either through an oil company, or the UN, which offers posts to Spanish and French translators. I talk to him like a Dutch uncle, and later ring George Ivan Smith at UNESCO…

16 October. Airgraphs from abroad. John Fig complains about the "shallowness" of life in Mona, "without the dimension of God". Nchami finds he must work 3, even 4 years, at Iowa for his degree. Agbonkonkon has failed the University scholarship he hoped for, and will concentrate on "recognition"… Asante thinks of giving up poetry, "which does not pay."

17 October. At Wokingham, I take a taxi, via the Pinewoods sanatorium, where the Selvon family, Sam, wife, and baby, are lying. It is a French Canadian foundation, lying just beyond Caesar's Camp. He looked pale, but otherwise quite strong, and with his pride, refused to take any fruit or chocolate, saying that his brother Dennis looks after him very well. He can only see his wife once a week. The attendant said

he was making slow progress, and has an even chance of a complete recovery. I felt miserably inadequate, leaving him a single *Lilliput*.

19 October. [Henriette gives birth to the couple's first child] I did not learn until well after 1800 that Baby arrived at 14.47, a fine boy of 7lb 4oz., kicking lustily. After a flurry of telephoning, I went to see her in the Anne ward. Baby has a big head, a sloping brow, rather cross in repose, a strong resemblance to Sam, very delightful. [...] Henriette is radiant; in the words of Lamming,

> Tending her orchid of flesh,
> The frail filament of her fibre...

22 October. At the studio Keane reads five lesser poets from the Southern Caribbean quite brilliantly, a different approach for each. He has just returned from touring with his band, as far West as Haverfordwest, as far North as Inverness. An angry letter from the British Council man in Kumasi (Groves) complaining of our "intellectual cossetting" of MacNeill Stewart, and his "tendentious" "Ode to Dr Nanka Bruce"... Adisa Williams has written to congratulate us on the same item. Certainly, if one applies absolute standards it is no great thing ("His home a people's hermitage" etc), but then, if one did, there would be nothing to put in the programme at all. JGW was more concerned with a report in the *Evening News* about a delegation to meet Cheddi Jagan, the Marxist victor in Guiana. They included Frank Pilgrim, and Peter Kempadoo,* "a member of the BBC's West Indian Service"...

23 October. A young German, anti-Nazi, Janheinz Jahn, writes from Frankfurt. He has translated half a dozen poems from *African Affairs*, and wants permission to include them in an anthology he is bringing out, called *Black Orpheus*. I suppose he should be given permission even though he excludes Lasebikan and Babalola. Why is it that it is a German who does these things? JGW is relieved to learn that Pilgrim and Kempadoo were sent by the Labour Party to try and wean Jagan from the Communists.

30 October. Pilgrim, Pauline and Gordon read an extract from "Canje, the River of Ocean," by the strange Wilson Harris: a page and a half of prose introduction, eight pages of epic. Achilles, Tiresias, and Ulysses appear on the Canje River (returned soldier, logman, fisherman).

31 October. Up at 0730, dusting, cleaning, shopping for the Great Day, the arrival of Rainer-Martin in the world.

3 November. The papers talk about Churchill's view, "atomic bombs as a moral deterrent". This is what I tried to put in ethical terms in 1945, only to have the ms returned by Connolly. I suppose it is really not a very elaborate idea – a Jamaican had it in a poem years ago. At the Langham, Ekwensi reads a story about old days in Abeokuta, "The Olumo Rock", by a young man called Wole Soyinka.* It is clumsy, but memorable, much better than the usual run.

4 November. Mercedes with a *Diary*, as usual tilted against religion. We argue about *Geneviève*, which she "adores". Salkey reads an Anancy story, "The Rains Will Come," rather too obviously aimed at Bustamante.

10 November. Joan Silverman cheers me up with a wonderful misprint for Mittelholzer's *Weather at Middenshot*: she types it "Middenshit", no bad description of too much of him.

11 November. Death of Dylan Thomas. The papers treat him as a major poet.

12 November. Young Brathwaite makes a series of poetry recordings: a "Report on a Village" by Neville Dawes, and poetry of various kinds and excellences: a long "Legend" by Roach, a collection of four minor poets, with Margaret Lee.*

13 November. "Notes" most of the day, ending with various Mau Mau atrocities. Gordon came to read an amoral Jamaican story, "Ganja," by L. Sylvester Small.

20 November. Adisa tells me that Cyprian has sold his novel *People of the City* to the new publishers Andrew Dakers. JGW shows me an application for a Guggenheim Fellowship put in by George Lamming, who wants a reference from him. [Barnabas] Ramon Fortune "thanks the programme" for providing him with the money to buy a typewriter. Cedric Lindo says that St. Lucian meanness has prevented Walcott from going to study at Bristol. Such is our tiny world.

24 November. Martin's breakfast is a moveable feast, between 0400 hours and 0700 hours...Today it was early, which gave me a bad temper, made worse by Noel Vaz, who mucked up a story "Seven Voices of the Rainbow," by the brilliant, sick, mind of Barry Reckord, who hates the Negro race so much. We had to cut out a sentence at the end, (caked dirt falls between the toes of the hero's mother, as she serves him with food). [...] At 1700, Neville Mittelholzer, a brother Edgar never

mentioned, although he has been here since 1945.

26 November. Those whom the gods would destroy they first make mad. The *Mail* has a leader, attacking the hysteria of the USA, writhing under the coils of the appalling McCarthy. Yet on the same page, they give details of what is happening in Kenya, an officer, infuriated by the hamstringing of his horse, tells a Sergeant Major to kill *anyone* black. He does so, shooting in the stomach a group of harmless forestry officials at a road block. They cry out in Swahili for God to put them out of their agony. Later evidence reveals that 10/- prizes are offered for Mau Mau deaths by competing units, with a barometer in one mess showing "official" deaths on one side, and "unofficial" on the other. On the other side of the medal, no "person of colour" is invited to the dinner offered the Queen in Bermuda. The British world Empire is no more, we are pursuing the shadow of a shade. Neither creative, nor dominant, minority...

27 November. Back to record G. Woolford in a story by Cyril Charles, "The Maker of Men," a substitute for the embarrassing Reckord piece. He has been visiting Oxford with an anarchist friend called Ostergaard, and was impressed by the fierceness of the young men he met. Willy Richardson brought in the sociologist Braithwaite, who remembered me from the Fabian conference at Clacton.

4 December. At lunchtime, a recording of four poets, including Brathwaite, by Pauline and Keane. The latter comes armed with two works by Gide in translation, and a French blonde girlfriend, who makes intelligent comments on the tapestry by Jean Turcat, presented to the BBC by the French Government. I also learn that Jan Carew is in a Surrey mental home...

7 December. A good start for the week. Tony reports a conversation with Joan Liverman, who, she suggested, might take the place of Sylvia's secretary, who is leaving. "No, I'd rather kill myself with Mr Swanzy. I learned twenty new words in the last batch of letters that we did". The *News Chronicle* is running a series of rave articles on Schweitzer. A piece from James Cameron (the man sacked from *Picture Post*, for describing among other things the child brothels run in Korea for the GI defenders of freedom). Roy Fuller deals with a collection by Clare McFarlane, unexpectedly good, much better, he says, than new verse sent him by the *Listener* for review. They are heavily influenced by Yeats.

> These are the poems I built
> Out of what remained
> After the dreams were spilt –
> Like that poor, feeble-brained
> Man who found it gone,
> The cottage of his hand,
> A wife and only son,
> Burned by the King's command;
> Who took the precious loam
> Of carbonated life
> And built another home
> To mitigate his grief;
> A garden where alone
> He heard at times afar
> The winds assume a tone
> Dear and familiar.

We went on to discuss Africa, where R. Fuller has published some pieces in the ephemeral *Equator*. In the evening, ministered to Henriette and Martin, and type a cross notice on the bad collection of West African fables, produced for Penguin by Currey and Phebean Itayemi.

10 December. Miss Felhoen Kraal, from the Tropical Institute in Leyden, and the review *West Indische Gids*, to obtain details of Caribbean writing in English. She is a pretty creature, not too starchy although she is a Doctor, read Law, worked in Surinam. Needless, to say, she already knows far more about the West Indian literary situation than anyone among the shabby ranks of British academics…

11 December. The 21st anniversary of the Overseas Service. […] Back at the Langham, Frances Quarshie-Idun reads a story by Martha Bello, "My First Baby", in a sexy voice.

12 December. Letter from Efua, who is trying to lead the literary life, and has met a young American called Sutherland. Dennis Selvon reads some uninspiring memories of Christmas. He says that Sam is having his infected part removed by surgery on the 19th. Leaving the studio, we meet Gordon, and are all photographed for the TV programme they are making on the coming of age of External Broadcasting.

14 December. At the Langham, Spike Hennessey calls from Mycenae Road, with an extraordinary article, for *West Africa* [magazine], on the West African service. I am an "intellectual giant", "obsessed by West

Africa". I am also, with Mary and Sheila, "an agent of MI5..."

15 December. Seth Jectson reads a Christmas pot boiler, the young singer Rudette an unmemorable story by one Connie McTurk... Lunch at the School of African Studies with Lyndon Harries, the Swahili specialist, depressed by London, and regretting Mikindani. The nice schoolmaster Hollingsworth was also there and they approved a vague idea for an *East African Voices* programme. The cultural sources would "very likely" be far *richer* than in West Africa, although hardly directly in English!

1954
[Swanzy begins 1954 with a six week trip to East and Central Africa]

1 January. The visit to East and Central Africa, six weeks, ostensibly to prepare a GOS programme on Uganda, which the Queen is visiting later in the year, actually, as editor of *African Affairs*, to see a little of the reality that lies behind my back-room burrowings.

2 January. I am met [at the airport in Entebbe, Uganda] by Graham Phillips, the Chief Engineer to the Uganda Broadcasting Service, (seconded from the BBC) and Mrs [Lena] Jeger and Parry, the assistant PRO, who conveys greetings to me from Andrew Cohen. It is hard to absorb after the anomalous life in London. But the fifteen miles into Kampala bring one down to the slower pace in Africa. [...] The Philipses live far out on the East, towards Jinja, behind the Kaloleni Hill, which is the main European residential quarter. [...] GP plunges almost immediately into an account of the progress in building up the new station, at the incredible cost of £84,000, which includes transmitter, mast, a studio block. [...] Phillips is particularly proud of a control panel which he designed and built, with his assistant Stephenson, for £720, instead of the £40,000 charged for standard Marconi equipment. [...] It is all rather intoxicating, the creative side of colonialism, the belated effort which *should* have been made after the end of the first war [...]. We call on the Stephensons, a tall owlish man, a large wife, a nice little boy. Inevitably, there is tension. Stephenson, I was told, is going on leave, after a long tour of three years [...]. I take to him, for he is passionately interested in local music, and it must be galling to come under someone without African experience, straight from Cyprus and the Middle East...

4 January. In the evening, supper with Audrey, handsome in green silk. The others there: a red-bearded Professor of English called Warner,

and Vowles, the Registrar, a young man with a sharp nose and grating voice. They had with them their respective wives, and the conversation was academic politics. They were all reading *The Reason Why* (the account of the Charge of the Light Brigade) but did not like it when I said that Phillips was also reading it. [...] Towards the end, partly to get them talking, I raised the gambit of a literary programme for East Africa from London. They hummed and hawed, and I can scarcely blame them. The Warners are the backbone of the Literary Club, composed almost entirely of Indians, given to hot debates of T.S. Eliot...

[On the 13th January, Swanzy flies from Uganda to Kenya]

14 January. I took a taxi at the Overland Garage, crowded with white girl staff, to go to the suburb of Kabete, where Cable and Wireless run their broadcasting station. A very English scene, but for the passers-by. A fine new church with high tower and vast windows, built by the Church of Scotland. Parklands, unpretentious European bungalows, with gardens full of flowering shrubs. [...] Many signs of the emergency: barbed wire, look-out towers, RAMC lorries. The Kikuyu are not so ugly as I had expected, although it is painful to see their women, straining forward with vast headloads, held by a strap around their brows. Finally, Kabete and Electra House, a bungalow manned by Coulthard, and a staff of four Europeans and two Indians, who provide six hours broadcasting a day. [...] They rebroadcast the "whole range" of BBC programmes, apart from the Third, and "talks on African politics"... They put on no straight plays, because they have no rehearsal studio. The operation is financed by 30/- licences, with some 17,000 subscribers, mostly European since the Indians are difficult to check, and exchange sets... The Indian programmes use commercial film music and Voice of America transcriptions. Their franchise lasts until 1956. There was a scheme to expand services with £100,000, but London has "gone sour". Of our shortwave output, he only "willingly" relays the World News. Four years ago, he tried to stop *Calling East Africa*, but was compelled by pressure from the Colonial Office to renew it. It is still "unsatisfactory," because of the content, "English details", and the reception, which is bad. None of this is particularly interesting, or surprising.

14 February. The last of Africa, a dark road by a dune. I wonder how long it will be before I return.

16 February. Back at the Langham, very deflated. [...] [JGW] for his part, heard my travelogue, but showed not great interest in any follow up. Reception conditions, programmes, he simply does not want to

know about. Perhaps this is to be expected: but he does not even want a report. As for the idea of an East African literary programme, he dismisses it out of hand. The overmighty subject. Otherwise, it can all be regarded as 'experience'.

17 February. The afternoon spent in getting on top of *Caribbean Voices*. One detects the influence of the gifted Walcott on less gifted rivals, who are very flatulent. In a Trinidad office drama: "Go on, apprise me of the total tally of my shortcomings and indebtedness". A Jamaican writes of "the elemental orchestration of the zodiac". Another soars even further. "Haughtiness of laughter swelling in hollow windpipes, and curbed only by thoughts of halitosis". All these remind me of myself. It was a relief to find E.M. Roach on a dead poet friend. "He lived half mortally".

18 February. Jan Carew reads a memory of childhood, "Death in a Stone," and told me he has been acting as adviser on Guiana affairs to Jennie Lee and the Bevan group, five days a week – Kingsley Martin took an article for the *New Statesman* without reading it through first. He (Jan) is going to Vienna in a week invited by a publisher. Depression in the afternoon. The African tour was pitiless in showing up my shortcomings, technical and managerial, and moral...

20 February. Household chores once more, and Eddie Brathwaite records in the morning, a story "Hurricane Season," by Edgar Mittelholzer. George Lamming looks in rather *farouche* again.

24 February. Mercedes with a *Diary,* the metronome recommences. It is curious how little work there is to do on the West African programmes. Perhaps JGW is right, it is too early to trawl for African creativity in such a new field.

6 March. At teatime, Willy came, to invite us to a large party he is giving. This was a great occasion, and we did not leave until well past two in the morning. All the West Indian talent in London seemed to be there: Boscoe Holder to sing calypsos, culminating in the shocking "Saxophone"; Willy to sing the more respectable verses, "Many a plain woman"; Edric Connor with a series, "The bridegroom was taken into custodee"... How I wish I could see Carnival with my own eyes! George Lamming was in great form, flushed by a good reception from Joyce Cary, and Walter Allen's praise of his second book, *The Emigrants*. Gordon acted as MC, AET heckled. The Crosses, who have shaken the dust of Trinidad from their feet, and are probably going to West Africa, where

he hopes for a legal post. I danced cheek to cheek with the enchanting Lesley – oh dear, what charm there is in smiling Chinese eyes...

9 March. At the office, J.D. Ogundere reads some recent poems by Babalola, both charming, in spite of (or perhaps because of) the difficulty of the word "wasps", which he surmounted on the run-through, only to produce "wapses" in the recording. A very different recording by Vidia Naipaul, with a very sharp sketch "A Family Reunion", an old Hindu matriarch dying of dropsy, and the relatives covertly quarrelling over her money. I asked him back to supper, where Henriette remembered that, being a Brahmin, he cannot eat meat or egg. [...] On Trinidad, he confirmed that his father was a Brahmin from Nepal, his mother from South India. He is trying for a teaching job in Ankara. The insurance company will not pay him any insurance for the dead Seepersad, who left a good deal of debt.

16 March. On to Hans Crescent, to deliver a talk on African writing to the Circle, attended by half a dozen Africans assembled by John Akar, as well as Henriette, JGW, Mercedes, Marj, Featherstone, Hugh Paget and a few more. Cyprian Ekwensi took the chair. For the record, I started with the Bemba hand-piano, then read the following: A Zulu poem by Vilakazi ("Africa," April 1946). A memoir of S.E.K. Mqhanzi by A. C. Jordan ("Outlook," September 1945). These, really, as a kind of "control", an example of work helped by intelligent Europeans. For West Africa a debate on the use of English in the old *Eastern Mail*, under Clinton in Calabar, and a comment on the culture of Freedom in the *People* (August 1951). Then a reading of the first page of Nigerian publications, received from Ibadan in 1950-2. The winning poem, by David Carney, in the 1951 Festival of Arts. An extract from a story in the *University Herald* (July 1948). "The Song of the Matchet," by Epelle, in *African Affairs* (October 1952). A part of the amusing story, "Okoro's Order" by Nchami, the tailor who orders a girl as well as her dress (March 1950). A part of Phebean Itayemi's brilliant "Soup" (August 1949). A part of Ekwensi's "Bananas" in Cullen Young's *New African Writing* (1947). The first two paragraphs of Ekwensi's *People of the City*, which arrived in proof today... "Talking Drums" (*African Affairs* July 1953). The whole of Enitan Brown's "blooming flowers of Lagos on parade" (*African Affairs* for July 1949). Then in the search for the "real quality of the African imagination", Lasebikan in *African Affairs* (July 1949), Babalola's "When I First Heard of Forest Farms", "The Son of Abuteni," (*AA* October 1950), and the "Genuine Gentleman" (*AA* April 1953). Then the very interesting transliteration of a Mbale story, word for word, in "Kongo Oversee." Then, as an example of failure, "A Foolish

Vow that was Not Kept," in the disappointing Penguin, the one thing to reach the British public so far... Finally, a long reading from *The Palm Wine Drinkard*, the great exception to every rule. An indigestible evening perhaps, but pioneering, which provoked some discussion. Afterwards, drinks with Hugh Paget, that kindly, watchful man.

22 March. Frances Quarshie-Idun, that elegant sprig of the Gold Coast *haute bourgeoisie,* reads an extract from the Akinsemoyin novel, *The Seed Eternal.* She contributes memories of Lagos Mayfair: an aunt who dressed in high collars and high boots, Moslems [sic] stuffing themselves with food before dawn in Ramadan, Syrians pouring dirty water form windows on noise makers in the streets. An airgraph from Edwina Melville, far up on the Rupununi savannahs of Guiana, forced to boil water, since it is the season for the Indians to poison it for the fishing. Lloyd Reckord, in to argue about his brilliant, sick-minded brother's play *Adella.* Edward Brathwaite, writing to ask for a reference to the British Council, and quoting recent poems, "restore them to forever life"...

2 April. Increasingly, sex rears its ugly head in the *Voices*. Salkey reads a story by Neville Dawes, "Ta Ta Small," about incest, a typical poet's piece of prose, all images, and no articulation. He was followed by Gordon Bell reading Telemaque's "Betrayal," a coward who claims to be an arsonist, in order to impress a girl, beautifully and indirectly described, "a cough, a sharp face". Salkey, incidentally, is now a waiter at the Sugar Hill, a new night club, where George Lamming ordered champagne four nights running for a girl called Jennifer. I could wish he would pay back the £8 he still owes me...

14 April. At 9, recorded the half-yearly summary on the *Voices*. I opened by recalling the death of Seepersad Naipaul, with his "sensitive sense of humour and of honour," then the waning of the St Vincent school. Then an attack, on *The Baths of Absalom*, by James Pope-Hennessy,* who laments the Philistinism of Trinidad, the provincialism of Castries. Did he know anything of Selvon, or Walcott? But, is he more to blame than the men who withhold the fare money that Selvon wanted to return to the sun (he is now in a sanatorium), or that Walcott wanted to come to Bristol? "Sometimes one thinks that the West Indies do not deserve well of their creative people." After this, a reference to Mittelholzer's two new novels, and George Lamming's *Emigrants* with [Barnabas] Ramon Fortune, and "The Kite," chosen by *London Calling* for the 21st anniversary of the Overseas Service... Then one plunged into the bulk of the actual items broadcast, grouping, first, into the emerging comment on race differences; Vidia Naipaul's "Epicurean Service," Reckord's "Seven Voices

of the Rainbow," Roach's "Legend of Daaga": "The guns saluted his contemptuous heart". After this, the leisure class, "the most difficult of all strata to make agreeable in art". Gloria Escoffery, Ken Maxwell, with his "Uncle Charlie" who, "believes in an occasional dose of salts for internal complaints, and cold cream for external ones", and leaves half-hunter watches to people who pre-decease him. Then the many varieties of dialect, especially Robinson's "Shirt Apiece," with Fred, the chicken owner, collecting the corn thoughtfully provided by the sect, The Children of the Earth. "That's habit with him, if he's got anything not so important to do, he'll do it with his left hand, leavin' the right free for brainwork". In poetry, described, at length, Forde's drama about Susanna and the Elders, "The Plot in the Garden", and the Yeatsian lines by R. L. C. McFarlane,* already quoted in this diary.

21 April. Olumbe Bassir,* the biologist, who has never shown the slightest interest in literary work, comes with a request to forage in the five years' collection of *West African Voices,* to select items for an anthology. I make a guarded reply. If he had ever taken part in them, or contributed…

23 April. Bassir rang up at 1300 to ask if he could look in for fifteen minutes, to collect the thirty scripts he had decided he wants to use. This was against the arrangement I had made, a preliminary survey, a final approval from JGW, when he returns. If in fact he ever does publish, I am certain he will not consult the authors, or get their permission. […] Two more macabre *Voices.* Gordon reads "The Red Penny," by Naomi Gibbins,* a murder by razor, and Pauline "The Sign" by Lloyd Clarke,* a haunting. Both contain racial undertones. Something is going sour with the programme, it was better in the old days, with clumsy peasant stories, honest to God protest? Yet perhaps these were a mask too, acceptable to the latter-day Imperialist…

5 May. Mercedes comes for a *Diary,* after visiting some of the 700 Jamaicans, who have just landed in the weekend from a Dutch ship… Women in little round felt hats with feathers, clutching crocus bags… She found them installed in Brixton, eight to a room. What will happen to the poor dears when there is a slump? She had a cautionary story of a white girl at J. Lyons, caught in the act with a number of Coloured boys. In consequence, the firm have discontinued taking Coloured people. The migration brings jobs to some – yesterday she was talking to a member of a legal firm which is specialising in prosecuting stowaways. (He thought Kingston was in West Africa.) One trouble is the way the Foreign and Commonwealth Relations Offices hamstring the attempts by the Home Office to control or lessen the immigration, for Imperial reasons.

12 May. A letter arrived today from Efua, who is marrying the young Afro-American Sutherland in ten days' time. One should not monkey with other people's lives. If things had been different, if, for example, I worked on the Gold Coast, if I had been unmarried when I met her, I might have taken the plunge, and damned the consequences. But as it was. That is not the point, of course, nor even the further thought, that she was, in many ways, already very complicated in her emotions, the long Cape Coast history, the European Morgue, a Governor in the days when Frank Swanzy married Efua Ketse, by local custom. To this day, we have never talked to each other entirely honestly. At least (what a comment), the relationship has given rise to poetry of quite a different emotional order to the usual material from the Coast...

13 May. Frank Pilgrim, delightful as ever, reading a story "Sugar Cake," by Naomi Gibbins, one of the legion of anonymous Caribbean writers.

1 June. John Akar reads his own story "Bokari's Fi[?]" about a Sierra Leone houseboy. When I suggested his trying Television with his play, he told me a surprising story. He sent another, better play, about an American woman who does not know if her child is black or white, to the head of the TV drama script department, Sir Basil Bartlett, the husband of Mary Malcolm. In due course he was summoned to an interview, where they were surprised to find him Coloured, and went into details of casting. He then received an invitation to visit Bartlett for a cup of tea in his flat in Bayswater. There certain proposals were made. "I could make you. I made Gordon Heath." (The young American Negro actor). He escaped by dialling the number of the flat, and pressing the button... The manuscript was returned next day, and he has never since been offered a part of any kind. My attitude to commercial TV is slightly altered...

2 June. I told the Akar story to JGW, who had heard a similar tale about another Coloured actor from Reggie Smith. He will speak to Bob McCall, now No 2 to George Barnes... Pauline read "The Triumph," an alarming sketch of Jamaican peasants by A.K. Elliott.* What vast numbers of unknown names! She says that the two *Adella* rehearsals, for which Lloyd is claiming extra money, were actually full-length readings, in the hope of a stage production... I had it played back. Not so disagreeable as on the second hearing, but still a mess at the crises.

9 June. Annual interview with Warren McAlpine [Director of the BBC's North American Service], who is retiring next January... He was kind enough to say that he would have liked to have known me better, "one

of the liveliest minds in the Overseas Service". I rehearsed my usual plaints, but they make little impression on men who know little or nothing about the RAS... What do I want? More involvement in the BBC machine. "But meetings are so boring." After the stocktaking of my own limitations after the Africa tour, I am a little more reconciled to my own limitations, and the bitterness is, for the moment, past.

10 June. A key day in my life. At 11 in the office of JGW, James Millar casually asked me if I would come out to the Gold Coast, for two tours, as Head of Programmes. The idea seemed even more attractive an hour later, when I saw the *Times,* which doubtless he had already seen. They have given the [inaugural Rhodes Chair of Race Relations] at Oxford, not to Mason, not to Little, not to Trevor, not to me, not, I am sure, to a great many other deserving people, but to Kenneth Kirkwood... At any rate, the invitation from JGW softens the blow considerably. When I got home, I found Henriette enthusiastic, so long as the climate on the Coast is not too difficult for Ba [their son, Martin], and he will not need too many "pricks". She is sorry for her father, as I for Q, who will miss her grandson. Another to suffer, perhaps, will be Jonah [John, son of Eric Ravilious and Tirzah Garwood]. But, after all, the absence will only be for 18 months, with a 6 month leave in 1956, and then another spell, in a place where I have so many connections. A new place, which I only know on paper, at a historical moment, the first handing over of power in British Africa. And oh, the *relief,* from the grinding ten-year labour at the Royal African Society!

11 June. James Millar brings the Colonial Office application form, which I fill in with the old *Curriculum Vitae,* so often entered in the past, in vain. What of the consequential changes? Perhaps R. Oliver might take on editorship – he has the proper academic base, denied me. Perhaps Vidia [Naipaul] might be persuaded to produce *Caribbean Voices* as a stepping stone to the wider world (far more appropriate than the Home Civil or a British Council job in Ankara). One cannot think of anyone for *West African Voices,* but this is a growth market, and perhaps they could find an *African?*

18 June. JGW decrees that Bassir must be left alone with the files of *West African Voices.* After all, they are not our property, and he must get the writers' approval, if he does not want a law suit. But, all the same, I am doubtful. It is in the highest degree unlikely that they will know anything about it... Gloria Vaz reads the sketch, "The Voice", by Edwina Melville, describing the reception of one of her broadcast stories, on the lonely ranch Emprensa on the remote Rupununi plateau. It starts

with the whispering thatched roof, and the great dome of the sky full of voices; and it dies away, at the end, to the silent thatch again... True art, if artless. I sent the script to *London Calling*. It is the most vivid thing I have ever seen on GOS.

22 June. Lunch for Sam Selvon, with Willy Richardson, at Freddy Mills. I give him the advice that is given unavailingly to me. "Go out and meet people. You can't expect the world to come to you." etc etc. But that is precisely what the artist does expect. Sam is still pinning his hopes on the Indian Service, or perhaps on Stanley Best in the British Council. I wish I were more useful. In a sense, the programme lured Sam to the metropolis; and since he arrived, it has done very, very little for him – although the list of stories used is really quite a long one, over the years.

28 June. The Millars come to supper. He is very cagey – Henriette says "another JGW", but I say that he is Scotch. At least he is a gentleman. Doubts about Margret dispelled as the evening wore on, especially after Martin has thawed her reserve. Not much talk about the larger implications of a radio service underpinning an emerging independent state.

29 June. Eileen Ormsby Cooper, that figure of the past, reads some Jamaican poetry, including offerings from herself, then Frances [Quarshie-Idun] comes with a German friend, to cope with a story, "The King's Last Wife". She is going back to the Coast in a fortnight, and hopes to work in radio. Her father is presenting her with a large house, which she does not know what to do with. They stay for lunch and Frances says she has read *Four Guineas* [: *a journey through West Africa* by Elspeth Huxley (1954)], which annoys her, but which she agrees with...

4 July. Read up [on] the Gold Coast, without the neuralgic pains of the last month. [W. Walter] Claridge is absurdly prejudiced in favour of the Ashanti against the Fante [in *A History of the Gold Coast and Ashanti: From the Earliest Times to the Commencement of the Twentieth Century*], perhaps with good reason, they are at least independent. Swanzys come and go, more often indeed than the index indicates.

6 July. Gordon sends in three chapters of a novel, somewhat disconnected, the first humorous about a salesman on his round, the next a painful family scene, the third an even more painful interview with a psychiatrist. All no doubt autobiography. At lunch with George Lamming and Jan Carew, meet Wilson Harris. A fine young man, with fine brow, hooded eyes, a moustache, looking like a tall Mahratta. Most of his conversation

was with George whom he has not met before, with prompts from the producer. The general approach, idea and philosophy, against the particular approach of word and sensation. In fact, anti-phenomenal, not a very good formula for literature, I would have thought. (Thinkers are normally, in our world, not stylists.) They ended with Martin Buber, *I and Thou*. Harris (what an inappropriate name for this phenomenon) spoke at immense length, pleasantly punctuated now and again, by a fresh breath, and the words 'In short'. It was all immensely stimulating, and I cannot remember who it was, who threw out the remark, which may be profound, and again may not: "Communism only provides a faith for those who have never lost it."

We drifted down to Trafalgar Square, still talking, poor Jan Carew rather swamped. His sundry references to "lecturing in London University" are not, however, wishful thinking. He is really taking a class at the LSE in race relations. This through his contacts with the Bevanites. I returned to Seth Jectson reading a story by Tutuola, "Totofioko and the Active Skull," not a bad description of the past two hours.

7 July. Perhaps I am too literal in this diary... *What Katie did next*, in my case, *met next*. I never re-read what I have written, so that I do not know if norms and standards emerge, from the crowding detail of day-to-day. But today, I suppose, I should note another climacteric: a formal severing of my links with the RAS. Needless to say, this ended not with a bang, but a whimper, a Finance and General Purpose Committee too small for a quorum, consisting of JGW and [Sir Charles] Ponsonby [of the Royal African Society], the twin poles of my existence [...]. Pons must have been told by Heather what was in the wind, for he spent a quarter of an hour first talking to JGW about his recent experiences in Kenya [...]. He was surprised when I told him that it is James Millar who is "bringing *me* to the Gold Coast", and not the other way around. My lack of worldliness of a perpetual surprise to the old politician...

13 July. The agreeable Ekpunobi, whose voice was deemed too sibilant, re-emerges after two years, to read a romantic story, "The Juju Rock" (at Jebbe in the Niger) by Nchami. At the end, he attacks me about the BBC "always favouring the Gold Coast". He even says, "You all go there, never to Nigeria." I point out that the new Head of the Light Programmes, [Tom] Chalmers, was Director of the [Nigerian Broadcasting Service] NBS for nearly three years. "Well then, he was the only one." I then quote the dozens of other seconded staff. "But you never train the staff." I quote the batches who have been coming over. [...] Opposite the Francis Edwards bookshop, I even bumped into someone known

from that distant time, Diana Athill, the bright Colonel's daughter, now working in Andre Deutsch, who does more in a year for original letters than George Weiden[field] has done since he began.

16 July. At the Langham, a long, cordial conversation with James Millar, who says that [Jimmy] Moxon wants the Head of Programmes to be out by September. He thinks that JGW will postpone it to December, if only because of the problems of replacing me under my various hats, Caribbean, West African, Mauritius, Colonies.

19 July. Lunch given by James Millar to Robert Gardiner and his wife, JGW and myself. JGW in good form, recalling visits to the Northern Territories [...]. Both Gardiners very mellow – he is now a high official in Accra, and could prove helpful. I tried to be as tactful as I could, while JBM [Millar] expatiated on his plans. This meant, I kept silent.

23 July. At the office, JGW also continues his life-pattern. James Millar, just back from seeing Kodwo Mercer, was absolutely flabbergasted to learn that seven Gold Coast senior programme staff are to come for training in London, at the beginning of September. (All the papers were stuffed away in JGW's drawer.) For his part, JGW was annoyed by a letter written by JBM to Leslie Perowne in Nigeria, offering him the post of Head of Programme Training – in Accra. From all this, one escapes to *Caribbean Voices,* for once interesting, Vidia Naipaul, that remarkable young man, with a sharp and bitter family sketch "My Aunt's Gold Teeth." He came in a new suit and new tie, "presented by an admirer", from his digs in Paddington Street, "a terrible place, where men urinate in public". He describes a conversation with a match salesman, a Swede, who asks him his politics. "Not a Communist, if that's what you mean. I hate oppression and injustice." I had to edit the story, with a homily on *agape*, since it was very savage, a fat, repellent old lady, taking up Christianity, and having the horrors, including seven snakes, against which she invokes the Virgin, and Rama.

26 July. In the evening, Gold Coast radio documents. It certainly looks as though it would not be difficult to provide a better line of programme than that given at the moment. One note: the role of Deputy Director, which is being given to an African, could very well be vital from my point of view.

29 July. *Caribbean Voices* still shows a little spark of life from time to time. Edwina Melville's piece is printed on the front page of *London Calling*. *Bim* has a flattering reference from Frank Collymore...[Herman] Stephens,[*]

the Antiguan poet, reads some poems by Archie Lindo and Aston Mullings.*
Perhaps I could continue like this till the cows come home...

30 July. News of Sam Selvon, who has given up his clerks job in the Indian High Commission, in order to finish his novel, which still has 40,000 words to go. His speech is still slow and slurred, as he reads a pot boiler, "Water for Veronica." Words fail to express the admiration which I feel for him.

13 August. In the afternoon, a slight pang, recording the brilliant Wilson Harris, with an impressive "Statement," very impressive indeed, although very hard to understand, even by himself. He and Malcolm de Chazal, sundered by the South Atlantic and Africa and the Indian Ocean, are strangely alike, in their organic approach to Nature. Both see Man as *primus inter pares,* but not basically divided. They are the most interesting minds I have encountered in the eight years of my stewardship. The only man to measure up to them, George Lamming, is reflecting, rather than reflective. It seems a pity to leave it all for geese that are almost certainly not swans.

19 August. To the studio, to produce Eddie Brathwaite, reading two short stories, quite unmemorable, one by Karl Sealy, the other by J.M. Hewitt* (Barbados). He has not yet heard from Adisadel, and talks of trying to join the Gold Coast Educational service, as a village schoolmaster, or inspector. He has a feeling for "Africa", and it will be nice to share the new experience with him, a man who has given me something, as well as possibly receiving it.

24 August. Today the Millars should have arrived at Takoradi. I think of them from on the top of the bus, from which eight Jamaicans, just off the boat, are staring at the West End shops. An Empire, even in its decline, especially in its decline, is a very odd thing. Routine back at the office.

26 August. In the evening, to see Cyprian Ekwensi at his digs in Ladbroke Road. As always, I admire his style (on a par with his beautiful, finicking writing). Poor rooms, very poor, but a real writer's corner. His wife sweet and pale, with her paralysed mouth. The baby Papando (Star) extraordinarily tough. I was plied with gin [...] and other drinks, all from bottles that were quite new. Rather distractingly, the radio was kept on, *Calling West Africa* and *Of Human Bondage*, while we discussed pharmacy, his novels, marketing boards. He showed me a book of poems a long way after Belloc, by "Jonathan Husk", actually Curling, dedicated

to "Cyprian Ekwensi, a coming West African writer". The most fascinating things were his photograph albums, an extraordinary Ibo mirror world. His father, a fierce old white-haired professional elephant hunter, now living in Jos. A tough brother who is a cinema projectionist, another who owns the *Kaduna Express*, a very pretty sister Kathy, who is a nurse, another sister, Emily, married to a doctor.

1 September. In the afternoon, a little man called Olowu reads "The Curse of Bada" by Tim Aluko. A novella by Eddie Brathwaite, *The Boy and the Sea*, a picture of Barbados, wonderfully sensitive, not always easy to understand. There is a great talent there, struggling to get out, mostly emotional. Wind, salt water, sun, quite different from Lamming, by whom it is no doubt influenced.

2 September. Gordon Woolford reads the first chapter of his novel, *On the Rocks*. As its name implies, it is not very gay. [...] At the BBC, I had a drink with Willy Richardson, and handed him selected manuscripts from *Caribbean Voices* to consider for publication.

10 September. Why do we always holiday out of season? This year, because of the long delay over the Gold Coast, which has still not vouchsafed a reply. Can there be some political objection? I can see myself *persona non grata* (a) bearing my name (b) for some piece of maladroit honesty in the [*African Affairs*] Journal. Kind letters from the Millars, who are enjoying Cantonments life...

7 October. Michael Joseph sends me a copy of *The Emigrants* at last, and I read the first section in the evening. Artificial sentences and paragraph structures, women pervading everything, more control and less poetry than the first book, but the same power.

9 October. In the evening, we go to a splendid farewell party, given for George Lamming by Pearl Connor in Compayne Gardens. It was the most brilliant party that I have ever attended. George was gentle and deprecating, in his large pullover, like a blackbird's egg. He had not asked the people, he is himself a perpetual guest. Absentees included Sam Selvon, whom he is seeing tomorrow, and Mittelholzer out of town, with Carew, AET, Padmore, Willy Edmett, JGW. But almost every other West Indian of talent in London was there. Edric Connor, back from playing Dagoo, in Huston's *Moby Dick*, being made at Fishguard and Youghal, with typical lavishness. [...] Denis Williams, putting on weight in both senses, no longer a disciple of Wilson Harris, reading mathematics, in intervals of painting and teaching at the central School.

[...] A marvellous young Negro dancer, all powdered gold. Politicians like Albert Gomes, fat and sardonic, and a small man with a hearing aid, neat and precise, Eric Williams, the Robespierre of the coming Trinidad revolution... Others one can only mention: Willy Richardson, Douglas Hall, the bitter and ambitious Clifford Sealy, who is not making the grade and blames it on the wrong thing. No Vidia Naipaul, too young, no friend of the Negro race.

12 October. In the afternoon, two of the Gold Coast ladies, Doris Tamakloe and Susie Laryea,* record some simple Ashanti stories by Charles Owusu. There is, I am afraid, an anaemia of the spirit in the Gold Coast, in contrast to the ebullience of Nigeria. (Compare also the contrast between Ibo Trinidad and Twi Jamaica?) Maybe it has something to do with scale... If I ever get there, I should like to put on a weekly programme, called "The Singing Net," after Mary Kingsley's minstrel mnemonic...

14 October. Edward Brathwaite reads a portrait of F. R. Leavis. Lunch at Schmidts to Vidia Naipaul, who says he has had seventy letters of rejection, obtained one short temporary job at the National Portrait Gallery, and is kept alive only by food parcels from a girlfriend in Birmingham. Clearly, he should be asked to take on my job as editor of the *Voices*, even though he might not want to do the production.

15 October. Victor Sassoon came for drinks in the evening, in good form about Manipur and Bangkok, where he teaches English in the University, at £1800 a year. I brought along Vidia, and they seemed to get on, especially since they were both at Univ... VN was inclined to talk *de haut en bas*, "I don't want to come to India, the best intellectuals live in Worcestershire." But I think that Victor saw the tension lying underneath. In the evening, a party given by Dorothy Brooks for Cyprian's novel. The publisher was there, a boyish face and grey hair, named Ludovici. Mercedes and Rosey Poole, a large number of Whites of the *avant garde*, who belong to the West African Arts Club, but know nothing about either, except that they are currently fashionable.

18 October. At long last, a communication from the Colonial Office, signed by one Balls, offering me secondment for two tours of service with the Gold Coast Broadcasting Service, at £1850 per annum, with no interruption of my BBC pension rights. I told the Admin man, Charles Curran, that I would take the plunge. Then, a recording by Carew of his own story "The Hunt," good second-grade stuff. He has with him a copy of Jahn's anthology *Schwarzer Orpheus*, which looks well presented, and very handsomely printed and designed. Oh, these Germans!

29 October. Record my swansong, the last six monthly summary. One can scarcely admit that the programme is so close to the bottom of the barrel, but one can hint at it. I pity those that have to follow. As it is, there is the appearance of the extraordinary Wilson Harris in person, the development of Salkey, the re-emergence of that great spirit Sam Selvon. Barry Reckord may one day produce a three-act play, which will get into the canon, if he can heal himself in doing so. Eddie Brathwaite, Nadia Cattouse, the world may hear of them. Above all, Vidia Naipaul, for whom JGW promises to make some provision. Dear Ramon Fortune as well. By and large, I feel like Moses, who will never himself cross over Jordan.

3 November. All day with my Gold Coast colleagues to be. The two ladies largely silent. Acquah, Charles Assinor and Abdulla not very vocal. The running made by the handsome young Ewe, Roland Agodzo, and Yeboah, whom I like less and less the more I see him. A great deal of their talk was about staff grievances, basic pay £280 per year, poor equipment, opportunities. It does seem unfair that the expatriate, who receives at least eight times more pay, is also given a very cheap house, subsidised by the Government, while they have to hire their houses at the appalling Accra prices [...] As to programmes, the main difficulty is to combine six linguistic divisions, Twi, Fante, Ewe, Hausa, Dagbani, with English and the normal radio break-down by function. [...] At least we got to know each other better.

4 November. A young Jamaican sociologist, Stuart Hall,* comes in with a Canadian girlfriend, to read some of his own rather derivative (Walcott) poetry, "New Landscapes for Aeneas".

11 November. A suitable person, Willy Richardson, reads a suitable script, my last item in *Caribbean Voices*. A piece on the future of the Caribbean by Richard Gayeaux, "Water Lies Down, Water Stands Up."

14 November. A lovely autumn morning, clear and only very slightly cold. Mercedes, who has really been exceptionally kind and sympathetic, drives us down to Heathrow, with Johan following on his cyc-auto. [...] There is a lot of work for poor Henriette to do before she is able to follow me with the Babe. Then a hurried summons. Flight 310 to Accra is departing by Number 7 gate. The little group stands waving to the very end.

15 November. Condensed milk in the coffee, peppery smells outside the window, we are certainly in Africa. Everyone on the plane is very

friendly as we fly over the brown ribbon of the Volta, the featureless Accra plains. I rehearse the pretty speech I will make to the reception committee (James has promised a red carpet and the Radio Band). The new-old firm of Swanzy and Millar, the dress of Efua's infant, the sense of "coming home", if only to a place I have "lived in" for the last ten years [as Editor of *African Affairs*], among so many others. But I might have saved my breath. There was no reception committee, no red carpet, no band, only the thin, elegant, charm of Jack Lawton [on secondment from the BBC]... As Jack drives us in his little car down the broad Dodowa Road, over the treeless downs, towards Accra, nothing he says suggests that this "reception" is "accidental" [...] After some miles, we come to a clump of trees, on a little rise to the right hand of the road where there is a formless white tower, and a flagstaff. This is Broadcasting House [BH2], at the end of a short avenue, along which new bungalows have been run up. To the South, one can just see the first houses of Accra along the Ring Road, on hills to the West, the huts of a very large location, Nima, the haunt of thieves, which "the police do not like patrolling". The radio masts lie on the South, 5kw, 1½kw. Other senses beside sight: smells of flesh, of a woodfire, sounds of many birds, and the hammering of carpenters. I meet Bill Busby, the Chief Engineer [on secondment from the BBC], a long, lanky man, with a small head, and mild brown eyes, under a sold cranium. A large, worried man called Hayfron, a Programme Engineer, in the process of being passed over. Frances Quarshie-Idun, delightfully cool and stylish in a frock from Paris. The insinuating little Ewe, Emmanuel Senayah. "Pleased to meet you." "Say that after two months, and I will believe you." James Millar arrives after an hour – he explained that he has been meeting the wrong plane [...] James plunges into our immediate headaches. There is a crisis between [Prime Minister, Dr Kwame] Nkrumah and the Asanteman Council. All news stories have to be passed by the Chief Regional Commissioner in Kumasi – only to be killed, through [Jimmy] Moxon, by the Information Minister Archie Casely-Hayford, and the Prime Minister's Office.

17 November. Back at Dodowa Road, for the regular Programme Meeting held every Wednesday morning and including most of the senior staff on the creative side – a splendid institution, allowing everyone to feel a part of each other. Jack Lawton presides and I talk little, but study the faces. The squinting eyes of the tough Joe Ghartey, who talks bitterly of the British Council, and generally shows himself hostile to change. Beside him, his erstwhile girlfriend Marian Smith-Mensah, a pretty woman with a broad chestnut face, who is said to manipulate the all-powerful Staff Union. The amiable face of Ben Gadzekpo. The boyish,

moustached face of James Arthur, a former Policeman now in charge of the Gramophone Library. Ghartey takes me and Ben Gadzekpo up to the airport, to say *au revoir* to Len Pearce who goes on leave. Ben is too shy to come into the bar of the Lisbon Airport Hotel to get a drink; but I have lunch with Joe. He seems more and more a Lion on the Path (he tells me that "Ghartey" means Lion, the name of the ruling dynasty in Winneba). For eighteen years he was in the Administration, a clerk in the Brong areas of Western Ashanti from 1929-43. Then thanks to some sentimental book he wrote called *A Basket of Leaves,* he got transferred into radio. He still has eight unpublished books with the Literature Bureau. He makes it fairly clear that he does not encourage experiment; but leans heavily, but benevolently, on all. In particular, he supports promotion by seniority. Any break of the order and one will hear from the Union, which he sees an "an arm of the Civil Service."

18 November. There is a need to staff our Kumasi office with someone wielding authority, a kind of Viceroy. It is, after all, the key town in the whole of the Gold Coast, on the verge of independence. Why not send Joe Ghartey, the veteran, experienced in Ashanti, and not very keen to introduce new things under BBC direction? James thinks that this is a rather good idea. He has already felt the impact of Joe's "stone bottom".

19 November. A long talk with Tweedledum and Tweedledee, Ghartey and Gadzekpo, on programme exchanges between language groups, hybrids based on local reports and music. Clearly difficult, if not impossible. What should be the language of the narrator? Ghartey stressed the dangers of broadcasting local news, unless vetted by a Government official. In Cape Coast, for example, any reference to the Fante word for nose is synonymous with the *Oguaahene* [Paramount Chief of Cape Coast], who is gifted with an unfortunate example. At least the discussion was interesting, for personal reasons. I much prefer Ben Gadzekpo, light and anxious, making charming use of the word "perchance". Perchance to dream.

27 November. Two tantalising letters from Henriette, full of love, but reporting problems getting rid of the flat, which no one seems to want, at least in the winter. Work in the morning on [40] letters soliciting contributions to the projected literary programme, *The Singing Net.*

18 December. 167 miles to Sekondi, for the naming ceremony of Efua's daughter, Essie [Esi] [...] Finally, I find Efua in Effiakuma, in the second of a line of five white bungalows [...] A sweet little baby, very pale. A

husband called Bill Sutherland, with a charming weak face, round, receding chin, strong American accent, the sort of person who would not be out of place at an Oxford [University] party. [...] Later things improved, as Efua takes me through some manuscript poetry by a friend of hers in Kumasi, Archie Winful.*

22 December. The Programme Meeting, which is to be held an hour earlier, at 10. Arrangements for Christmas and New Year, the launching of *The Singing Net,* a New Year party to be given by me.

23 December. At noon, Nkrumah to record a short New Year message (not more than one minute). He was charming, even deferential, saying that English was, of all languages, the most difficult to read aloud. I explained to him the principle of grouping passages round one vital word, that stops the flow, like a stone on a mountain stream. This does not seem to help him much in his endeavours. But the talk went very well, in his high, gravelly voice. James showed him the site of the new radio complex [BH3, the current site of the Ghana Broadcasting Corporation], to be opened in 1957 or 1958, and crowned possibly with a bandstand, Frewen's suggestion.

29 December. Strange news from London. Shortly before Christmas, JGW died at his home of a heart attack, at the age of 52. My feeling is mainly regret. Perhaps, when all is said and done, I *have been* ungrateful, suspicious, unyielding. I owed to him early encouragement, first when I came from the Dominions Office in 1941, later when he read the epic on the RAF, finally in 1944 when he brought me over as a kind of dogsbody.

30 December. In the evening, [Komla] Gbedemah [Minister for Finance] arrives five minutes before the broadcast on premium bonds, and executes it impeccably. He was cold and distant, despite the letter I presented from A.G. Fraser. Ten minutes after he left, Nkrumah arrived, and paid me the compliment of rehearsing his entire statement on Ashanti. He reads the last two pages with emotion, very well; and I believe that *these* were the pages he had written himself, refuting charges of "dictatorship". The thing that emerges is the promise of a Regional Council for Ashanti. I must say, I found him a most charming man.

[From VOLUME 5: 1st January 1955 – 15th February 1957]

1955

5 January. In Cape Coast with Philip Gbeho.* [...] A large man with a benevolent face, Osei Badu, takes me along to see Kobina Sekyi,* in a white chamber in a sunny street. He is all that I expected: grey-haired, finely proportioned, flat nose, deep eyes, grey moustache, dressed in blue and gold, right shoulder bared, as is the custom, amid a fine collection of books and ancient photographs. A feeling of age and disillusionment, a very honest eye. He is not to be drawn on a talk on the 1886 plan for Fante Union, or even to send manuscripts for *The Singing Net;* and he agrees only to "look at" the music list. He leaves an odd feeling of greatness.

17 January. At 11, a very bright young man, with a thin, fanatical face, comes in with a short story, and a recommendation from Robert Baffour [OBE, Permanent Secretary of the Ministry of Transport and Communication]. His name is Frank Parkes,* and he is the grandson of a West Indian who joined the Sierra Leone administration around the turn of the century, in the Bai Bureh rebellion. [...] The story, which is set in the "Weekend in Havana", had definite atmosphere, and Mr P. seems someone who might be more useful inside the organisation than outside it.

19 January. At 1600, Andrew Opoku* and the seventh Twi lesson (*Adesua* 7). He looks well, even glistening, after a month in the country at Aburi, and I suspect that he has his sights on a job in Broadcasting. (He only gets £600 on contract from the Literature Bureau, where most of his manuscripts are still awaiting publication.)

21 January. Two hours with Frank Parkes, running through his drama "Snuff and [the] Ashes". Kofi, a clerk, tries to seduce Afie, the friend of his friend Ebow, who finally keeps her, through a love potion brought by a witch-doctor, produced by Kwesi, another friend, a reporter on *The Graphic*. The trouble, as with other Gold Coast writers I know of, is that FP is far too much concerned with technique to lose himself in the story, as the more unsophisticated Nigerians often succeed in doing. After a detailed criticism, we plunge into some of the 25 stories broadcast last year, from the 275 submitted for the radio competition. The young man did not like this, and his glands ran. [...] In particular, he disliked being told how often West Indians redraft their work.

27 January. Parkes looks in, with stories much improved. Gadzekpo

reports a proposal by young Roland Agodzo, for talks put out at dawn, the "hour of truth" in Eweland. I listen with him to music played by James Arthur, for a possible theme [tune] for *The Singing Net,* which starts tomorrow. The most attractive is an odd, haunting little wandering song, *Yehwe Ono Ara* (We See Our God), sung in Twi by [Oto] Boateng, with J.H.K. Nketia accompanying on the piano (Disk 519B). It contains the line "O listen to what I have to say."

28 January. At tea, Ben [Gadzekpo] and Bankole Timothy* discuss a literary discussion for *The Singing Net,* whose first number passed off quite well, although rather too much crammed into the fourteen minutes.

29 January. Frances criticises the first number of *The Singing Net.* "Too many words and too much Swanzy."

30 January. At last, around 14.30, the disagreeable young beach master takes me down to the surf boat, and I am paddled out to the ship – the *Nigerstroom* [on which his wife, Henriette, and his son, Martin, have arrived], past canoes and lesser ships, by twelve boatmen, each with a blue and white headband, and a singlet marked "Rose's Lime Juice", wielding most beautiful paddles, tridents painted silver, flashing in the sun. It takes half an hour, racing another boat that contains a cheerful African customs officer in a huge sun-helmet. [...] Over the side, many heads, one very fair, besides a Catholic White Father, another very small, with long ringlets drooping from a little sun-hat. A scramble up the ladder, and the curious joy of reunion, a feeling of circles, another life enfolding me, gentler and more personal, and oddly phantasmagorical.

4 February. Joe Sackey* reads poetry by himself, Joe de Graft,* [Amu] Djoleto* in *The Singing Net.* Henriette finds him sympathetic.

25 February. In *The Singing Net,* [Sam] Amarteifio* introduces some poems in English and Hausa, read by Danbani.

11 March. Rehearse Sam Amarteifio and Susie Laryea on Efua's latest poems, glorifying the lovely girl who would not marry. "The gun is silent in the stream." One voice, another voice, two voices in unison. It came off rather well.

25 March. Sam A. reads MacNeill Stewart's poem on Oterkpolu, which has nice lines, "in the glimmering folds of morning", an accurate description, as I know, having seen it.

8 April. In the evening I work on six plays sent in by Albert Kayper-Mensah,* the young poet who works in Wesley College in Kumasi. They are interesting documents of the muddle we are creating in Africa. Set in a never-land, they revel in unreal emotional situations and vast discussions on Art and Life. Sometimes, they show a real talent in recapturing overheard conversations, especially from medical men.

9 April. A fruitless trip to Achimota [School], to try and find Philip Gbeho, and ask if he would act as Chairman in the first discussion in *Seconds Out!* I was lucky, however, since I caught Nketia, on the point of going on trek to the Afram plains in Ashanti, to record hunters music, on tapes loaned by WABU [West African Broadcasting Unit]. He showed me the proofs of a fascinating book he has produced on Twi [funeral] dirges, along with photographs of drums and drummers, and a transcript of the most famous of all drum beats, containing the stanza on the path and the river, quoted in Rattray [*Religion and Art in Ashanti* (1927)]. Wonderful material for *The Singing Net,* with even the English strangely haunting and hypnotic. At the end of each stanza: "I am learning; let me succeed".

29 April. Another Feature, this time Flo Prah's* effort on delinquent children, rejected by Gytha in her day of power. I included it in *The Singing Net,* since it was a work of art rather than a documentary. [...] Needless to say, it was wrecked on transmission. Since Florence had drafted no announcement, nor given any details to Programme Parade, I had a separate announcement made, and delivered to the Presentation hut at 14.00. The Continuity Sheet contained the usual phrase: "See separate sheet". The engineers at WABU, of course thought that this referred to Prah's original script for the feature. So they played the tape *without* announcement, and all the listener heard was the signature tune. To make matters worse, Control Room then panicked, and cut to WABU. As a result, the wretched programme was jerked into the second sentence in the opening narration, rendering everything that followed unintelligible. A post-mortem was held with JBM, Akester, Leo, Sam Amarteifio, and produced the usual crop of excuses.

2 May. Frank Parkes gets through his first day [working at Broadcasting House].

4 May. A new idea for a programme starting on 5 June, *Music at the End of the Morning*, when people are relaxing. Kpohanu gives a preliminary report on his Accra survey, with only 106 replies and 30 by post, out of a sample of 350, 10% among the 3552 boxholders... It shows at least

one interesting thing: 25% rise at 05.00, 19% by 05.30 i.e. nearly half are up by dawn...

6 May. Back to record Nketia and *The Awakening,* with drum beats interpolated, a beautiful little arrival in *The Singing Net.* Yet another Nigerian transcription proves a dud. What on earth can they do in that magnificent Broadcasting House all day, beyond impress the visiting fireman from London? Sam Selvon sends his second novel from England, *An Island is a World.* A triumph of courage and sheer guts. Andrew Opoku annoyed that neither I nor James are coming to the Twi lessons.

7 May. Re-record the Nigeria slow speech transcriptions, for Roberts' teachers in training. At BH, a meeting with James over Kpohanu's Listener Survey – the sample is much too small. Why not try a small market town like Nsawam? Two young men look in from Takoradi, Eddie Brathwaite, and an unlovely Jamaican called Probyn Marsh, with discontented, ambitious eyes. Eddie says, "I hear you are running a programme called *The Singing Gnat.*"

13 May. For *The Singing Net,* a strange, rather gifted story, by one Adolph Agbadja,* an Ewe. It is called "Heaven is a Fine Place", and it has a very original idea, well carried out. A young illiterate hears a preacher talk about getting a passport, a license, to go to Heaven, and he sets about trying to get them, with comic results, in Government office and police station. He finally finds Heaven in a spiritual lodge in Koforidua [in Ghana's Eastern Region], where the incumbent asks, "What do you want, you son of a bitch?" It is hard to say whether the story is written sincerely or sarcastically. Frank Parkes, who reads it, thinks it may even be political. But it certainly has force, and vivid detail – it talks about "worm-like velvets", etc. As we went in to record, we met another possible writer, the Fante [Samuel] Otoo* of the Vernacular Bureau, who is starting a fishing series with the graphic title, *Nworaba,* the Stars. He has an extraordinary account of how the fishermen listen for the various calls of fish, their hands cupped over their paddles...

9 June. Over luncheon, a heavy storm with the usual crackle of the leaves, and the line cloud coming out of the sea. In the midst of it, I record Nketia – an astonishing moment, light, smell, sound, things I will remember all my life. Otoo, the Fante writer, in *People in the News,* where Frances for once exerts herself, shocked by the decision to remove her.

19 June. In the evening, work with James on applications, cut down

to 90 for PA [Programme Assistant], 43 for JPA [Junior Programme Assistant].

30 June. Frank Parkes back from Ho with good soundpicture, drums, high life, the Prime Minister's speech opening the postal agency at Kpedze, a village in the hills. The coming of the midgets [recorders] has revolutionized our work, and the skill of untrained people like Frank is remarkable. I think the public nature of the recordings appeals to their outgoing natures, the general desire to astonish, entertain, show-off... The report was put out after the midday news, in the midst of a violent rainstorm. In the afternoon, Ben assists with interviews for JPA.

8 July. In the afternoon [...] record Henry Ofori* on his story of escaping the Ashanti, sent in for the film competition.

10 July. *Sunday Magazine* full of colour, Parkes on a youth conference at Anoma, Baffour on the Elmina Festival ("Fish in the Omanhene's net, a good year for Elmina"), Sam interviewing John Hatch the Leftist commentator, Frances on Frafra drumming and singing. *The Critics* followed, and *O Come Let Us Sing* from Swedru, so awful that James [Millar] and Leslie [Perowne, Head of Programme Training, on secondment from the BBC] rang up to complain. In the afternoon, the Americans, as well as the British Council, ruffled by an attack, "Who Do They Think They Are?" in the *Sunday Mirror,* by Henry Ofori, alias Carl Mutt.

15 July. In the afternoon, an unfortunate *contretemps* at tea. Henriette has invited her Dutch friend from the shipping line, with the ugly baby. Henry Ofori also comes, *en route* to record a piece for *The Singing Net.* The Dutchwoman is quite panic stricken. In seven years on the Coast, she has never talked to an African, except as a servant. Later, Henriette gallantly gets up to entertain James on the line about the by-election, a defeat for the CPP. "I think we should play it down. Do you think we should mention it at all?" "Sam Morris is a CPP partisan, he won't put a foot wrong." "Yes, I'm sure he will be fair (sic), but we don't want to trail our coat. It wouldn't be appreciated". So much for the sentiments enunciated at the Achimota Conference. He says he will "balance" it by trying to get Kofi Baako, the Chief Government Whip, to talk about Saltpond Flood Relief.

29 July. The last day of interviews, extending to 14.30, with old Ben in great form. "If perchance you joined the Department, what would

your father say?" He was beautifully poetic on the Dagomba [Albert Bako] Derimanu. "I found him outside the Government Office in Tamale. Something was lost, a valuable thing."

1 August. The new era starts. A purely local civil service [...]

5 August. "Ivan had been courting a young radio announcer, by name Vanilla." This story, by a schoolboy, is, so far, the one unsolicited contribution sent it to *The Singing Net* in the last two months.

19 August. Joe Ghartey, down from Kumasi, wanting to double programme time there, and more than double staff. One can see his dream: build up an independent organisation, in close touch with NLM [National Liberation Movement], and when it scoops the pool... James is diplomatic. I have to leave after an hour, to rehearse Ben Gadzekpo, in an interesting talk on Ewe poetry by a friend of his, Israel Kafu Hoh,* who works in the Education Department. The poems are quite different from anything I have seen so far, Chinese or Japanese in texture. (Afubaka, The Lagoon).

> Glide on steadily, that we reach home early,
> Good marketing and fishing vessels.
> In the twilight is the setting sun.
> The winds are cold, and my pores are sealed.

An odd thing for Africa.

22 August. As for the Gold Coast, a gull in Togoland bought an electric toaster from a crook for £1020, under the impression that it was able to print £1 notes. An allegory of Empire and Commonwealth? We hold a microphone test for the PAs and JPAs selected and two more fall by the wayside, the scornful Mrs Ayeh, and Miss Amissah of the scarlet lips. Albert Sam comes in, to complain about the way English programmes get all the peak times. Why no evening broadcasting?

24 August. Rather a painful Programme meeting. Which lasted until 12.30, and discussed innumerable things, but only one useful one, the addition of a Vernacular half hour, *Akwasida*, to the Sunday morning schedules.

1 September. In the afternoon, more creation. Frank Parkes recording a story, "Money Sweet" by Adolph Agbadja, which sailed too close to the wind, I thought, even subconsciously. A dictator comes from abroad, and possesses himself of a magic bank. Frank stayed on for drinks, then for supper, and we had a regular palaver about the state of the compound.

10 September. The fine ravaged head of Matson, the Permanent Secretary at the Ministry of Education, a historian, who tells me of the existence of a third Select Committee report, this time in 1865. I found myself sounding the BBC trombone. "Radio unites the three streams of the modern world: admin, technology, aesthetics." [...] Eddie Brathwaite brought Efua for a short time, and I took her back to the Raos via WABU. [...] Edward stayed the night.

11 September. Edward in good form. On the Africans: "They prefer to live rather than to think." He has written a good story on the fetish incident on the beach for *The Singing Net,* which is landing some excellent catches. Andrew Opoku, a long saga about an early cocoa farmer (stiff with proverbs) who decides to venture to new lands across the Densu, Agbadja with a story about a wizard in the dells below Aburi, who feasts on virgins' hearts, I.K. Hoh with more Ewe poems, and translations, like this of a vulture: "I learned to hate men/ Before they hated me". The fifteen poems have something of the quality of a Japanese *haiku.* In the afternoon, we took Edward to the beach, where Ba [Martin] was contemptuous of other people's castle walls.

13 September. Eddie Brathwaite leaves. On this last morning, he says how unhappy he is in his Technical Institute. I promise to show the story of the fetish to Sean. I doubt if there is much chance for him in radio.

21 September. At the Programme meeting, many items, notably a wave of demands for more indigenous music, whether orchestrated or not, who can say.

28 September. Tension at the Programme meeting on the vexed problem, vernaculars versus English. Protests at fetish music on Sunday mornings (*Kwasida*). Ben Gadzekpo clashes with Sam Morris, that good Christian, then with Leslie, then suggests that the mid-week service should always be broadcast in a local language, Sam ripostes by asking for Children's programmes in English...

4 October. I feel like showing [T.W.] Chalmers [Swanzy's replacement as BBC producer of the *Calling West Africa* series] the magnificent seven-page poem on the [River] Afram in four-line stanzas, in Twi and English translation, just handed to me by Andrew Opoku. "River, I am passing..." It is by far the finest things I have seen from a West African source, of whatever kind, and it justifies the 28 episodes of *The Singing Net* that have now gone out.

8 October. Saturday. James is unusually warm on the broadcast of the "Afram River", the "best thing I have heard since coming to the Gold Coast". He heard it at the Roger Club, where two others, Africans, were "glued to the microphone". We have spent nearly a year to achieve this; but it is pleasant, for all that.

28 October. In the afternoon, the [National] Theatre Committee meets in grand surroundings, Daniel Chapman [Nyaho]'s office [Permanent Representative to the United Nations] in the Prime Minister's department, with [Archie] Casely-Hayford [Minister of the Interior] in the Chair, and very reasonable. I suspect he sees it as a field for son Beattie. [...] I had to leave for the reading of the poetry for *The Singing Net*: the Squire of Oterkpolu [McNeill Stewart] at his most fleshy, a local Nsawam bard eulogising his father, the "Prince of Larteh", who once photographed the Prince of Wales. Frank introduced Gilly Jones-Quartey, and the young cripple E.D. Ofori reads the offerings.

17 December. Perhaps it is depression [...] but I am upset by the headlines in the *Ghana Evening News*, over an article by the dishonest Padmore. "BRITAIN PREPARING TO DOUBLE-CROSS THE GOLD COAST."

1956

4 January. A Programme Meeting three hours, too full of Europeans, I think: myself, Leslie [Perowne], Len Pearce, Jane London, David Rees, six against eight Africans (including Sam Morris, midway between the worlds). No striking change in December expenses, apart from an increase in Vernacular outgoings, probably because of Christmas. A sub-committee was set up to consider problems of music copyright. I also give an account of the eleven stations known to be putting out their own programmes. Also a report on the entries so far received for the radio-play competition: 30 in Twi, 23 in English, 20 in Ewe, 13 in Fante, 11 in Ga, 3 in Dagbani (schoolboys) and none in Hausa...

14 February. Later, [Michael] Dei-Anang* delivers an impossible script, written in over-ripe Whitehallese by Ivor Cummings, whom he calls "Old Ivory" [Cummings was a Colonial Office worker who worked with Nkrumah to train the first generation of Ghanaian diplomats]. "To the end, full implementation is being sought, albeit only in the initial stages." Dei-Anang, with his humorous, glancing eyes, read it all as it should be read, like a prose-poem.

19 February. Morning visits. Adolph Agbadja, the young Ewe short-story writer, whom I would like to bring into broadcasting in some way, although his one technical accomplishment is an ability to type. Robert Gardiner [Permanent Secretary of the Ministry of Housing] brings back the Swanzy manuscript [that Swanzy is writing on the nineteenth-century Swanzys for the journal *Transactions of the Historical Society of the Gold Coast and Togoland*], which he thinks is unkind to the dead (Letitia Elizabeth Landon?) [English poet who died at Cape Coast as wife of the Scottish merchant George Maclean]. He also thinks that I should "go into it more deeply". I say that I will visit the Public Records Office on leave in the summer.

23 February. Independence plans go forward. [...] I rehearse Albert Sam, reading "Ohia and the Thieving Deer", then work with Frank on the script on Niger. At 11.30, a state visit from the new Minister [of the Interior], and his unsmiling Deputy Nylander. Ebenezer [Ako-Adjei] is a sharp little man, who worked with Nkrumah on a paper in Chicago. They certainly make a stranger team than the Hon Archie [Casely-Hayford] and his assistant; and Frank says that they are good friends of his. Thursday lunch with Len, including wine, then sleep, then a summary of the first fifty programmes in *The Singing Net*.

9 March. The arrival of [Bidi] Setsoafia, the new Ewe SPA [Senior Programme Assistant], whom Ben [Gadzekpo] doesn't seem to like – a man who has written a great many textbooks. A JPA meeting. S.K. Otoo reads "A Day in the Life of a Fisherman", in which he again makes the extraordinary claim that Fante sailors can hear the cries of fish by listening with their hands cupped over their paddles, and even, he says, distinguish between shoals of herring and mackerel.

15 March. I attend the play-reading organised by [Geormbeeyi] Adali-Mortty*: Henry Ofori, Pauline Clark, Beattie, a pleasant man called Francois, in whose house in Korle Gonno the reading is held. They are balanced between *The Importance of Being Ernest* and *Brer Rabbit*. I bring the script of *Ignorant Love,* the prize-winning play, preach the gospel of the Caribbean [writers], and bring in Andre Obey and John Drinkwater for good measure. The trouble is, I really do not know enough about it never having taken part in drama, at school or university.

27 March. In the afternoon, a call from Archie Winful, back in Accra, in the Establishment Secretariat. It is just possible that he might be the answer to our need, to have someone local in Programmes, with a horizon built on Higher Education.

19 April. A busy morning. The endless question of fees. The printer. A script by R. Baffour. Ian [Wilson] on the Whitepaper on Federation. News from Kumasi: Len has fallen down a storm drain near the resthouse and cracked a rib. Someone has nevertheless "told the remainder of the team (James Arthur and Owusu Akyem) to proceed to Navrongo." [...] Drinks with Gerry. Then a late rehearsal with the Adali-Mortty group, this time at WABU, for a casting of [Albert] Kayper-Mensah's *The Rescue*, rather more sophisticated than *Ignorant Love*. I make a self-denying ordinance, and give the main juvenile part to someone other than the charming Edith Nortey, who "starred" in the first play. Rather than the second run though, they disperse at 20.30. When I get home, Ba [Martin] woke up crying for Henriette, who had gone for drinks at the Browns. Tactlessly, I went round there, with the babe in arms. Henriette forgave me. After all, today I put in ten hours, the longest day I have had in West Africa. In this climate, it is killing. They say that in the last half-year of a tour, you only do about two hours *useful* work a day.

12 June. In the afternoon, I have to inform poor [Bidi] Setsoafia that he is being transferred from Grams Library. [...] I think that he realises I try to help him, so far as I am able. He has, after all, several plays up his sleeve. A call from someone very different, the little clerk, Archibald Aikins, disgruntled, with a story about "John Bully", full of the most charming misprints: "he was shocked as an infuriated loin advanced at a furious pace to where he was hiding" [...] [Stephen Bekoe] Mfodwo [who will become Director-General of GBC in the 1970s] hands in the epic poetry drama, "The Dawn of a New Era", by a follower of Nkrumah, living beyond Takoradi [J. Aggrey-Smith]...

21 June. At 5, I turn up at WABU, to see the production of "The Dawn of a New Era", which has tricky points of censorship – the character of "statesman" is far too close to that of Kwame Nkrumah. But Mfodwo, the producer, does not want me in the control room. "It is better without your august presence." I decide to comply with this request, not knowing whether the adjective was intended rudely or not, after the young man had agreed to change the character "statesman" to "linguist". On the news, a sad item. Kobina Sekyi, the paladin of the past, has died at Cape Coast...

27 June. The minutes take up most of the afternoon, until 1700, when I listen to the Mfodwo production of "The [Dawn of a] New Era", from which I was barred. I do not think it is pique that makes me think it badly handled, apart from the rich voice of Osborne [Kwesi] Brew, and the historic powers of O.K. Dako, as a drunkard.

[Swanzy completes his first tour and visits Morocco on his way to Europe for five months leave ending in London.]

27 September. Gil Saunders has given me a number of up-to-date Bulletins, which allow me to keep up with developments in Accra. A glow, as I read James at the laying of the Foundation Stone [for the new Broadcasting House, BH-3]. "A radio service is not only bricks and mortar, but essentially programmes. Programmes like *Seconds Out!*, *The Singing Net*, *Gold Coast Theatre* – all channels for the creative energies of the people." Ah ha...

23 November. Lunch at Venezia for Mary, Sheila, and Di Athill, who was interesting on the state of the London book trade. Only three firms are now still independent – Heinemann, Deutsch, and Weidenfeld and Nicolson... George [Weidenfeld] recently approached André [Deutsch] with a proposal to form a merger, and was 'tearful' when the latter suggested the name 'Deutsch and Weidenfeld'...

6 December. [Lands in Accra early in the morning] The peppery smell of Africa, so well-remembered. [...] It is interesting to see how the town is being tarted up. Owen's Folly is being reconstructed, the charming round huts have been replaced by hideous Army sheds, the Bank has had a new coat of paint, flowers are planted at selected corners. The most striking new erection, a kind of Arc de Triomphe on the way to the Castle, not far from the crossroads, where the fatal shot was fired in [February] 1948. [...] Finally BH and a welcome which warms the heart. One never knows with these things, but they all seemed pleased to see me.

15 December. Frank Parkes' two historical features, one in July, another in September, a little clumsy, a little wordy, but all the same, with the root of the matter in them, and all derived from documents... James criticized the first 'severely'; but changed his tune when the Prime Minister rang up to congratulate the Service... [...] The only other talent near Frank, Andrew Opoku, has also done very good work in the Twi 'Discovering the Past.'

17 December. At the office, relations with James are much more relaxed, since I am determined to prove my worth in providing features, mostly historical; and planning, to the smallest detail, the coverage for six weeks of Independence. Sam Morris is to prepare a programme on [J.E.] Casely-Hayford, Frank on [Sir Frederick Gordon] Guggisberg, Ben on Togbi Sri II [Awoamefia of Anlo, CBE], H.S. on the Northern Territories, as well as [George] Maclean. One problem is Ashanti – the Lion, down

from Kumasi, is still adamant that he will only commemorate King Ghartey. Could Nketia oblige? [...] Botsio is worried about the chances of delay still occurring before Self-Government arrives on 6th March. There is much confusion about the adjective "Ghana". Three memos came from the Prime Minister's Office within 24 hours. Should it be Ghanean, Ghanaian or Ghanese? Adjololo was summoned by Nkrumah, who repeated over and over and over again: "Ghanean Navy, Ghanean Navy". This seems interesting to show how his mind is working. He is to have a yacht for state visits, and there will be a small flotilla of coastal defence vessels at Takoradi.

1957
23 January. Plans for the week before Independence (24th February). A special edition of *Sunday Magazine*. In place of *Nigerian Notebook*, a "meditation" on the *Eve of Independence*. Readings from pioneer Gold Coast authors in English and in the main local languages. On Tuesday 27th, a production of [Isaac] Dadson's* "Journey to Independence", which works in a good deal of useful quotations and talk by a lawyer on the legal aspects of independence, status, etc. On Wednesday, the poem by [Frank Kofi] Nyaku,* in Ewe and English: "We Are All But Brothers". In *Seconds Out!*, a rather forlorn discussion idea, Should the Commonwealth Be More Closely Organised? [...] Other items include the talk by Robert Gardiner, "The Meaning of Independence". One fears that this may arouse suspicions among the ranks of the CPP?...

10 February. The afternoon spent typing out a summary of the second year of *The Singing Net*, which will appear in the *Graphic*. (They like the articles since they are free.)

11 February. James is now at grips with the Prime Minister's Office, about the new title of our organisation. Nkrumah wants Ghana Radio, on the Asian model. We, of course, want Ghana Broadcasting Service. Someone ([Geoffrey] Bing?) proposes Ghana Broadcasting System, on the American model. It looks as though this will be the title adopted...

[From VOLUME 6: 16th February 1957 – 15th July 1959]

19 February. A Senior Staff meeting, mainly on Independence, with Joe Ghartey, finally established in Accra. Tea at 61 Seventh Road for Joe Ghartey, who showed signs of animation when the advertisement for Deputy Director was mentioned...

21 February. I walk to WABU [West African Broadcasting Unit], for the recording of Robert Gardiner's think-piece, "The End of the Campaign". A little later, Ben [Gadzekpo], Rose [Djabanor], and Halm read a "meditation" I have concocted from poems by [Michael] Dei-Anang, [Frank Kofi] Nyaku, Israel Kafu Hoh. No rest for the wicked – at 1000, recording of [Isaac] Dadson's feature, "The Journey to Independence", beginning with the gunfire at the Christiansborg Crossroads in 1948, and helped by the recorded reminiscences of McNeill Stewart. Jack [Lawton] takes the part of Superintendent Imray, but does not like it – "it opens old wounds". I fill my fourth role as a Governor, the inept Gerald Creasy.

26 February. Work on the Commonwealth messages, to be co-ordinated. The Prime Ministers of Pakistan and Ceylon [Sri Lanka] have recorded talks, the Foreign Ministers of Canada, Australia and New Zealand (including Mike Pearson and R.G. Casey). Only India plays it down, with some subaltern official, a woman secretary, whose script is full of digs against Imperialism, and trots at racialism in South Africa. It also contains a reference to poor old J.B. Danquah. The Rajah is obviously hedging his bets.

3 March. James has decided, rightly, that all six tickets for the presentation to the Duchess [of Kent] should go to Africans, and I go to the Catholic Church to inform Sam Bannerman, and to Commodore Street to inform Ben Gadzekpo, whom I found brooding over "insults" yesterday at the hand of Gerry Brown. Back at the Office, a call from Jack, in Liaison. The time for the presentation has been altered, and, at the Duchess' special request, attendance is unrestricted. So Henriette and I go up to the Castle, under a pretty green and white awning, and into a cool reception room. [...] The Duchess was delightful, not as tall as I had imagined, with a sad face, and large painted mouth. [...] At drinks, John Redfern, Basil Davidson, the young Cameron Duodu,* a gifted boy in the Basel mission bookshop, whom we want to attract to radio work. [...] This morning at the airport, the American Nixon went round with Nkrumah shaking hands at random with the crowd. "We must speak to our customers." He thinks that the gentle Duchess is cutting no ice, the cheers are only for Nkrumah. "They should have sent the Queen Mum, a real market mammy" ...

5 March. University Convocation, Procession of Floats, Opening of National Museum, Wreath at the Memorial, Reception at the Supreme Court, Civic Luncheon, Regatta, Unveiling Arch, Fireworks, Pageant, Speaker's Reception, Legislative Assembly, Midnight and INDEPENDENCE,

addressed by the Prime Minister on the Old Polo Ground. [...] I was up at the office at 06.45 to collect John Hammond, narrator of the Salute Programme, from his home at the extreme end of the Korle Gonno Estate. [...] John was splendid, with his magnificent *March of Time* voice, doubly so since he was on the late night shift, working up to 01.00 this morning, and never complaining... After six hours, a late lunch, a siesta, some more recording. Henriette goes off with Margaret to see the unveiling of the National Monument, while I look after Ba, and his new nanny, a neat, savage little girl called Vinolia, from Amedzofe. We caught a glimpse of Miss Ghana, the handsome sempstress from Kpandu, as she rode in triumph through Persepolis. [...] Then up the steel ladder, Ba held tightly, with Vinolia following, to see the fireworks from the roof. [...] I fell asleep during the Watch Service, but was woken at midnight by the hooters in the harbour, to hear Frank *ad libbing* for a quarter of an hour, before the voice of Nkrumah, breaking with emotion in front of a crowd of perhaps 100,000. "At long last, the total liberation of the African continent." Then the Anthem, twice repeated. From neighbouring Nima, no drums, no cries, complete silence. So Ghana is born.

6 March. Independence Day. Arden Clark, now Governor-General, fakes the Oath of Office, Parliament is opened by the Duchess, State Drive, Garden Party at the Castle, Pageant at the Stadium, Prime Minister's Reception and Ball at the State House. At the office, Frank almost breaking down with nerves, looking at the photographs of the leaders on the Old Polo Ground, their faces tense and distorted. [...] Later, in the review of the day's events, Frank skips the State Opening, and spends twenty minutes on the scene at midnight, imitating the characteristic candescence of the Prime Minister, and adding for good measure reference to "the hauling down of that symbol of tyranny, the Union Jack". The rest of the programme is made up of five minutes of Owusu Prempeh from Kumasi, with a recording of A.C. Russell, and Ankrah massacring McNeill Stewart's poem on the Duchess. [...] A really first class "Women's Half Hour", very well conducted by Rose Djabanor: discreet music, discreet interviews, a brilliant use of the memoirs of old Mrs Fraser, a poem beautifully read by Adali-Mortty. To complete my discomfiture, Jack says that our boys are abusing their [press] passes, and turning up at ceremonies to which they have not been assigned.

10 March. At 20.15, to BH, to read the summary of the second year of *The Singing Net*. The recording staff are cold and in the middle, I suddenly find myself wondering: What the *Hell* am I doing here? Four days after "Independence", and the *Oburoni* [foreign/white person] still infesting us!

13 March. In the afternoon, as I mull over the minutes, James comes in with a long face, and hands me two pieces of paper, saying "the first fruits of freedom". One is a curt note from little Jilly Wilde, forwarding an even curter memorandum from Ako Adjei. No BBC news of any kind to be rebroadcast, the Hausa programme is to be jammed, an Overseas Service begun from Accra, the name to be Ghana National Broadcasting System, or more popularly Radio Ghana. The changes seem to be to me reasonable enough, apart from the denial of BBC World News. It is the manner which is nasty, given our three year effort, leaning over backward to see all points of view.

22 March. James purring – he had "a *very* successful" interview with the PM. The title is altered, for the third time in a week, to the Ghana Broadcasting System, the GOS [Ghana Overseas Service] World News is restored to 0700. "I reminded him that it was his [Nkrumah's] own interview with Reith in 1952 that led to the invitation to the BBC. I said I would assist him to the utmost of our powers. I then asked him candidly if he wanted us all to leave. When he said no, I explained that he could not expect so much assistance in building up an External Service." [...] At 16.30, to see the brilliant young writer, Cameron Duodu, at the offices of the *New Nation,* the religious paper, overlooking the harbour. He does not wish to leave the "work of Christ" for a reporter's post at 5 guineas a week: but he asked about the chance of freelance work. Back to the studio for Efua's free adaptation, very free, of Agbaja's "Heaven is a Fine Place." [...] The cast came from the *évolué* circle: Mrs Easmon, Dr and Mrs Anfom, Kwesi Brew, Archie Winful, with the main part taken by Ralph Blavo. The effects were poor, but the production by Sam Bannerman, has a remarkable impetus.

24 March. I leave [home], to see again the young Duodu, who is "biting". A year in News would disillusion him. But he is very talented – "Encounter with a White Man", quite brilliant for a boy of 19.

5 April. James comes in with Geoffrey Bing, who is going to London to consult his friend Plummer on commercial "spots" [advertising]. I console myself with a rather beautiful poem by Kayper-Mensah, "The Ghosts", set in Kumasi, awaiting Doomsday. A young man in a taxi receives messages from two men, who died long ago. Adali-Mortty reads it beautifully, aided by music from John [Hammond] and Ephraim Amu.

20 April. At the studio, I produce an Easter poetry programme for the *Net,* beautifully read by Efua and Adali-Mortty, who says, I think sincerely,

"You will be remembered for what you are doing with this kind of thing."

14 May. I hand over informally to Joe Ghartey [returned from Kumasi to take over from Swanzy as Head of Programmes]. It is awkward, since Gerry makes a point of coming to consult me, on all sorts of matters, in the presence of the Lion. I then play back a number of our show-pieces to [Henry] Straker, who appears to admire them, although James Arthur plays havoc with the level of "Heaven is a Fine Place", and cuts the last five lines of Kayper-Mensah's "Ghosts", so beautifully read by Adali-Mortty.

12 June. Wednesday, and the Programme Meeting, at which I raise my voice for the first time in several weeks. Silence is rather silly, and patronising, to old Joe. [...] Adolph Agbaja, who is now a Programme Assistant, complains that we have not paid him for the one short story used in the *Net* in the last half year. The whole object for his appointment was that he should have a secure base to deliver his scripts.

30 July. The news at BH is that within two days we are to be put under a Ministry presided over by Kofi Baako. [...] Another visitor, a bearded young traveller from Longmans [British publishing house], interested in seeing scripts from *The Singing Net*.

31 July. Our new master, Kofi Baako, makes an appearance on the compound at 08.25, before either Bill [Busby] or I have arrived; and rebukes Owusu Akyem (a former classmate) for putting out a tactless interview in "Akan Magazine", in defiance of a warning by [Roland] Agodzo, that handsome, devious young militant. The interview actually suggested that market supplies were running short!

3 August. Saturday [...], Henriette and Clare [daughter, born 15th July] to see Miss Dittuck at the Maternity Clinic in the old Technical Institute on Seventh Avenue. [...] It is a pretty scene: mothers of all races, African, Indian, Syrian, European. Later, fetch Efua from the new bungalow on the Lagostown Ridge. [...] She records some poems by the younger generation, people like [Osborne Henry] Kwesi Brew.

11 August. Letters to John Fig, and Vidia Naipaul, whose *Masseur* is entirely charming, and for three-quarters of the way, promises to be more than that.

13 August. Some paperwork follows, above all a memo on an anthology

I propose to make of the first three years of *The Singing Net*, to be produced in time for the first anniversary of Independence [...] and fleshed out with some of the critical writing in *Sound Judgement*.

5 September. Wonderful news, the Ministry accepts the idea of a literary anthology, the first in the history of the country.

13 September. Sam Bannerman, in a state, after a row with Efua, who kept back the script of [Henry] Ofori's amusing [play, "The] Literary Society" for two weeks, and clearly intends to engross it. I do not like pushing on with the literary anthology on my own (the letter went out today to fifty people), but I am certain I am right. Like all writers, she only likes people who write like her... Cf. Vidia, when he took over *Caribbean Voices*.

17 September. A good programme, at last, on the box, Henry Ofori's satirical sketch, "The Literary Society": at times extremely funny, capturing the pursuit of culture under difficulties in a small provincial town. Production by Sam Bannerman, with "support" from Efua.

3 October. Ben shows me his notes on the Programme Meeting yesterday – short and succinct, and more than adequate. There is a "famine" in radio plays, a competition should be mounted as soon as possible.

20 October. I am put out, the literary dictator, by the arrival of Efua, who comes to say that she intends to present an anthology, hand-written, to the Prime Minister. I try to put myself in her place. She must have been upset by the circular letter [which Swanzy sent out to fifty writers of his own choosing]. After all, in 1955 it was she who gave me a list of possible authors for the *Net*. It is not her fault that only one, Kayper-Mensah, has proven of any use, besides herself. But if I had set up a selection committee [as Sutherland had suggested], remembering the Arts Council, and her own handling of fellow authors in the features, what squabbles there would have been! She never listens and has no box [radio]. Names like [Andrew Amankwa] Opoku and Israel [Kafu] Hoh mean nothing to her.

23 October. From Adali-Mortty, fresh stories about Efua, the Swan of Volta. On Sunday, through the Arts Council, she is organising a meeting of writers. A week ago, as I recall, Beattie asked me for a list of authors and their addresses (used for the invitation to the anthology) without saying what it was for. Andrew Opoku expresses sympathy, but he does not tell me of his own invitation for Sunday. How silly all this intrigue is!

2 November. Saturday and early to the [Maternity] Clinic. [...] Goodland, the intelligent Extra Mural Lecturer, comes in, to announce a Literary Conference in the New Year. I suggest inviting Ulli Beier from Nigeria, and possibly [Adeboye] Babalola, and he shows me the first number of the expensive quarterly, *Black Orpheus,* published in Lagos in September. It contains, without acknowledgment, many of the things I broadcast in *Calling West Africa* nearly ten years ago, like "Kujowu and the Elephants." [...] I am stupidly hurt, as ever. Nothing of the magnanimity of Frank Collymore to be found in this harsh continent. But, as the Jesuits say, what a lot of good *can* be done in the world, if you don't want to claim the credit.

4 November. I spend a long time talking to James about my future. An African expert with the GOS? They would not wear it. Perhaps it might be better to try as External Service Officer in Belfast. [...] Joe Ghartey will take on the job of HOP in February, and I can go, in March or April, early mainly because of Henriette's state of health.

9 November. Henriette more and more sunk in gloom. The abscess will not resolve itself. [...] I have asked [B.B.] Quist to make a tentative booking to sail on the *Apapa* on the 9th April. That might allow me time to see the anthology through the press, the last thing, as is fitting, I will do for Ghana...

26 November. Much of the day with Henriette, who talks of cancer, and pegging out alone. At the same time, she is eating heartily. I had time to go down to the Government Printers, to see how they were getting on with the anthology. They have completed five galleys, in Roman, when italics were asked for. [...] The man in charge is an amiable Creole called Penney, who talked of "other priorities". I doubt I will ever see it completed on African soil.

6 December. James announces the latest promotions: Amenuyeawu, Vida Koranteng-Asante, Asiseh and Crentsil. What we are doing is strengthening the Twi component of the service, since the language is the only possible alternative to English as a *lingua franca* [due to more than 50% of the population speaking Twi].

1958
3 January. I went up to the New Year School at [the University of Ghana] Legon, to listen to a seminar conducted by Goodland, and one Maxwell, from Londonderry [Ireland]. [...] They read, and analysed, Peter

Abrahams' *Wreath from Udomo*. Among those taking part, Joe de Graft, beautiful and assured, Geormbeeyi Adali-Mortty, Israel Hoh, uncomfortable in a cloth cap, and Efua, with whom I had a short chat. She explained that she "had only just thought" of the literary exhibition, and the anthology was not a *comprehensive* anthology. The request for a list of names by Beattie was "a simple coincidence." [...] In the evening, I turn to my last: the twenty English plays sent in to the competition. They seem heavily influenced by [Henry Ofori's] "The Literary Society" and [Bidi Setsoafia's*] "I Married a Been-To". The best, on first sight, by Addow, the man in Effiduasi, whose entry for Sean's film competition yielded six programmes for the *Net* in 1956.

9 January. A visit from a queer character, Ulli Beier, the editor of *Black Orpheus*. He is from Ibadan, a tall, young German Jew, an émigré from Berlin. [...] He does not tell me much I do not know about the Nigerian literary scene; except that the villain Olumbe Bassir, who plundered *West African Voices,* has finally got the University Press to publish an anthology, which will include poems by Efua Sutherland, without her knowledge.

11 January. I find to my delight the proofs of the anthology waiting on my desk, and spend all afternoon correcting them. The actual printing is not at all bad.

13 January. News of my departure is voiced abroad, and reporters come from the *Graphic* and the *Ghana Star*. Work on the proofs; and find James immersed in *his* proofs, the 24-page brochure on Ghana Radio, for the opening in March. Poor radiologists, with their desire for paper immortality!

14 January. A hilarious day at the Ministry, all morning, all afternoon, on a committee chaired by Iddrissu, with Robert Baffour, [Michael] Dei-Anang, and two regional representatives, Andoh and Kaleem, to consider the entries for the words for the National Anthem. We have 361 versions, [...] most of them delightfully bad, in fact, so bad we are continually laughing, much to the annoyance of the surrounding bureaucrats. [...] At least twenty typed out the original words by Philip Gbeho and his friends, with variations – "thorn of a new day" instead of "dawn". At the end of the day, we kept four, not as a whole but for their parts. [...] One, I knew, was by Kayper-Mensah, another by McNeill Stewart and Tetteh Larteh, another, just possibly, by Frank Parkes. They, at least, could be *sung* to the music, by the long enduring Ishmael [Addams, leader of the Damas Choir]. [...] Back until 23.30, to work on the

page proofs. The book comes to around 225 pages, leaving out Robert Gardiner's article on Independence, and some poems by Hoh, Winful and Parkes. This suggests that the estimate 80,000 words is not too badly out.

16 January. The morning spent on proofs, which I deliver to [Malcolm] Ray [of the Government Printers] in the afternoon, under the title, *First Folios from Ghana*. Then I have cold feet. This is too precious. It must be the dull but accurate, *Voices of Ghana*.

22 January. Final details of the radio play competition: 46 Twi entries, 36 English, 28 Ewe, 24 Fante, 13 Ga, 6 Hausa, 2 Dagbani. The Twis report that thirteen of their scripts are up to standard. The Ewe entry was very poor, and deserves only a single consolation prize.

28 January. The Cabinet consider the report of the panel of judges for the words for the National Anthem. I went with Gerry and Ishmael, with the tapes of the three versions, recorded by the Damas choir. [...] The Ministers were all in short sleeves, apart from Nkrumah. Gerry played the three versions. [...] Then Gerry played instrumental music, to accompany Dei-Anang's version [submitted yesterday], which Ishmael seemed to have difficulty in singing. [Kofi] Baako was about to say something, when he was silenced by the Prime Minister. "We don't want politics, Kofi. Walls have mouths," looking significantly at me. [...] The audience had lasted a little over twenty minutes.

3 February. Rusty Westmoreland rings up to say that the Cabinet have accepted my proposal to cannibalise the best entries for the National Anthem; and they ask the Ministry to set up a small panel to do the work, this will consist of Robert Baffour, Ishmael Addams and myself, but not Dei-Anang, since he put in an entry. In effect this means that I will be responsible as the other two are almost certain to agree with what I put up – neither are writers and both are going on trek.

6 February. [George] Padmore is enthusiastic for the Anthology to be circulated in time for the Pan-African Conference in April, but he wants to see the galleys – there is an objection to the ideological contribution, "The Meaning of Independence" by R.K. Gardiner.

7 February. ...some more work on the cannibal pot for the Anthem. This time, a possible first verse, the first and last two lines by myself, and five others cobbled from Wallis of the Ministry of Housing (English), Leonora Evans-Anfom, now in Tamale, the Colemans of the Catholic

School of Hohoe, Ashun of the Government Agent's Office at Kibi, and MacNeill from the House of Swanzy...

9 February. Sunday. Two calendar months, and we will be sailing from Takoradi. It is hard to imagine. Do I want to go or not? In some ways, Yes. In some ways, No. I cannot help feeling that if I go, I shall never again be given the chance of doing the sort of relevant, creative work that I have been doing *faute de mieux* in the last year. If there were a different set of power-holders in Ghana, I could always perhaps switch to a firmer cultural base, ensconced somewhere at Legon.

27 February. Henriette to get a medical certificate of pregnancy, finally confirmed by Dr Bannerman, who says she is twelve weeks gone [with Andrew], and the confinement will be some time in September. It is wonderful news.

28 February. The secret crown of my work in West Africa. Just before noon, Rusty Westmoreland rings up to enquire if the composite version of the Anthem has been recorded by the Damas choir. A few minutes later, we are summoned to the Cabinet. I am in my oldest clothes, and there is no car available, since Henriette is at the dentist. Sam Amarteifio brings me, horn blaring, as fast as possible, with Ishmael, and the tape and tape machine following. [...] It is clear that they have accepted the new version, and they listen with nodding heads, to the tape, played by Ishmael. [...] There is only one outstanding problem, the last line. "And tell the nations that the world is one" is not liked, for several reasons, and I am asked to provide an alternative, to be submitted to Baako. Gbedemah, as ever, makes a verbal proposal, which does not even rhyme: "And pay our homage to the new born babe." Kwame Nkrumah is very kind. He is the only one to notice us as we pack up – the others have turned to the next item in the agenda. He even thanks us. For a moment, I feel a certain poignancy. How nice it would be, if the sentimentalists were right, and we were all, Whites and Blacks, working loyally for the edification of a new State, out of the wrecks of the ugliness of the former years!

25 March. Hints in the press that the National Anthem words contain "a lot of secret history". One wonders if old Philip [Gbeho] has been talking out of turn. My conscience is clear [...], the version is good enough to be going on with, although inevitably limited by time. Probably in ten years, the words will change – as Kwame Nkrumah extends his empire or is toppled from power. My other concern is the Anthology, on which I spent most of the morning.

29 March. Saturday, and a surprise from Malcolm Ray, who delivers the anthology in its coat of buff and brown, with bold green print over all: VOICES OF GHANA.

2 April. At 0845, for my final act in Ghana, the presentation of the *Voices* to His Excellency the Osagyefo, the Hon. Dr Kwame Nkrumah. At Elliot's request, there are no photographers present, and the "ceremony" took five minutes. Oddly gentle and even vague, he took the book, asked if the poem by [Prince Haasnem] Nehrbot ["Ode to the Hon. Dr Kwame Nkrumah"] was "really good", asked if he could treat it as a work of reference. I asked for an inscription in his *Autobiography*, which I had brought. He complied and asked for something in the *Voices*. [...] I was feeling glum at the last Programme Meeting. [...] Depression heightened by a Senior Staff meeting, followed by a group photograph, and a party, attended by only 33 of the 54 programme staff. [...] The presents were numerous, too numerous. [...] In return, in accordance with Akan custom [...], I presented Ben, on behalf of the staff, with a copy of *Voices of Ghana*, and this was photographed by a man from the *Graphic*.

7 April. Cameron Duodu, with an embarrassing rave article about me, starting with the multi-voice reading of Sherlock Holmes. [...] My main interest is to see that the *Voices* are given as wide a coverage as possible – 3 copies to all contributors, literary editors and papers and colleges and universities all over the world.

9 April. Duodu's article placarded in the *Graphic*, with an unfortunate photograph, a curriculum vitae of "Henry", and at least half devoted to praise of James, a "marvellous boss" to help the "energetic genius", etc etc. [...] We drive to the quay, where the *Apapa* slowly noses in, 11,000 gleaming tons. Henriette in a state again, but a drink settles her. Lunch and Jack [Lawton] says good-bye. The first to meet us in Ghana, the last to leave. [...] At 1500, through customs. We file on board, and are sitting in the cabin, when we hear voices. A delightful surprise for in bursts Ishmael, smiling from ear to ear, and others from the choir, who are on the musical trek to Tarkwa, and thought they would make the detour to say farewell. They make one feel that, after all, I have not been a total failure.

APPENDIX:

Aarons, R. L. C. Jamaican short-story writer, born in 1905. Aarons worked in the Jamaican Civil Service and served in several cultural groups and associations on the island, including the Jamaican branch of PEN. His short stories were published in local papers and magazines and also featured in *14 Jamaican Short Stories* (1950) and the *Independence Anthology of Jamaican Literature* (1962). His collection, *The Cow that Laughed and Other Stories*, was published in 1944.

Ablack, Robert Kenneth. Trinidadian broadcaster and first-class cricketer, born in 1919. He appeared for Northamptonshire County Cricket Club between 1946 and 1949. He remained in Britain, working with the Caribbean section of the BBC. He returned to Trinidad in 1962, eventually becoming Chairman of Trinidad and Tobago's National Broadcasting Service. He died in 2010.

Adali-Mortty, Geormbeeyi. Born in 1916 in the Ewe village of Gbledee on the Ghana-Togo border, Adali-Mortty was educated at Achimota and worked as a teacher for nine years after leaving school. In 1946 he became a social worker before transferring to the Institute of Extra-Mural Studies in 1949. Adali-Mortty wrote many articles on education for newspapers and bodies like UNESCO, as well as working to record and study Ewe poetry. As a poet, he was inspired by his travels in Europe, North and South America, and Asia, as well as by the themes of Ewe traditionally storytelling. Adali-Mortty wrote and produced radio plays in Ghana and contributed his poetry to the first literary radio programme, *The Singing Net*. He edited *Okyeame: Ghana's literary magazine* with Efua Sutherland et. al, was on the advisory committee of the international literary journal *Black Orpheus*, and his writing appears in anthologies of West African verse.

Adoki, G. E. Nigerian author who was part of a literary group working out of Lagos in the late 1940s and early 1950s that included Cyprian Ekwensi (see entry, below). He contributed short stories to *West African Voices* and his work was featured in *African New Writing: Short Stories by African Authors* (1947).

Agbadja, Adolph Kwesi Afordoanyi. Agbadja was born in 1928 in the Ewe town of Dzodze near the Ghana-Togo border. Educated at Roman Catholic and Methodist missionary schools, he worked as a colporteur for the popular magazine *Psychology,* and took a correspondence course. Agbadja has said that it was listening to the B.B.C.'s *West African Voices* and particularly the writing of Cyprian Ekwensi that inspired him to begin writing short stories in 1954. He joined Radio Ghana's Programme Unit in 1956 and had 18 of his stories in English and Ewe selected for broadcast over the next two years. In addition, his short story "Heaven is a Fine Thing" was adapted into a radio play by Efua Sutherland. Agbadja's stories have been published in various literary journals and anthologies, including the first anthology of Ghanaian writing *Voices of Ghana: Literary Contributions to the Ghana Broadcasting System, 1955-57* (1958).

Agbonkonkon, Peter. Nigerian writer whose work featured regularly on *West African Voices.*

Akar, John. Sierra Leonean writer, actor, and diplomat, born in 1927. He was educated in Sierra Leone, the U.S., and Britain. He appeared on stage in London and on Broadway and was both a reader on, and contributor to, *West African Voices.* Returning to Sierra Leone, in 1960 he became Director of Broadcasting of the Sierra Leone Broadcasting Services and, in 1963, founded and directed the Sierra Leone National Dance Troupe. He later moved to Jamaica, where he was active in journalism and broadcasting. He died in 1975.

Akinsemoyin, Kunle. Nigerian writer who was a frequent contributor to *West African Voices* as both an author and reader. His books include the collection of traditional Nigerian folktales *Twilight and the Tortoise* (1963). He seems to have produced a novel that he passed on to Swanzy, titled *The Seed Eternal*, but it is unclear if this was ever published.

Akiwowo, Akinsola A. Nigerian poet and renowned sociologist, born in 1922. In the late 1940s and early 1950s, Akiwowo wrote poetry that featured on *West African Voices* and was published in *African Affairs* and *Phylon: The Atlanta University Review of Race and Culture* (Akinwowo studied at Morehouse College, Atlanta in the early 1950s). He is best known as a sociologist whose important work explored the theoretical and practical uses of sociological knowledge in Africa and the necessity of what he called the indigenization of the sociological enterprise. He died in 2014.

Aluko, Tim. Nigerian novelist and short-story writer, born in 1918. Educated in Ibadan, Lagos, and London, he trained as a civil engineer and town planner and held positions as director of public works for western Nigeria and as a faculty member at the University of Lagos. His first novel, *One Man, One Wife* was published in 1959. Prior to that, he had regularly contributed short stories to *West African Voices* and also served as a reader on the programme. He died in 2010.

Amarteifio, Sam. Worked in broadcasting with the Gold Coast Broadcasting Service during the 1950s and 1960s. In 1951, ahead of the major employment drive in 1955, he was selected to receive programme production training with the BBC in London. Whilst there, he worked on the *Calling West Africa* series and his duties included performing poetry and short stories for *West African Voices* and presenting various features. When he returned to Broadcasting House in Accra, Amarteifio developed new programming and was known for presenting the fortnightly discussion series *Seconds Out*.

Arthur, William. S. Barbadian poet, writer, social commentator, and educator, born in 1909. He served as headmaster of Buxton Boys' School where he called for school texts to be written with local themes, imagery, and nation language. He contributed articles to Barbados's *Herald* newspaper and *Forum* magazine. His poetry and fiction appeared in *BIM*, and he had numerous pieces broadcast on *Caribbean Voices*. Arthur also published three volumes of poetry, including *Whispers of the Dawn* (1941). He died in 2011.

Auguste, Rose. St Lucian writer who had one short-story broadcast on *Caribbean Voices* – a historical tale of seventeenth-century St. Lucia. She also appears to have published a book locally in Castries, *Gifts of Heaven*.

Babalola, Solomon Adeboye. Born in Ipetumodu, Western State, Nigeria in 1926, Babalola was a writer, academic, and teacher. Educated in Nigeria, Ghana, and Cambridge, England, Babalola earned a Ph.D. at the University of London. He is known for his translations of Yoruba oral poetry, which were broadcast on *West African Voices*, as well as of numerous folk tales. His important study and anthology of ìjálá poems (hunters' songs), *Content and Form of Yoruba Ijala*, was published in 1966. After returning to Nigeria, Babalola held positions as lecturer at the Institute of African Studies, University of Ife; principal of Igbobi College, Lagos; and professor of African languages and literatures at the University of Lagos. He died in 2008.

Baker, Flora. Baker lived in Trinidad and contributed two poems to *Caribbean Voices*.

Barrow, Raymond. Born in Belize (then British Honduras) in 1920, Barrow had an illustrious career as both an attorney and a poet. He contributed four poems to *Caribbean Voices* and also featured in *Poetry of the Negro* (1951), by Langston Hughes and Arna Bontemps. In a 1951/52 special issue of *Caribbean Quarterly* on British Honduras, editors Philip Sherlock and Andrew Pearse described Barrow's verse as "often quiet and unpretentious, although some of his latest poems show a pretty turn of violent metaphor." He died in 2006.

Barsoe, Elsie. Jamaican editor, journalist, critic, and actor, born in 1915. She edited, contributed to, and published *Pepperpot*, an annual Jamaican Review, for 21 years. Barsoe also played a significant role in the development of Jamaican drama with her theatre group "People's Theatre." She was an actor herself on both stage and screen, starring in *A High Wind in Jamaica* (1965). As Margaret Cezair-Thompson has noted of Barsoe: "Her home was a publishing office, literary salon, guesthouse for arriving and departing writers, and the venue of many parties at which politicians, actors, poets, and painters ate, drank, argued, and inspired one another." She died in 1974.

Bassir, Olumbe. Nigerian scientist and academic, born in 1919. In 1957, he published *An Anthology of West African Verse* with Ibadan University Press. Earlier he had contacted Swanzy with a request to view a collection of *West African Voices* scripts to gather material for an edited collection of verse. He was told he would need to seek the authors' permissions, but in the diaries Swanzy includes a note that his suspicions regarding Bassir not seeking permissions from the *West African Voices* contributors were justified. Bassir died in 2001.

Bell, Gordon. Barbadian writer and critic, he was a regular reader on *Caribbean Voices* and an integral member of the programme's Critics' Circle. In 1934, he published the satirical book *Wayside Sketches: Pen Pictures of Barbadian Life*.

Bennett, Louise. Major Jamaican poet, folklorist, writer, and educator, born in 1919. One of the most influential figures in Jamaican culture, her poetry was instrumental in showing that Jamaican Creole could be the medium of significant art. She spent significant periods of time in Britain, working for the BBC at various points. A number of her poems were broadcast on *Caribbean Voices*, some of which were read by herself. She also acted as a reader on the programme. Her poems were collected in *Jamaica Labrish* (1966) and much of her work remains in print. She died in 2006.

Bennett, Wycliffe. Pioneer producer and director, born in 1922. He is widely considered a founder of the theatre movement in Jamaica. He was Chairman Emeritus of the Ward Theatre Foundation and life member of the Little Theatre Movement. He also served as General Manager of the Jamaica Broadcasting Corporation. His book, with Hazel Bennett, *The Jamaican Theatre: Highlights of the Performing Arts in the Twentieth Century* was published in 2011. He died in 2009.

Blackman, Peter. Born in Barbados in 1909, Blackman was a poet, Communist activist, anti-colonial campaigner, and broadcaster. He came to Britain in 1937 and became involved in a range of organisations: the Negro Welfare Association, the League of Coloured Peoples, the Committee for West Indian Affairs, and the League Against Imperialism. Throughout WWII, he broadcast regularly on the BBC to the Caribbean, but in the post-1945 context of the Cold War Blackman was virtually banned from the corporation. His poetry collection *My Song is for All Men* was published in 1952. A posthumous collection, *Footprints*, was published in 2013. He died in 1993.

Bolton, Valerie. Jamaican actress who trained at RADA in London and served as a reader on *Caribbean Voices*.

Boyce, Edgar E.. Trinidadian short-story writer who had over a dozen stories broadcast on *Caribbean Voices*.

Braithwaite, R. B. E. Short-story writer from Trinidad, who contributed several short stories to *Caribbean Voices* in the late 1940s.

Braithwaite, E. R. Born in Guyana in 1912, E. R. Brathwaite was a novelist, teacher, and diplomat. He served in the RAF in WWII and in 1950 became a school teacher in London, the experience of which provided the raw material for his well-known novel *To Sir With Love* (1959). Other published work includes, *Honorary White, Reluctant Neighbours* and *A Kind of Homecoming*. His fiction has been widely anthologized and *To Sir With Love* was adapted into a successful film starring Sidney Poitier. He died in 2016.

Brathwaite, Kamau. Originally L. Edward, Brathwaite was born in Barbados in 1930 and was one of the Caribbean's most significant literary and intellectual figures. A poet, historian, philosopher, and editor, his landmark works include *Creole Society in Jamaica 1770-1820* (1971), *The Arrivants* (1973), and *History of the Voice* (1984). He read History at Cambridge between 1950-53, and received a PhD at the University of Sussex in 1968. He worked in Ghana between 1955-1962, while during his time in the UK in the mid-1960s he was one of the key figures in the founding of the *Caribbean Artists Movement*. He was a regular contributor to, and a reader on, *Caribbean Voices*. He published over twenty collections of poetry between *Rights of Passage* (1967) and *The Lazarus Poems* (2017) He died in 2020.

Brew, Osborne Henry Kwesi. Brew was born in 1928 at Cape Coast to an elite Fante family and orphaned at an early age. With the support of a British guardian, Brew completed school and became one of the first to attend the University College of the Gold Coast (now University of Ghana). While studying for his degree in English, he played the lead in Marlowe's *Doctor Faustus;* wrote prose, poetry and drama; and won a British Council poetry competition. In 1953, he was recruited into the Civil Service as part of the decolonisation process. Having worked for the Foreign Service in Britain, France, Germany, India and the USSR, Brew served as Ghana's Ambassador to Mexico, Lebanon and Senegal. Upon return to Ghana he established a flour milling company and died as a celebrated Ghanaian poet in 2007. Brew's poetry was broadcast on Ghana's national radio service, appeared in various national and international anthologies and literary magazines, and in published collections – the first of which was *The Shadows of Laughter* (Longman, 1968).

Brown, Enitan. Nigerian poet. A member of the pioneering generation of Nigerian poets writing in English that included Dennis Osadebay and Adeboye Babalola. His work was published in *African Affairs* in the late 1940s and he contributed to *West African Voices*. His verse was also included in *African Voices: An Anthology of Native African Writing* (1958).

Brown, Marjorie. Jamaican writer who had several stories recorded for *Caribbean Voices*. She is one of a number of women writers whose work Swanzy was evidently impressed by, but whose output has garnered little critical comment.

Browne, Michael. Short-story writer who had four pieces broadcast on *Caribbean Voices*.

Bunting, J. R. Poet, educator, and civil servant. Born in England in 1929, Bunting lived in Jamaica for many years and identified closely with the country. He was an early contributor to the arts journal *Focus*, established a literary club in Jamaica, and had over a dozen poems broadcast on *Caribbean Voices*. He worked as Headmaster of Wolmer Boys's School in Kingston, before becoming Education Officer in Nigeria. Later, he became a consultant to the British publishing firm Evans Brothers and was involved in a large number of publications relating to the Caribbean and West Africa.

Burke, Terry. Jamaican writer. She was a member of the Jamaican branch of PEN and was literary editor of the magazine *Madame* (1946-50), established by Helen Violet Ormsby Marshall (see entry below). Her work was anthologized in *14 Jamaican Short Stories* (1950) and she was both a contributor to, and reader on, *Caribbean Voices*.

Cain, Henry Edney Conrad. Born in Belize (then British Honduras), Cain joined the civil service in 1940, retiring from the position of Accountant General in 1976 to become Managing Director of the Monetary Authority of Belize. He subsequently served in a succession of high-profile diplomatic roles. Long interested in music and the arts, he was a member of the St George's Literary and Debating Society and was for many years the treasurer of the annual National Festival of Performing Arts which flourished in Belize in the 1950s and 1960s. He had two poems broadcast on *Caribbean Voices* and published a collection of verse in 1948, which was reprinted alongside a number of later compositions as *When the Angel says: "Write!"* in 2001.

Calder-Marshall, Arthur. English novelist, essayist, critic, travel writer, and biographer, born in 1908. A member of the British Communist Party and of the left-wing Readers & Writers Group, his visit to Trinidad in 1938 to investigate social conditions and the recent labour unrest was documented in his book *Glory Dead*, reissued by Peepal Tree Press as a Caribbean Modern Classic in 2022. He was a frequent speaker on *Caribbean Voices*' Critics' Circle. He died in 1992.

Campbell, George. Jamaican poet, born in 1918, who worked as a journalist and critic on the Jamaican *Daily Gleaner* and on the opposition *Public Opinion*. He was heavily involved in the nationalist movement and, with Edna Manley, co-founded the magazine *Focus*. His collection *First Poems* appeared in 1945, a selection of verses from which was read on *Caribbean Voices*. It was reissued as a Caribbean Modern Classic by Peepal Tree in 2012. He died in 2002.

Campbell, Owen. St. Vincentian poet. Together with Shake Keane and Daniel Williams, he was known as one of the 'trio' of St. Vincentian poets, whose work appeared regularly in Caribbean literary journals including *BIM* and *Kyk-over-al*. He was also a significant contributor to *Caribbean Voices*, with over twenty pieces broadcast on the programme. As with the other members of the trio, Campbell's poetry is distinguished by a sense of local commitment.

Carberry, H. D. Born in Canada of Jamaican parentage in 1921, Carberry was a poet and barrister. A well-known collector of Caribbean literature, he was a member of the circle of nationalist writers and artists in Jamaica that included George Campbell and Edna Manley. He is most famous for his much-anthologized poem "Nature." He had several poems broadcast on *Caribbean Voices*. A collection of his poetry, *It Takes a Mighty Fire* was published in 1995. He died in 1989.

Carew, Jan. Guyanese novelist, playwright, poet, painter, and educator, born in 1920. One of the Caribbean's great polymaths, Carew was the author of numerous works of fiction, including *Black Midas* (1958), *The Wild Coast* (1960) and *The Last Barbarian* (1960) and historical essays; he was also a political activist, socialist, and pan-Africanist described by Ambalavaner Sivanandan as heralding and helping to shape "the cultural revolution against colonialism and racism." He was a significant contributor to *Caribbean Voices* as a writer, reader, and critic. A collection of his poetry, *Return to Streets of Eternity* was published in 2015, the same year as his memoir, *Episodes in My Life*. He died in 2012.

Carr, Ernest. Trinidadian poet, short-story writer, essayist, and folklorist. Born in 1902, Carr was an early member of the literary group of the 1920s associated with *The Beacon* journal. An influential figure, he was considered the 'elder statesman' to George Lamming and others of the new writers in the islands at the time. He contributed several stories and poems to *Caribbean Voices*. He died in 1975.

Cattouse, Nadia. Belizean singer and actor, born in 1924. She first came to Britain during WWII and trained as a signals operator in Scotland. After the war, she worked as a teacher in Belize before returning to Britain in the early 1950s. She served as a reader on *Caribbean Voices*. Her television career began in 1954 and saw her appear in such shows as *Play for Today, Dixon of Dock Green*, and *Freedom Road: Songs of Negro Protest*. Cattouse was also an important figure in the folk-song revival in the U.K. in the late 1960s and 1970s, recording several well-received albums. In 2003, The Windrush Foundation honoured Cattouse with the Lifetime Achievement Award for her contribution to the arts as a distinguished actress and singer.

Chang, Carlisle. Born in Trinidad in 1921, Chang was a significant painter, designer, and gallery owner – he was the first local artist to make a living solely from art. Trained in fine art in the U.K. and Italy, on returning to his native island in 1954, Chang combined his European training with Trinidadian folk-art forms. He went on to do artwork for Carnival bands and various dance and theatre productions. In 1958, he designed the Coat of Arms for the Federation of the West Indies. Although he did not have a solo exhibition until 1997, his work was widely on display in Trinidad in the form of murals at over a dozen public sites. He died in 2001.

Charles, Cyril. St. Vincentian writer who had nearly a dozen pieces broadcast on *Caribbean Voices*.

Chen, Bryan. Chinese-Trinidadian writer who contributed a short story to *Caribbean Voices*.

Clarke, Lloyd. Clarke contributed two short-stories to *Caribbean Voices* in 1954.

Clarke, Shelia. Trinidadian actress and dancer. The daughter of Kathleen Davis (see entry below), Clarke was the lead dancer in Boscoe Holder's the Holder Dance Company and later married Holder (see entry below). She featured in Holder's revue *Bal Creole*, which was broadcast on BBC television. In 1960, she and Holder put on a show entitled *At Home and Abroad* in Port of Spain, Trinidad, performed by local dancers and featuring dances based on Brazilian, Haitian and Trinidadian folklore.

Collymore, Frank. Bajan poet, teacher, actor, editor, and broadcaster. Born in 1893, he served as editor of the important literary journal *BIM* from the 1940s through to the 1970s. He published several collections of poetry and short stories, and his work has been widely anthologized. He was well-known for the fellowship, support, and advice he gave to his fellow Caribbean authors. In an article on Collymore in *The Caribbean Review of Books* entitled "The Godfather," John T. Gilmore writes: "As a lover of literature, he was also a dedicated and selfless encourager of the work of others, lending books to aspiring writers from their schooldays onwards, publishing their early work in *BIM* [...] and helping them to find other markets, especially through the relationship he established with Henry Swanzy, producer of the influential BBC radio programme

Caribbean Voices." Edward Baugh's biography, *Frank Collymore: A Biography* was published in 2009.

Collymore, George. Trinidadian jurist and author who served as a reader on *Caribbean Voices*.

Connor, Edric. Trinidadian actor, singer, song-writer, and folklorist, born in 1913. He arrived in London in 1944 and within a couple of years had become a household name as a broadcaster and singer. In 1951, Connor made his film debut in *Cry, the Beloved Country*. In 1958, he became the first Black actor to appear in a Shakespeare season in Stratford-Upon-Avon. His most significant contribution to *Caribbean Voices* was as a voice actor on Errol Hill's adaptation of Derek Walcott's play *Henri Christophe* in 1951. His autobiography, *Horizons: The Life and Times of Edric Connor* was published in 2007. He died in 1968.

Conton, Willy (William Farquhar). Sierra Leonean writer and educator. Born in 1925 in Gambia of Sierra Leonean Creole parents of Caribbean origin, Conton was educated in Sierra Leone and the U.K. He worked as a teacher in Sierra Leone and Ghana. His novel, *The African* (1960), appeared in the Heinemann African Writers Series. Simon Gikandi describes it as "one of the first attempts to reflect on the violence engendered by racial discrimination in South Africa and political violence elsewhere on the continent, and to imagine the possibility of forgiveness and reconciliation as the precondition for the emergence of a United States of Africa." He also produced a history of West Africa and a further novel, *The Flights* (1987). He died in 2003.

Crabbe, Neville. British stage and screen actor, born in 1923. He was a participant in the Negro Theatre Company, founded in 1948. He was best known for BBC *Sunday-Night Theatre* (1950), *Rheingold Theatre* (1953), and *ITV Television Playhouse* (1955). He was married to Pauline Henriques (see entry, below) and featured on *Caribbean Voices* as a reader. He died in 1983.

Currey, Ralph. South African-born poet and schoolmaster, born in 1907. He was sent to school in England at the age of 13 and continued his education there, publishing his first poetry collection, *Tiresias*, in 1940. His work was widely praised by such luminaries as T. S. Eliot and Ronald Blythe. He contributed as a critic to *Caribbean Voices*. He died in 2001.

Dadson, Isaac B. Born in 1920 at Kintampo in Ghana's Bono East Region, Dadson was educated at Mfantsipim School, and joined the Civil Service as an Accountant in 1930. In his biography for *Voices of Ghana: Literary Contributions to the Ghana Broadcasting System* (1958), Dadson writes about his translations of Shakespeare into the Ghanaian language of Fante, and his staging of *Julius Caesar* and the *Merchant of Venice*. His original play, *The Journey to Independence,* aired on the national radio service as well as being published in *Voices of Ghana* (1958). After independence, Dadson worked for the Ghana Broadcasting Corporation.

Davidson, Karl. Jamaican economist who contributed two pieces of travel writing to *Caribbean Voices.*

Davis, Kathleen. Born in Trinidad in 1903, Kathleen Davis was an actress and radio personality, also known as "Aunty Kay". She is best remembered as the long-time host of the popular children's programme *The Aunty Kay Show*, which aired from 1942 to 1985 on Radio Trinidad every Sunday afternoon. She came to Britain in the 1930s, where she studied medicine before becoming an actress. She featured alongside Paul Robeson in the London stage production of *Stevedore* and was cast in the 1936 production of C. L. R. James' play *Toussaint Louverture*. She also acted in several films, including a leading role in *Debt of Honour*, starring Leslie Banks. She served as a reader on *Caribbean Voices*. She died in 1996.

Dawes, Neville. Born in Nigeria in 1926 of Jamaican parents, Dawes grew up in rural Sturge Town in Jamaica. A novelist, poet, short-story writer, and critic who produced significant work on the development of Caribbean writing and the place of Africa in Caribbean culture. His published work includes *The Last Enchantment* (1960), *Interim* (1978) and a compendium of his poetry, short stories and critical writing, *Fugue and Other Writings* (2015). He was a regular contributor to *Caribbean Voices*, featuring nearly thirty times on the programme. He died in 1984.

De Graft, Joseph Coleman. Born in the Fante town of Cape Coast in 1924, De Graft attended one of the prestigious Mfantsipim School (est. 1876), where he later taught English and lead the Mfantsipim Drama Laboratory. De Graft helped shape the mid-twentieth century arts scene in Ghana. He staged a broad range of productions including Shakespeare, African dramatists such as Wole Soyinka, and his own plays. Moving to Accra, he joined the National Theatre Movement with Efua Sutherland and became the first Director of the Ghana Drama Studio, which Sutherland founded in 1961. De Graft was an actor, producer, director and playwright who worked on numerous plays for stage, radio and television. He also aided the development of theatre in Kenyan where he worked at the University of Nairobi as a UNESCO specialist in teaching English as a Second Language. In the year he died, 1978, he returned to Ghana as an Associate Professor at the University of Ghana's Institute of African Studies.

De Paiva, Lennox. Trinidadian writer who had four stories broadcast on *Caribbean Voices*. Several of his pieces focused on WWII and its impact on the Caribbean.

Dei-Anang, Michael. Ghanaian poet, novelist and civil servant. Born in the Easter Region town of Akwapim-Mampong in 1909, Dei-Anang studied at the prestigious Mfantsipim School and Achimota College before proceeding to the University of London. Returning to Ghana, he became a regular contributor and performer of literature for the national radio station. Dei-Anang held various ministerial posts in Dr Kwame Nkrumah's government and retired in 1961 as Ambassador Extraordinary and Minister Plenipotentiary to lead the African Affairs Secretariat for the Office of the President. Throughout his career he continued to write and publish collections of poetry and plays that explore Ghanaian myths and traditions. He also served as President of the Ghana Society of Writers. When Nkrumah was overthrown in 1966, Dei-Anang was briefly imprisoned and then relocated to America as a college teacher. He died in 1977.

Delano, Isaac Oluwole. Nigerian writer, linguist, teacher, and political activist. Born in the Yoruba village of Okenla in 1904, he worked for the British government in Nigeria before pioneering a movement to push back against the erosion of the Yoruba language, culture and history brought about by British imperialism. During the 1940s, Delano gained a scholarship to the University of London where he taught Yoruba and wrote a groundbreaking Yoruba dictionary. Having worked on the BBC's *Calling West Africa* series, Delano continued to work in radio broadcasting and as a newspaper correspondent when he returned to Nigeria. He died in 1979 and is remembered as an important nationalist in the Nigerian struggle for independence, a pan-Africanist, and an advocate for many social issues such as gender equality.

Djabanor, Rose. Radio announcer in colonial Ghana during the 1940s when the station was known as Station ZOY, and its primary function was to relay BBC programmes from London through Accra to wired relay stations across the Gold Coast colony. Her duties during WWII centred on the translation for broadcast of war news from English to Ga, which is predominantly spoken in Accra and the surrounding areas. In 1949, Djabanor was a member of the first cohort of programme staff who travelled to London to study radio programme production technique at the BBC. Upon return to Ghana, she was one of the earliest Ghanaian broadcasters to develop and present original programme content so that radio might be relevant for Ghanaian listeners at the end of Empire. Djabanor's work included compiling and presenting *Women's Half-Hour*, and performing literature for broadcast.

Djoleto, Solomon Alexander Amu. Djoleto was born at Somanya in Ghana's Eastern Region in 1929. He won a Government Scholarship to St. Augustine's College at Cape Coast in 1951 and spent his extracurricular time reading, taking part in the debating society, and as an unpaid reporter on the *National Times* newspaper. Having completed an English degree at the University of Ghana, he studied textbook production at the Institute of Education, University of London. He worked for Ghana's Ministry of Education as a teacher and education officer, edited the *Ghana Teachers' Journal*, and led the Ministry's publishing programme. Although a writer of textbooks, Djoleto is best known for his poetry, children's books, and novels, which include two Heinemann African Writers series titles: no. 41 *The Strange Man* (1967) and no. 160 *Money Galore* (1975). He died in 2012.

Drayton, Geoffrey. Bajan novelist, short-story writer, poet, journalist, and critic, born in 1924. In the early 1950s he worked as a journalist in the U.K., Canada, and Spain. His best known work, the novel *Christopher*, was published in 1959. There were two other novels, *Three Meridians* (1951) and *Zohara* (1961). He was a frequent contributor of both verse and short stories to *BIM* and had numerous pieces broadcast on *Caribbean Voices*. He died in 2017.

Dunbar, Rudolph. Celebrated Guyanese conductor, clarinetist, and composer, as well as journalist and educator. Born in 1899, he became the first black man to conduct orchestras in England, Germany, Poland, and Russia. He died in 1988.

Duodu, Martin Cameron. High-profile Ghanaian journalist and writer who worked in newspapers, radio and television in Ghana and Britain. Born in 1937 in the Akyem Abuakwa town of Asiakwa and educated in Ghana's Eastern Region, he taught briefly to fund his continued studies before moving to Accra in 1956. Whilst working on the religious newspaper, *New Nation,* Duodu sent literary submissions to the national broadcaster, including the short story "Tough Guy in Town" which was aired in 1954, anthologised in 1958, and reworked by Duodu into the novel *The Gab Boys* (1967). In April 1957, Duodu joined the news team of the Ghana Broadcasting System. During his time in radio, he contributed short stories and poetry to *The Singing Net* and plays to *Ghana Theatre* (formerly *Akan Theatre*). He was also an early member of the Ghana Society of Writers. Duodu became Editor of *Radio News* before becoming Editor of the Ghanaian edition of *Drum* magazine and then Ghana's best-selling newspaper, the *Daily Graphic*. Now based in Britain, he works as a freelance columnist.

Edmett, Willy (E. R.). British administrator and broadcaster. Edmett worked as a producer for the BBC's Colonial Service from the mid-1940s until the late 1950s. He served as one of the producers of both *Caribbean Voices* and *West African Voices* after Swanzy left for Ghana.

Ekwensi, Cyprian. Nigerian novelist, short-story writer, and children's author, born in 1921. Educated in Nigeria and the U.K., his early works include the novellas *When Love Whispers* (1947) and *The Leopard's Claw* (1950). A major figure in African literature – his novel *Burning Grass* (1962) followed Chinua Achebe's *Things Fall Apart* as the second in the Heinemann African Writers Series – Ekwensi's most successful book was *Jagua Nana* (1961). He regularly contributed stories to, and served as a reader on *West African Voices*. He died in 2007.

Elliott, A. K. Elliott contributed four pieces to *Caribbean Voices*. Swanzy categorizes him as one among the "vast numbers of unknown names" who featured on the programme.

Enwonwu, Ben. Celebrated Nigerian modernist painter and sculptor, born in 1917. A major figure in the Pan-African art world in the 1940s and 1950s, he won widespread critical acclaim across Europe and the United States. During Enwonwu's time in Britain in the 1940s, he became a close friend and correspondent of Swanzy. He died in 1994.

Epelle, Kiea. Nigerian poet, short-story writer, and editor. Epelle's work was regularly broadcast on *West African Voices*. His poetry was published in *African Affairs* in the early 1950s. He was involved in the publication of several volumes of folk-tales from Eastern Nigeria, including *Our Folklore and Fables* (1952-53).

Escoffery, Gloria. Jamaican painter, poet, short-story writer, and journalist, born in 1923. One of Jamaica's most outstanding painters, as well as an important art critic, she came to Britain in 1950 to study at London's Slade School of Art before returning to Jamaica, where she became involved in the independence struggle. She featured on *Caribbean Voices* as a poet and a critic and Swanzy was evidently very impressed by her artistic skill and critical acumen. A collection of her poetry, *Mother Jackson Murders the Moon* was published by Peepal Tree Press in 1998. She died in 2002.

Eweka, U. Nigerian poet whose work featured on *West African Voices* and in *African Affairs* during the mid- to late 1940s. He was based in Sapele alongside his fellow poet Yesufu-Giwa (see entry below). Noting the presence of both these writers in Sapele, an editorial in *African Affairs* from 1946 observed that "there seems to be a literary school [here] that might be worth investigating: at least the quality of its verse, however uneven, is much higher than any seen from 'older' areas like Lagos or the Gold Coast."

Eytle, Ernest. Born in Guyana in 1918, Eytle was a cricket commentator and writer. He served as a reader on *Caribbean Voices* and worked more widely across the BBC and other broadcasters. He published a biography of Frank Worrell in 1965.

Fágúnwà, Daniel Olorunfemi. A Nigerian chief and novelist, born in 1903 in the Southern Yoruba town of Okè-Igbó. His novel, *Ògbójú Ode nínú Igbó Irúnmole*, was the first to be published in Yoruba (trans. as *The Forest of a Thousand Demons* by Wole Soyinka, 1968). It established the literary style of employing African philosophy in moral tales, often with a hunter protagonist, and combines elements of Yoruba folklore – spirits, monsters, gods, magic, and witchcraft – with an exploration of the influence of Christianity. Fágúnwà wrote a number of further novels, short stories, and two travel books; and his writing has appeared on radio and in print. He continues to be the most popular Yoruba-language author and his influence on contemporary writers such as Amos Tutuola is now widely accepted. He was awarded the Margaret Wrong Prize for African Literature in 1955, an MBE from Queen Elizabeth II in 1959, and died in 1963.

Figueroa, John. Jamaican writer, poet, journalist, broadcaster, and educator born in 1920. An integral part of the post-1945 Caribbean literary scene, his writings include, in addition to poems and short stories, work in the fields of criticism, linguistics, education, and sport. He served as the first General Editor of Heinemann's *Caribbean Writers Series* and was an important participant in *Caribbean Voices* as a contributor and reader. Highly valued by Swanzy for his keen critical eye, he was also responsible for publishing two volumes of poetry from the programme entitled *Caribbean Voices*. His collected poetry, *The Chase*, was published by Peepal Tree in 1992. He died in 1999.

Forde, A. N. Born in Barbados in 1923, Forde was a poet, playwright, short-story writer, and editor. He was centrally involved in literary and cultural activities in Barbados, contributing some 21 stories to *BIM* between 1950 and 1973. His work has been widely anthologized. He was a regular contributor to *Caribbean Voices*, with over 20 pieces broadcast on the programme. In addition to his literary activities, he was a civil servant who worked as a diplomat for UNESCO and served as a permanent secretary upon his return to Barbados. He was also general manager of the Caribbean Broadcasting Corporation for a short period. A small collection of his poetry, *Canes by the Roadside* was published in British Guiana in 1951.

Fortune, Felix Ramon. Brother of Barnabas Ramon-Fortune, born in 1910. A Trinidadian probation officer, he visited Swanzy and left him "a sheaf of humourless religious verses." Only one of his poems appeared on *Caribbean Voices*. However, he did produce a series of plays, songs, and poetry. In 1959, his play *Talaq* was staged in Trinidad and, according to Reinhard Sander, was "perhaps instrumental in the repealing of the Muslim Marriage and Divorce Ordinance of 1950."

Foster Davis, (Ena) Noel. Jamaican musician and performer. One of three musically gifted sisters, Foster Davies was awarded a violin scholarship to Trinity College of Music, London, in 1936, before returning to Jamaica in 1939 to teach music with her sister Sybil at the then Foster-Davis Music Studio. The pair would tutor some of Jamaica's greatest singers and musicians. In 1950, Swanzy recorded a selection of Foster Davis's songs for *Caribbean Voices*. She died in 1985.

Fraser, Byron. Poet and policeman from Jamaican. He had some eight pieces broadcast on *Caribbean Voices*.

Fuller, Roy. British poet and novelist, born in 1912. He was associated with the post-war British poets known as the Movement. He was a regular guest on *Caribbean Voices*' Critics' Circle. He died in 1991.

Gadzekpo, Ben (Bernard Senedzi). Ghanaian broadcaster and writer, born in 1905. A pioneering broadcaster whose radio career began in 1943 when he was seconded to the government's Information Department to work as a vernacular announcer on Station ZOY. Five years later, he won a scholarship to train in radio programme production technique at the BBC. (It was here that he first met Swanzy, with whom he continued to correspond into the 1970s.) Upon his return to Ghana, he was appointed as programme assistant in the Broadcasting Department and rose to become Controller of Programmes at the Ghana Broadcasting Corporation. Gadzekpo also had his creative work broadcast on *West African Voices* and *The Singing Net*, including retellings of Ewe folktales. He wrote an as yet unpublished memoir, *Ghana Muntie: From Station Zoy to the Ghana Broadcasting Corporation*. He died in 1989.

Gbeho, Philip Comi. Ghanaian musician and music teacher best known for composing the music for the Ghanaian National Anthem. Born in the Ewe town of Keta in 1904, Gbeho studied at Achimota College (Accra) and Trinity College of Music (London). In London he staged African drumming and dance performances with a group of West African students, which led to regular contributions to the BBC's *Calling West Africa* radio series. Back in Ghana he led a national campaign through radio to popularise indigenous music and dance, and ensure its inclusion in the state school curriculum. In addition to the Ewe drum, Gbeho played European instruments such as the piano and violin. This led to his role in founding Ghana's National Symphony Orchestra and Choir in 1963. Gbeho died in 1976.

Ghartey, Joseph (Joe). Ghanaian playwright, poet, and broadcaster, born in 1911. In 1937, when broadcasting was started in Kumasi, he was put in charge of the local news bulletins in English, and began to develop other programmes. He also began writing and producing plays in Fante. In 1949-50, he was given a Government scholarship to the UK, where he took courses in linguistics and translation at the School of Oriental and African Studies, as well as working at the BBC Staff Training School. He later returned to Ghana and took over as Head of Programmes of the Ghana Broadcasting Corporation in 1958, following Swanzy's return to England.

Gibbins, Naomi. Gibbins contributed three short-stories to *Caribbean Voices* in 1954. Beyond that little is known of her; Swanzy refers to her as "one of the legion of anonymous Caribbean writers."

Giuseppi, Undine. Barbadian writer, educator and anthologist, born in 1917, whose anthologies, such as *Backfire, Sugar and Spice*, were widely used in West Indian schools. She taught for many years at St Augustine High School for Girls in Trinidad and was Principal of the University

School at St Augustine. She published an autobiography, *I Remember* in 2005, a year before her death in 2006.

Giwa-Osagie (Moru Yesufu-Giwa). Nigerian poet who contributed several verses to *West African Voices* and had a number of poems published in *African Affairs* in the late 1940s. There appears to be little further information on Yesufu-Giwa: *African Affairs* mentions he is from Sapele, and Isidore Okpewho in *Once Upon A Kingdom* suggests he was probably a "nationalist student" in the UK in the 1940s.

Gomes, Albert. Trinidadian poet, novelist, storywriter, editor, and politician, born in 1911. A prominent political figure well-known across the Caribbean, Gomes was also, according to Anson Gonzalez, "one of the giants, unacknowledged that is, of our literary world, who was making an effort to create a literary tradition not only for Trinidad and Tobago but for the entire West Indies." Gomes was a key figure in the artistic circle clustered around *The Beacon*, and also a tireless advocate of Trinidadian folk culture. He published a lively, partisan autobiography, *Through a Maze of Colour* in 1975, and a novel, *All Papa's Children* in 1978. He died in 1978.

Gordon, Jack J. Guyanese writer who specialized in short crime fiction. He had two stories broadcast on *Caribbean Voices*, as well as work published in *The Trinidad Guardian* and *Chronicle Christmas Annual* (Guyana) in the late 1940s and early 1950s.

Goveia, Elsa. Guyanese historian considered one of the founders of modern Caribbean historiography. Her books include the seminal *A Study on the Historiography of the British West Indies* (1956) and *Slave Society in the British Leeward Islands at the End of the Eighteenth Century* (1965). She was the first female Professor at the University of the West Indies. She died in 1980.

Grant, C. E. L. (Cy). Significant Guyanese actor, singer, and writer, born in 1919. He acted on stage and screen and was the first black artist to appear regularly on British TV, singing the daily news on BBC's "Tonight" programme in the 1950s. In 1973, he co-founded the Drum Arts Centre in London. He produced several poems, one of which appeared in John Figueroa's anthology of poetry from *Caribbean Voices*, and also published the memoir *Blackness and the Dreaming Soul* in 2007. He died in 2010.

Grason, Doreen Goodwin. Antiguan writer who contributed to *Caribbean Voices*, primarily as a reader.

Grenfell Williams, John. A South African, born in Johannesburg in 1903, who qualified as a lawyer. With the outbreak of WWII in 1939 he joined the Ministry of Information and there met the then controller of the BBC Overseas Service, who offered him the post of director of the new African Service. He became head of the Colonial Service in 1946. He died in 1955.

Hall, Stuart. Born in Jamaica in 1932, Hall was a major academic, writer, and cultural studies pioneer. He was Director of the Birmingham Centre for Contemporary Cultural Studies and Professor of Sociology at the Open University. The first editor of *New Left Review*, he was also founding editor of the journal *Soundings* and author of many seminal articles and books on politics and culture. He acted as a critic on *Caribbean Voices*, but also had several poems recorded for the programme. A hugely influential thinker, he died in 2014.

Harris, Wilson. Born in Guyana in 1921, Harris was one of the Caribbean's most distinctive and formidable novelists, poets, and intellectuals. After serving as a land surveyor in Guyana, he moved to the UK in the 1950s to pursue his writing career. His earliest publications were collections of poetry, *Fetish* (1951), *The Well and the Land* (1952) and *Eternity to Season* (1954). After *Palace of the Peacock* (1960) the first book in the *Guyana Quartet* with *The Far Journey of Oudin* (1961), *The Whole Armour* (1962) and *The Secret Ladder* (1963), Harris went on to write a further 20 novels, the last being *The Ghost of Memory* (2006). His early critical writings, including *Tradition, the Writer and Society* (1967), *History, Fable and Myth in the Caribbean and the Guyanas* (1970) and *Fossil and Psyche* (1974) had a profound effect in challenging the inherited, colonialised assumptions of Caribbean thought of both Left and Right. He was knighted for his services to literature before his death in 2018.

Haweis, Stephen. English visual artist. Born in 1878, he moved to Dominica after losing much of his inheritance in the 1929 stock-market crash. Here he studied and painted tropical fish and wrote for local newspapers. He also contributed articles and poetry to *The Beacon* in Trinidad and had three works broadcast on *Caribbean Voices*. His book, *Mount Joy* (1968), is an account of his time in Dominica. He died in 1969.

Hazell, Vivian. Jamaican poet who fought in WWII. He served with 576 and 101 Squadrons as a Flight Engineer on Lancaster bombers and was decorated for his heroism. Before joining the RAF, he worked as a typesetter at the *Gleaner*. In 1943, during a wartime broadcast, he delivered a message to his mother in Kingston that, as James Procter notes, included an impromptu performance of "After the Raid," a poem he composed following his return from the major bombing raids over Berlin. His work was also broadcast on *Caribbean Voices*. He remained in Britain following the war, working in London as a typesetter. He was the author of two slim, self-published, volumes of poetry, *Poems* (1956) and *First fruits of me* (1965).

Hearne, John. Jamaican novelist, historian, teacher, journalist and social commentator, born in 1926. He was the author of six highly praised novels, including *Voices under the Window* (1955), *Stranger at the Gate* (1956), *The Faces of Love* (1957), *The Autumn Equinox* (1959) *Land of the Living* (1961) and *The Sure Salvation* (1981), all of which are being republished by Peepal Tree Press. He was well-known as a provocative commentator in the Jamaican press. Together with Morris Cargill, he wrote three James Bond-style thrillers under the name John Morris. He died in 1994.

Hendricks, A. L. (Micky). Jamaican poet, writer, and broadcasting director, born in 1922. The younger brother of Vivette Hendricks, he produced numerous collections of poetry throughout his lifetime, including *On the Mountain* (1965), *These Green Islands* (1971), *Muet* (1971), *Madonna of the Unknown* (1974), *Islanders and Other Poems* (1983) and *The Naked Ghost and Other Poems* (1986). Several of his poems were featured on *Caribbean Voices*. He died in 1992.

Hendricks, Vivette. Jamaican poet, born in 1925, whose worked appeared in the *Independence Anthology of Jamaican Literature* (1962) and John Figueroa's edited collections *Caribbean Voices Vols. I and II*. She was a regular participant on *Caribbean Voices*, both as a reader and contributor of poetry.

Henriques, Pauline. Jamaican screen and theatre actress. Born in Kingston in 1914, she moved to London at the age of five. In the 1940s, she became a regular reader on *Caribbean Voices* and was one of Swanzy's most valued contributors. In 1946, she became the first black actress to appear on British television when she starred in Eugene O'Neill's *All God's Chillun' Got Wings*. In 1966 she became Britain's first black woman magistrate and was awarded an OBE in 1969. She died in 1998.

Henry, A. E. T. Jamaican journalist, humourist, storywriter, and columnist for *The Gleaner* and *The Star*. Born in 1911, he lived in London for a long period and worked regularly for the BBC. He contributed numerous short stories to *Caribbean Voices*.

Herbert, C. L. Trinidadian poet, teacher, and land surveyor, born in 1926. Herbert was an early contributor to the journal *BIM* and a close friend of George Lamming (it is said that he paid half of Lamming's boat-fare to England when the novelist first left the Caribbean). A gifted poet, Herbert's work featured in *Kyk-over-al* and *Caribbean Quarterly*, and he had a dozen or so poems broadcast on *Caribbean Voices*. *The Poems of Cecil Herbert* were edited and published with an introduction by Danielle Gianetti, circa 1979, in Trinidad.

Hewitt, J. M. Bajan writer (and cricketer) who contributed several short stories to *Caribbean Voices*. His work also featured in the journal *Bim*.

Hill, Errol. Born in Trinidad in 1921, Hill was a significant playwright, actor, and theatre historian. Regularly referred to as one of the pioneers of Caribbean theatre, his plays include *The Ping-Pong*, *Broken Melody*, *Man Better Man*, performed in the West End and during the Commonwealth Festival of Arts in Britain in 1965, *Wey-Wey*, *Strictly Matrimony* and *The Square Peg*. He was an actor and announcer with the BBC in the early 1950s and contributed regularly to *Caribbean Voices* as both a writer and reader. He wrote two important studies: *Trinidad Carnival* (1972) and *The Jamaican Stage, 1655-1900*. He died in 2003.

Hoh, Israel Kafu. Ghanaian poet born in the Ewe village of Afiadenyigba in 1912. He completed Teacher Training College in Akropong and became a teacher in 1933. Working at various schools in the Volta Region, he rose to Headmaster in 1945 and became an Assistant Education Officer alongside Frank Kofi Nyaku in 1953. Hoh had begun writing poetry at the age of 17 and became a regular contributor to the Gold Coast Broadcasting Service's flagship literary programme *The Singing Net*. Swanzy states that the programme relied heavily on the quantity and quality of Hoh's poetry. He also wrote plays and published his poetry in *Okyeame: Ghana's literary magazine,* which was edited by Efua Sutherland, Geormbeeyi Adali-Mortty and others from the Accra literary network that grew out of Radio Ghana.

Holder, Boscoe. Trinidadian painter, musician, dancer, and producer of Caribbean dance revues, born in 1921. Holder was one of the Caribbean's leading painters. He travelled to London in 1950 and in the same year a version of *Bal Creole*, a revue that he had produced for Trinidad Carnival, was broadcast by BBC television. It featured Holder and his wife, Sheila Clarke, and introduced the steel drum to British audiences for the first time. Holder died in 2007.

Howard, O. M. English writer resident in Jamaica. She had four short-stories broadcast on *Caribbean Voices*, as well as work published in *West Indian Review* in the late 1940s.

Hutton, Albinia. Born in 1894 in Kingston, Jamaica of Scottish parentage, Hutton was a white Creole poet. Her collection *Poems* appeared in 1912, followed by *Hill Songs and Wayside Verses* in 1932. Her work was included in *A Treasury of Jamaican Poetry* and she had six pieces broadcast on *Caribbean Voices*.

Hutton, Elsie. Jamaican poet. A white Creole, Hutton was part of The Poetry League of Jamaica. Her poems appeared in the *Year Books*, published by New Dawn Press. She was a regular contributor to *Caribbean Voices*, with some twenty poems broadcast on the programme.

Itayemi, Phebean. Nigerian educator and writer, born in 1927. She was educated at Queen's College, Lagos and St. Andrews University, Scotland. She is now regarded as the first published Nigerian female writer: her short story "Nothing So Sweet" won a British Council competition in 1946 and was published in *African New Writing*. In 1953, she published *Folk Tales and Fables* with P. Gurrey, a collection of traditional stories from across West Africa. She served as an education officer in Nigeria throughout the 1960s and 1970s and, as an educationist, is best known as the co-author of the secondary school textbooks *New Practical English* and *Brighter Grammar*. Her book of memoirs, *Up-Country Girl*, appeared in 2013. She died in 2020.

Jakes, Bob. St. Vincentian writer who had two pieces broadcast on *Caribbean Voices*.

Jarvis, Euton. Born in Tobago in 1941, Jarvis worked as a reporter on the *Chronicle* and then became clerk for the Water Department in Tobago. He was a short-story writer who contributed several pieces to *Caribbean Voices*. Ronald Amoroso's play *The Master of Carnival* was adapted from a story by Jarvis.

Jectson, Seth. Ghanaian writer who provided factual programming to the BBC in the early 1950s, as well as contributing to *West African Review*. He was a regular reader on *West African Voices*.

John, Errol. Born in Trinidad in 1924, John was a significant actor, playwright, and director. He came to London after WWII where he found work in the theatre and, later, in television and film, securing roles in *The Heart of the Matter* (1953), *Simba* (1955) and *Cry, the Beloved Country* (1958). John's major career breakthrough came with the BBC's *A Man from the Sun* (1956), which led to him being cast in the title role in *Othello* at the Old Vic Theatre in 1962. His ground-breaking play *Moon on a Rainbow Shawl* was first performed in 1958. His other published play was *The Tout* (1966). He died in 1988.

Jones, Evan. Jamaican poet, playwright, biographer, screenwriter, and radio script writer, born in 1927. He produced an immense range of work. His film-writing credits include: the fantasy horror, *The Damned* (1962); the WWI drama, *King and Country* (1964); the spy spoof, *Modesty Blaise* (1966); the spy sequel to the Ipcress File, *Funeral in Berlin* (1966); and the WWII/sports film, *Escape to Victory* (1981). His stage and TV plays appeared in the U.K. and across the Caribbean. His poetry is much anthologized, particularly "Song of the Banana Man," and was broadcast on *Caribbean Voices*. He wrote several works of fiction for children, including *Skylarking* (1993), a collection of poems, *Understanding* (1967) and a novel, *Stonehaven* (1993). He died in 2012.

Jones-Quartey, K. A. B. Ghanaian scholar who was a fellow student of Kwame Nkrumah's at Lincoln University, Pennsylvania, USA. Together with Ako Adjei, they published a newspaper called *The African Interpreter* and founded the African Students Association in 1941. Jones-Quartey would go on to become a significant historian of the West African press and, in 1965, produced a notable biography of Nnamdi Azikiwe, the first president of Nigeria. He also served as the director of the Institute of Adult Education of the University of Ghana.

Kayper-Mensah, Albert William. Poet, playwright and teacher born in 1923 at Sekondi in Ghana's Western Region to a Shama family. Having schooled at Mfantsipim and Achimota, his prestigious education continued with a Masters in National Sciences from Cambridge and a Diploma of Education from London. In 1950, he became a teacher at Wesley College in Kumasi, Ghana. Whilst in Kumasi he sent poems and plays to the Programmes Unit at Broadcasting House in Accra, and his often nationalist-themed writing was regularly produced and aired. In 1956, Kayper-Mensah won the Margaret Wrong Prize for African Literature, and he continued to write prolifically resulting in such poetry collections as *The Dark Wanderer: Poems* (1970), *The Drummer in our Time* (1975), *Sankofa: Adinkra Poems* (1976), and *Akwaaba: a Collection of Poems* (1976) until his death in 1980.

Keane, Ellsworth McGranahan (Shake). Significant jazz musician and poet, born in St. Vincent in 1927. In the 1940s, the teenage Keane joined one of St. Vincent's leading bands, Ted Lawrence and His Silvertone Orchestra. In the early 1950s, he moved to London and soon became known in international jazz circles. His first poetry collection, *L'Oubli*, appeared in 1950. Several further collections followed, including the Casa De Las Americas prize-winning *One A Week With Water* (1979). A collected poems of six unpublished manuscripts *The Angel Horn* was published in 2005. His work was broadcast on *Caribbean Voices* alongside that of his compatriots and friends Owen Campbell and Daniel Williams – together they were known as the 'trio' of St. Vincent writing. He died in 1997.

Kempadoo, Peter Lauchmonen. Guyanese novelist, broadcaster, publisher, and teacher, born in 1926. After leaving school he worked for a time in a sugar factory, then as a teacher and later as a reporter in Georgetown. He travelled widely across the Caribbean, Africa, and Asia, acting as a consultant in rural development. He moved to the UK in 1953. His novel, *Guyana Boy*, was published in 1960 under the name Lauchmonen, followed by *Old Thom's Harvest* in 1965. He died in 2019.

Kent, Lena. Pseudonym of Lettice A King, Kent was born in Jamaica in 1888. Primarily a poet, she was a Medallist of the Institute of Jamaica and her work appeared regularly in the *Gleaner*. Her collections include *Spiritual Counsels for Young Christians* (1918). She contributed some nine poems to *Caribbean Voices*.

Lambert, Calvin. Born in Grenada in 1917, Lambert was a medical practitioner who, while at medical school, published two volumes of poetry, including *Selected Poems of a West Indian*. He was well-known to both Una Marson and Henry Swanzy, and in December 1947 he had a sequence of twelve poems broadcast on a single episode of *Caribbean Voices*. He died in 2000.

Lamming, George. Major Bajan novelist, poet, essayist, and intellectual, born in 1927. He emigrated to Britain in 1950 and in 1951 he became a broadcaster for the BBC Colonial Service. He was a significant and longstanding contributor to *Caribbean Voices*, both as a writer and a regular reader. His novels, which have remained in constant print, are *In the Castle of My Skin* (1953), *The Emigrants* (1954), *Of Age and Innocence* (1958), *Water with Berries* (1971) and *Natives of My Person* (1972). His essays in *The Pleasures of Exile* (1960) remain foundational documents of postcolonial Caribbean identity. He died in 2022.

Laryea, Susana. Worked for Ghana Broadcasting System from 1950, when it was the Gold Coast Broadcasting Service, until 1978 by which time it had become the Ghana Broadcasting Corporation. In 1954 Laryea was selected from the early Ghanaian programme makers to travel to the BBC in London to receive programme production training. Returning to the Gold Coast the same year, she rose through the ranks to complete her career in broadcasting as Head of GBC's External Services.

Lasebikan, E. L. (Tunde). Nigerian poet and scholar. A specialist in Yoruba poetry, Lasebikan worked at the School of African and Oriental Studies in London in the late 1940s. He was a key contributor to *West African Voices*, featuring as a critic on its first broadcast. His scholarly works include *The Tonal Structure of Yoruba Poetry* (1956).

Le Page, Robert (Bob). British-born sociolinguist who was an eminent scholar of Creole linguistics and co-author of the *Dictionary of Jamaican English* (1967). He taught for over a decade in Jamaica. He featured on *Caribbean Voices* as a critic. He died in 2006.

Lee, Margaret. Guyanese poet, critic, and teacher. She was involved in the Guyanese literary scene in the late 1940s, contributing reviews to *Kyk-over-al*. She had five pieces broadcast on *Caribbean Voices*. Lee taught at Bishops' High School in Georgetown.

Levy, Eric. Levy had one short poem, "Confessions of a Hermit", broadcast on *Caribbean Voices*.

Lincott, P. D. Penname of the Trinidadian writer P. D. [Patrick] Chookolingo who was a major voice in the development of a popular and idiosyncratic Trinidadian journalism, including the scandalous scourge of the political elite, *The Bomb*. He had one short story broadcast on *Caribbean Voices*.

Lindo, Archie. Jamaican poet, short-story writer, novelist, playwright, broadcaster, critic, and photographer, born in 1908. A well-known playwright in the 1940s whose work included an adaptation of H. G. De Lisser's *The White Witch of Rose Hall*, Lindo also published several poetry and short-story collections, including *Bronze* (1944) and *My Heart Was Singing* (1944) and contributed over a dozen pieces to *Caribbean Voices*. He worked for Jamaican local radio and was art critic for *The Star* newspaper from 1960. His photographs are part of the National Gallery of Jamaica collection. He died in 1990.

Lindo, Cedric. Regional representative for the BBC in Jamaica. Alongside his wife Gladys, he was involved in gathering and selecting submissions for *Caribbean Voices*. He was a regular contributor to *The Gleaner* and in 1962 co-edited *The Independence Anthology of Jamaican Literature*.

Lindo, Gladys. Literary agent for the BBC in Kingston, Jamaica. Alongside her husband Cedric, she acted as the first point of contact for Swanzy in Jamaica and was instrumental in selecting submissions for *Caribbean Voices*.

Lloyd, Harrison. Penname of an anonymous author. Lloyd had one story broadcast on *Caribbean Voices*, but the general consensus amongst those involved in the programme seems to have been that his work was of very poor quality.

Lockhart, Emily. Better known as Lily, Lockhart was a member of the well-known Dominican Lockhart family and the cousin of Jean Rhys. Based in St. Lucia in the 1930s, she edited and published *The West Indian Enterprise* to which she contributed her own stories. Lockhart wrote poems and calypsos in nation language, including one called "Creole Song" that referenced "the gold Sargasso Sea" and provided the title for Rhys' most famous novel. By 1950, Lockhart had moved to London, where she had two pieces, "Bird of Gold" and "A West Indian Symposium," broadcast on *Caribbean Voices*. She died in 1972.

Loewenthal, Enid. Trinidad-based writer who had five pieces broadcast on *Caribbean Voices*.

MacJajah, N.O.M. Nigerian writer who claimed to be the founder of the United African Academy of Drama and Social Services. He first approached Swanzy in the late 1940s with various manuscripts. Swanzy was keen to see MacJajah's work featured on *Calling West Africa* and later recorded his plays for transmission on *West African Voices*. MacJajah's play, *The Trial of the Wizard*, which is based on Opobo beliefs, was published by Swanzy in *African Affairs* in 1951.

Mackay, Mercedes. English journalist, critic, broadcaster, and novelist. Despite the paucity of critical commentary on her life and work, Mackay was widely regarded in the 1940s-1960s as an authority on West Africa. Born in Cornwall, she was educated in Sussex and at the Central School of Speech and Drama in London. In her twenties, she married an engineer and subsequently spent time in Quebec and Tanganyika before moving to Nigeria for eight years where she ran a radio station in Ibadan. She joined the BBC in the 1940s and made weekly broadcasts to West Africa for the BBC Overseas Service. Her *West African Diary* was a staple feature of *West African Voices*. She was also an incredibly prolific reviewer for *African Affairs*. In 1954, her first novel, *Black Argosy*, was published. She produced three further novels, as well as articles on traditional African music. She was greatly valued by Swanzy as a knowledgeable and reliable colleague.

Mais, Roger. Jamaican novelist, poet, playwright, and journalist, born in 1905. Described by Swanzy as a "stormy petrel," Mais' narratives of working-class life in Kingston were the literary adjunct to the anti-colonial energies of the mid-twentieth century. He published two collections of short stories, *Face and Other Stories* (1941) and *And Most of All Man* (1943) and three novels, *The Hills Were Joyful Together* (1953), *Brother Man* (1954) and *Black Lightning* (1955). His criticism, prose, and poetry all featured on *Caribbean Voices*. He died in 1955.

Majekodunmi, N. C. Born in Nigeria, Majekodunmi was a doctor who hailed from a famous Abeokuta family. His work appeared on *West African Voices* and his poem "1944" was published in *African Affairs* in the late 1940s.

Manley, Carmen. Born in Panama in 1931 of Jamaican parents, Manley was a well-known scriptwriter, actress, and broadcaster on TV and radio. She spent some time in Britain where she met Swanzy and contributed as a reader on *Caribbean Voices*. She died in 1975.

Manley, Michael. Jamaican politician, labour leader, author, and intellectual, born in 1924. Manley served as Prime Minister of Jamaica from 1972 to 1980 and from 1989 to 1992. Manley's first job after graduation from the London School of Economics & Political Science was as a broadcast journalist with the External Services of the BBC. He first met Swanzy in this period and acted as a reader on *Caribbean Voices* in the late 1940s. In addition to a number of political works, he wrote a well-received *History of West Indian Cricket* (1995) Manley died in 1997.

Marson, Una. Major Jamaican broadcaster, poet, playwright, and activist, born in 1905. She worked as the assistant editor of a Jamaican political journal before, in 1928, launching her own magazine, *The Cosmopolitan*, which dealt with local, feminist and workers' rights issues. In 1930 she self-published her first collection of poems, *Tropic Reveries*, followed by *Heights and Depths* (1931), and her first play, *At What Price*. In the 1930s, she moved between Jamaica and England, working as a journalist and writing further plays and poetry. During her stay in London between 1938 and 1945, she became centrally involved in the BBC's *Calling the West Indies* programming and was instrumental in the creation of *Caribbean Voices*, serving as the programme's first editor. She returned to Jamaica in 1945 and later spent time in the U.S.A. *Una Marson: Selected Poems* was published in the Peepal Tree Caribbean Modern Classics series in 2011. She died in 1965.

Martins, Orlando. Yoruba Nigerian film and stage actor, born in 1899. A pioneering figure in British film, he arrived in London in 1919 and went on to star in numerous stage and cinematic productions from the 1930s to the 1950s, including *Cry, the Beloved Country* (1954) and *Simba* (1955). In the late 1940s, he worked with Swanzy as a reader on the BBC's West African programmes. He died in 1985.

Maxwell, Ken. Jamaican broadcaster, journalist, radio personality, poet, and short-story writer who worked for the Jamaican Broadcasting Corporation in the late 1950s and 1960s. He had over a dozen pieces broadcast on *Caribbean Voices* and also served as a reader on the programme.

McBurnie, Beryl. Renowned Trinidadian educationalist, choreographer, and pioneer of Caribbean dance, born in 1914. After studying in the U.S. and working on Broadway as an understudy to Carmen Miranda in the 1930s, McBurnie returned to Trinidad in 1940 and established the legendary Little Carib Theatre. The Theatre became the focus for Trinidad's dance and drama and had a significant influence on the development of Caribbean theatre. Judy Raymond's biography, *Beryl McBurnie* was published in 2018. She died in 2000.

McFarlane, Basil. Jamaican poet, journalist, film and art critic, and broadcaster, born in 1922. The son of J. E. Clare McFarlane, he was one of the early poets to be included in the arts journal *Focus* and a regular contributor to *Caribbean Voices*. His poetry collection, *Jacob and the Angel and other poems* was published in British Guiana in 1952.

McFarlane, J. E. Clare. Jamaican poet, essayist, anthologist, critic, born in 1894. He was the founder of the Jamaican Poetry League in 1923 and his *Voices from Summerland* (1929) was the first anthology of Jamaican poetry. He made several contributions to *Caribbean Voices*, although Henry Swanzy remained sceptical about the quality of his work. His poetry collections include: *Beatrice: a narrative poem in ten parts* (1918), *Daphne, a Tale of the Hills* (1931), *The Magdalen* (1957) and *Selected Shorter Poems* (1954). He died in 1962.

McFarlane, R. L. C. Jamaican poet and educator, born in 1925. The son of J. E. Clare McFarlane, his poetic works were regularly published from the 1950s through to the 1990s; they include: *Hunting the Bright Stream* (1960), *Poems in Three Phases* (1976), *Suddenly the Lignum Vitae: poems 1976-78* (1978)

Meikle, Rupert. Jamaican writer who ran a cultural club in Port Maria and was strongly invested in the Harlem Renaissance. He was a frequent correspondent of such African American authors as James Weldon Johnson. A friend of Una Marson, Meikle consistently championed her work.

Melville, Edwina. Born in Georgetown, Guyana in 1926, Melville was a poet, short-story writer, and journalist. After her marriage to Charles Melville in 1950, she settled in the Rupununi savannah, the subject of much of her work. Her poetry was published in *Kyk-over-al* and *New World*, as well as in A. J. Seymour's *A Treasury of Guianese Poetry*. Her illustrated story collection *This is the Rupununi: A Simple Story of the Savannah Lands of the Rupununi* appeared in 1956. She later became an MP for District 9 (Rupununi). She died in 1993.

Mendes, Alfred. Born in Trinidad in 1897 of Portuguese parents, Mendes was a novelist, short story writer, and editor. Along with C. L. R. James and Albert Gomes, he was a significant force in the "Trinidad Renaissance" of the 1930s. He edited the literary magazine *Trinidad*, published the novels *Pitch Lake* (1934) and *Black Fauns* (1935), and contributed some 60 short stories to magazines in Trinidad, London, New York, and Paris. Some of these were collected in *The Man Who Ran Away and Other Stories* (2006). He featured as a critic on *Caribbean Voices*. He died in 1991.

Millar, James. Born in Scotland in 1909, Millar worked for the British Foreign Office before joining the BBC in 1946. He was the Director General of the Gold Coast Broadcasting Service from 1954 to 1957 and the Director General of the Ghana Broadcasting Corporation from 1957 to 1960. He died in 1986.

Milner-Brown, A. L. Ghanaian writer whose work was recorded for *West African Voices*. His poem "Who Knows?" was included in *Poems from Black Africa*, edited by Langston Hughes. There the "Notes on Contributors" refers to him as a "freelance writer, newspaper man, and teacher living in Accra."

Milton, Beau (H. M. Beaufoy Milton). British actor and writer, born in 1907. He was a regular reader for *West African Voices* and *Caribbean Voices*. He died in 1971.

Mittelholzer, Edgar. Guyanese novelist, short-story writer, and poet, born in 1909. Mittelholzer was a prolific author, producing some 22 novels, and a pioneer in the Anglophone Caribbean context as the first of his generation to emigrate to Britain to make a professional career as a writer. Arriving in the UK in 1948, he was contributor and reader on *Caribbean Voices*. From 1956 to late 1957, he also served as editor of the programme. According to an article in the *Guiana Graphic* following Mittelholzer's suicide in 1965, at the height of his career his novels were the "hottest sellers in the paperback market" and would sell an average of 8,000 copies. He published 24 novels, of which *Corentyne Thunder* (1941), *A Morning at the Office* (1950), *Shadows Move Among Them* (1951), *The Life and Death of Sylvia* (1953) and *My Bones and My Flute* (1955) have been republished in the Peepal Tree Caribbean Modern Classics Series, in addition to *Creole Chips and Other Writings : Short Fiction, Poetry, Drama and Essays (1937-1954)* which collects most of Mittelholzer's earlier uncollected writing.

Morris, Sam (Samson Uriah Morris). Grenada-born educator, anti-colonialist and civil rights activist, born in 1908. He came to London in 1939 and participated in several BBC programmes, including as a reader on *Caribbean Voices*. In 1953, he left for Ghana where he worked with Swanzy on the Gold Coast Broadcasting System. He served as a private secretary and press officer to Kwame Nkrumah for eight years, before returning to the UK in 1967. He died in 1976.

Morrison, Hugh. Born in the Panama Canal Zone of Jamaican parents in 1921, Morrison was a poet, essayist, short-story writer, critic, educator, and radio producer. He published short-stories and poems in Caribbean anthologies, magazines, and newspapers. He had one story, "Home is the Hunter," broadcast on *Caribbean Voices*.

Mulira, Eridadi. Born in Kamese, Uganda, in 1909, Mulira was a politician and publisher who wrote several books, poems, and plays. In 1950 the Fabian Colonial Bureau published his significant analysis of contemporary politics, *Troubled Uganda*.

Mullings, Aston. Jamaican poet who featured over a dozen times on *Caribbean Voices* in the mid-1950s. In introducing Mullins' poem "Sonata" in one broadcast, Swanzy made clear he was less than impressed by the poet's technique and colonial middle-class focus, describing his work as seeming "to belong to the veranda."

Naipaul, Seepersad. Trinidadian journalist and short story writer, born in 1906. Father of V. S. Naipaul and Shiva Naipaul, Seepersad worked as a journalist for the *Trinidad Guardian* – he was the newspaper's first East Indian reporter. His important short-story collection *Gurudeva and Other Indian Tales* was published in 1943 and a collected edition of his stories, including *Gurudeva and Other Indian Tales* and stories broadcast in *Caribbean Voices*, and *Seepersad Naipaul, Amazing Scenes: Selected Journalism 1928-1953* will be published by Peepal Tree in 2023. He died in 1953.

Naipaul, V. S. Major Trinidadian novelist, born in 1932. A significant and widely-known figure in world literature, Naipaul was knighted in 1990 and awarded the Nobel Prize in 2001. His early work, including some poetry, featured regularly on *Caribbean Voices* and in December 1954 he took over from Swanzy as editor of the programme until September 1956, a period discussed in Glyne A. Griffith's *The BBC and the Development of Anglophone Caribbean Literature 1943-1958* (2016). Swanzy admired the first three-quarters of Naipaul's first novel, *The Mystic Masseur* (1957), which was followed by a further eleven novels, including *A House for Mr Biswas* (1961), *The Mimic Men* (1967), *In A Free State* (1971), *Guerrillas* and *The Enigma of Arrival* (1987). Swanzy's regular contributor on *Caribbean Voices*, Arthur Calder-Marshall, is fictionalised as Foster Morris in *A Way in the World* (1994). V.S. Naipaul further published two collections of short stories, *Miguel Street* (1959) and *A Flag on the Island* (1967), which contains several stories first broadcast on *Caribbean Voices*, and fifteen works of non-fiction, of essays, memoir and travel writing. He died in 2018.

Nchami, V. C. Cameroonian writer who sold some twenty stories to the BBC and appeared regularly on *West African Voices*. His work also featured in *African Affairs*. He appears to have worked for a time in the Education Office at Buea in Cameroon, before moving to the Pharmacy School at Yaba near Lagos in Nigeria. He was involved in the establishment of the first English-language newspaper published in Cameroon in 1960.

Newton, Kenneth P. Trinidadian short-story writer whose work appeared in *BIM* and on *Caribbean Voices*.

Nicol, Davidson (Abioseh Nicol). Born in 1924, Nicol was a Sierra Leonean Creole academic, diplomat, physician, writer, and poet. He published a number of literary works, and in 1969 he was appointed

Sierra Leone ambassador to the UN and later served as chairman of the Security Council. A family friend and member of Swanzy's social circle, he was also the subject of a portrait by Swanzy's first wife, Tirzah Garwood. Nicol died in 1994.

Nketia, J. H. K. Significant Ghanaian ethnomusicologist and composer. Nketia was born in 1921 at Ashanti Mampong. Educated in Ghana and London, he went on to lecture and hold positions at prestigious universities across the world. A leading scholar on African musical traditions, he has published numerous books and articles, including *The Music of Africa* (1974), widely considered a definitive historical study. As a composer, Nketia has produced scores of pieces for choirs, instrumental groups, and solo voices, often combining African and Western instruments. Several of his early original songs were performed on Radio Ghana in the 1950s. One of them, 'Yehwe Ono Ara,' became the signature tune for the weekly literary programme, *The Singing Net*. Nketia died in 2019.

Nyaku, Frank Kofi. Born in 1924 at Ho in Ghana's Volta Region, Nyaku graduated from Achimota as a music teacher in 1949. In 1952, he was appointed Assistant Education Officer alongside Israel Kafu Hoh with a promotion to Education Officer in 1956. Nyaku wrote both fiction and non-fiction including school textbooks in Ewe; a biography of the first Vice Principal of Achimota College, Dr. James Emman Kwegyir Aggrey; the novel *Kofi Nyameko Nutinya;* and short stories and poems including two collections: *The Three Devils and Other Stories* (1981) and *The Marriage Experiment and Other Stories* (1984). His literary contributions to the national radio service include the humorous short-story *The Wrong Packing Case,* a poem metaphorical about Ghanaian national identity titled *Unity in Diversity,* and many original Ewe music compositions such as *Wo Bada Ku Badae* (*Horrible Death Usually Ends Reckless Lives*).

Ofori, Henry. Prominent Ghanaian journalist in the mid-twentieth century. Born to a Guan family in 1924 at Oda in Ghana's Eastern Region, he completed his secondary school education in 1943. Having worked at the R.A.F. Base in Takoradi and as a Soil Analyst for the West African Cocoa Research Institute at Tafo, Ofori attended Achimota College where he trained as a Physics teacher and won the college prizes for both poetry and prose writing. In 1950, the *Daily Graphic* newspaper was established in Accra and in 1955 Ofori left his teaching job to become an in-house columnist with the *Daily Graphic* and a contributor to the Mirror Group's sister paper, the *Sunday Mirror.* In the year of independence,

1957, he became Editor of the Ghana edition of *Drum* magazine, as well as writing for various African state-owned newspapers and serving as Secretary of the Ghana Press Club. Ofori often wrote columns under his penname Carl Mutt and was well-known for his uniquely humorous journalistic style. During his career, he continued to write fiction and his political satire was a regular feature on Ghana's radio literary programmes including. He died in 2013.

Onwuegbuzia, Christopher. Nigerian journalist who wrote for the *Comet* newspaper in the 1940s and served as a reader on *West African Voices*.

Opoku, Andrew Amankwa. Born in Ghana's Ashanti Region in 1912 to an Aburi family, Opoku began a teaching career in 1935 and became Headmaster in 1948. In 1951, he was seconded to the Vernacular Literature Bureau as Twi Language Editor before joining the Gold Coast Broadcasting Service in 1956. Opoku undertook international training in radio and then television. His radio broadcasting career included heading the Rural Broadcasting Unit, the Akan Section of Ghana Broadcasting Corporation's Radio 1, and the Education Department. Following training with the Canadian Broadcasting Corporation in 1963, Opoku became GBC's first Director of Television in 1970. A founding member of the Ghana Writers Association, he published four non-fiction books for the Vernacular Literature Bureau and contributed poems to Ghana's literary radio programme, *The Singing Net*. Some of his poems appear in *Voices of Ghana: Literary Contributions to the Ghana Broadcasting System, 1955-57* (1958) including "Afram" (sometimes "River Afram") which has appeared in a number of anthologies of African literature.

Ormsby Cooper, Eileen. Jamaican poet, born in 1926, who also served as PEN President on the island. A member of the well-known Ormsby family, her work is discussed by J. E. Clare McFarlane in his book *A Literature in the Making* in the chapter he devotes to "The Ormsbys." A dozen or so of her poems and short stories were featured on *Caribbean Voices*. Swanzy generally seems to consider her work as belonging to an increasingly outmoded tradition of Jamaican letters, one more in keeping with the tastes of the "withered ghost" of the colonial establishment, as he puts it in the diaries.

Ormsby Marshall, Helen Violet. Jamaican poet, short-story writer, compiler and editor, born in 1926. A member of the well-known Ormsby family, she compiled *Seed and Flower, An Anthology of Prose and Poetry* (1956), which featured work by several of the Ormsbys, including herself.

She was a feature writer for both the *Jamaican Standard* and *The Gleaner* in the late 1930s. She set up the journal *Madame* (1946-50) and established the Jamaican branch of the PEN club in 1948. She had five pieces broadcast on *Caribbean Voices*.

Osadebay, Dennis Chukude. Nigerian poet, politician, and journalist, born in 1911. One of the pioneering Nigerian poets writing in English, his collection *Africa Sings* appeared in 1952 and led to his work being generously represented in Olumbe Bassir's *Anthology of West African Verse* (see entry on Bassir, above). He was a significant contributor to *West African Voices*. During his political career, he helped to found the National Council of Nigeria and the Cameroons in the 1940s and served as both president of the Nigerian Senate (1960-63), and as premier of the newly created Mid-Western Region (1963-66). He is the subject of a sculpture by Ben Enwonwu (see entry on Enwonwu, above). He died in 1994.

Otoo, Samuel. A Fante civil servant from Ghana's Central Region who was employed by the Vernacular Literature Bureau. His former colleague at the Bureau was the radio and television programme maker Andrew Amankwa Opoku, and Otoo became a regular contributor to programmes on Ghana's national radio station. He was a panellist on talk shows such as *People in the News*, he started a series on fishing titled *Nworaba* (the Stars), and his creative writing was featured on the flagship literary programme *The Singing Net*.

Parkes, Frank Kobina. Born in 1932 in Accra, Ghana (then the Gold Coast) to a Sierra Leonean Father and Ghanaian Mother, Parkes worked briefly as a newspapers reporter and editor before undertaking a career in radio broadcasting. He also worked as a speech writer for Ghana's first president, Dr Kwame Nkrumah, and later obtained employment with NAFTI (Ghana's Film and Television Institute). As a Radio Producer, Parkes produced many popular Ghanaian programmes and is remembered for presenting the national radio coverage of the moment Ghana declared its independence on 6th March, 1957. He is best known as a poet whose most celebrated poem "African Heaven" was first published in *Voices of Ghana: Literary Contributions to the Ghana Broadcasting System, 1955-57* (1958) and then selected by Langston Hughes for inclusion in *An African Treasury* (1960). It has since been widely anthologised. Parkes also authored *Songs from the Wilderness* (University of London Press, 1965).

Phillips, George. Trinidadian short fiction writer who had four stories broadcast on *Caribbean Voices*. Swanzy was very impressed with his work, praising his "sharp sense of form and satire" in an article surveying Caribbean writing.

Pilgrim, Frank. Guyanese journalist, playwright, and broadcaster, born in 1926. A well-known worker in the field of culture in the Caribbean and Africa, Pilgrim travelled extensively. He worked as the Ghana correspondent for the *London Observer* (1962-66) and for the BBC. He contributed short stories to various newspapers and periodicals, while at least eight of his plays were performed in Guyana and broadcast on the radio, one of which *Miriamy* was published in 1955. He died in 1989.

Ponsonby, Sir Charles. Born in 1879, Ponsonby was a British Conservative politician who sat in the House of Commons from 1935 to 1950. In 1963, he became President of the Royal African Society having been on its Council for thirty-three years. He died in 1976.

Pope-Hennessy, Richard James. British travel writer and biographer, born in 1916. He spent a brief period in Trinidad in the late 1930s, serving as the private secretary to Hubert Young, the island's Governor. He published two books, *West Indian Summer* (1943) and *The Baths of Absalom* (1954), which drew on his experiences in the Caribbean. He died in 1974.

Prah, Florence. Broadcaster who travelled to London with Sam Amarteifio, Kobla Senayah, and Marian Smith-Mensah in 1951 to engage in radio training for programme production. She produced programmes and recorded literature by various African writers for the BBC's Overseas Service. Upon returning to the Gold Coast Broadcasting Service, Prah worked for the Programmes Unit preparing documentary features that were commended by Swanzy for the quality of her penmanship.

Quarshie-Idun, Frances. Ghanaian broadcaster, writer, artist, and gallery owner, better known as Frances Ademola. Ademola was educated in the UK and, in 1953, secured a place on a BBC training programme for colonial broadcasters. During this period, she wrote a play, *Squatters*, and was invited by Swanzy to become a reader on *West African Voices*, where, among other things, she translated, read, and provided critiques on Fante poetry. From 1954-1956, she worked as a producer for the Ghana Broadcasting Corporation, before moving to Nigeria to work for the Nigeria Broadcasting Corporation.

Ramon-Fortune, Barnabas J. Trinidadian poet, novelist, and short-story writer, born in 1917. He published verse in such journals as *BIM* and *Caribbean Quarterly* and contributed over thirty pieces to *Caribbean Voices*. He died in 2003.

Rattray, R. Carl. Jamaican lawyer and politician, born in 1929. Rattray was one of the founding members of the People's National Party and served as chairman of the Jamaica Council for Human Rights. He was also Attorney General from 1976 to 1980 and was elected as an MP in 1989, serving as Minister of Justice from 1989 to 1992. In the late 1940s he had several poems broadcast on *Caribbean Voices* and in 1951 his poetry collection *Firstlings* was published. In 2003, his collection *Poems of our Times* appeared with Ian Randle Publishers. He died in 2012.

Reckord, Barry. Born in Jamaica in 1926, Reckord was an important playwright, actor, and producer. Educated in Jamaica and the UK, he began writing plays as a student. By the late 1950s, his work was being staged at London's Royal Court Theatre (often produced by his brother, Lloyd). His most successful play, *Skyvers*, was first produced in 1963. He went on to write two television dramas for the BBC in the 1970s. In total, some 14 plays of his were produced in London, New York and Jamaica, where he was nationally recognised with a silver Musgrave medal. He had four works broadcast on *Caribbean Voices*, including his first play *Adella* (later staged at the Royal Court as *Flesh to a Tiger*). Other plays include: *You in Your Small Corner*, *Don't Gas the Blacks*, *A Liberated Woman*, *Streetwise*, and *Sugar D*. He died in 2011.

Reckord, Lloyd. Born in Jamaican in 1929, Reckord was an actor, film maker, and director. He left Jamaica for England in 1951, to join his brother, the dramatist Barry, who had already emigrated. Reckord trained at the Bristol Old Vic Theatre School and later joined the Old Vic Company. He went on to direct several of his brother's plays. He also starred in the West End production of *Hot Summer Night* (1958), which was adapted for ITV a year later He served as a frequent reader on *Caribbean Voices*. On his return to Jamaica, he founded the National Theatre Trust, producing more than 30 productions under that banner. He died in 2015.

Redhead, Eula. Born in 1917, Redhead was a Grenadian short-story writer whose fiction is distinguished by local knowledge and the use of patois. Although her work was often appreciated for its re-working of Grenadian folklore (including by Swanzy himself), she also produced more realist sketches depicting the history of, and everyday life on, the island. Eleven of her stories were broadcast on *Caribbean Voices* between 1948 and 1954. She died in 1983.

Reid, Victor S. Jamaican novelist, playwright, reporter, and editor, born in 1913. Reid began his career as a journalist, writing for *The Gleaner* among other publications. His first novel, *New Day* (1949), is a landmark of Caribbean writing, notable for its use of a poetic modification of Jamaican nation language as the language of fiction. His second novel, *The Leopard* (1958), has been called a major artistic statement of the Anglophone Caribbean's belated involvement with Africa. Reid contributed a number of fiction and non-fiction pieces to *Caribbean Voices*. He died in 1987.

Richardson, Willy. Trinidadian writer, broadcaster, and producer at the BBC. He was a regular contributor and reader on *Caribbean Voices*.

Roach, E. M. Born in Tobago in 1915, Roach was a poet who began writing in the late 1930s. His work appeared in numerous journals, including *BIM* and *Kyk-over-al*, and was widely anthologized. However, it was not until Peepal Tree Press's publication in 1992 of *The Flowering Rock: Collected Poems 1938-1974* that Roach's work was gathered in one place. He was a significant contributor to *Caribbean Voices*, with over 30 poems featured on the programme. Swanzy regularly referred to him as among "the best of the Caribbean poets." He committed in suicide in 1974.

Rose, Edgar. Grenadian writer who had two pieces broadcast on *Caribbean Voices*.

Sackey, Joseph H. Worked for the Gold Coast Broadcasting Service as a radio programme maker. As part of his duties, he performed literary pieces for the service's flagship English language literary programme, *The Singing Net*. As a writer, he also contributed his own literature to the programme. His works include the poem "The Hausa Trader", which was written in English and depicts the persuasive and enthusiastic sales technique of the "suave and cunning seller – bearded, tall, Hausa trader" who has travelled to Accra to peddle his wares.

Salkey, Andrew. Significant Jamaican novelist, poet, editor, broadcaster, academic, promoter, activist, and co-founder of the *Caribbean Artists Movement*. Born in Colón, Panama in 1928, Salkey was brought up in Jamaica and later relocated first to the UK and then to the U.S. He had numerous pieces broadcast on *Caribbean Voices*, and in the programme's final year in 1958 he served as one of its editors and presenters. His novels include *A Quality of Violence* (1959), *Escape to An Autumn Pavement* (1960), *The Late Emancipation of Jerry Stover* (1968), *The Adventures of Catullus Kelly* (1969) and *Come Home, Malcolm Heartland* (1976); three collections of short stories: *Anancy's Score* (1973), *The One* (1985) and *In the Border Country* (1998); four classic novels for children: *Hurricane*, *Riot*, *Earthquake* and *Drought*; and collections of poetry including *Jamaica: An Epic Poem* (1973), *In the Hills Where Her Dreams Live* (1979) and *Away* (1980). He died in 1995.

Sealy, Clifford. Born in 1927, Sealy was a Trinidadian poet, short-story writer, playwright, and editor. He was an early contributor to *BIM* and had several pieces broadcast on *Caribbean Voices*. He was a central figure in the Trinidadian literary scene in the 1970s, editing the journal *Voices* and managing The Bookshop in Port of Spain, which specialized in Caribbean books and literary readings.

Sealy, Karl. Bajan poet, short-story writer, and critic, born in 1932. His work appeared in several journals, including *BIM*, and was widely anthologized. He contributed over a dozen pieces to *Caribbean Voices*. He died in 1993.

Sekyi, Kobina. Born in the Fante town of Cape Coast in 1892, Sekyi was a celebrated nationalist, lawyer and playwright. Educated at Mfantsipim School and the University of London, Sekyi was called to the Bar in 1918 and established his law firm within the British colonial headquarters in the Gold Coast. Sekyi was President of the anti-colonial organisation the Aborigines' Rights Protection Society, as were his uncle and great-grandfather before him. He also fought for the rights of West Africans as an Executive Member of the National Congress of British West Africa and a member of the Coussey Committee, which drafted the constitutional change to end colonial rule in Ghana. His play, *The Blinkards* (1915), is well-known for satirising the way in which the Fante educated elite appropriated British culture. Sekyi died in 1956, the year before Ghana gained independence.

Selvon, Dennis. Brother of well-known Trinidadian author Sam Selvon, Dennis participated in *Caribbean Voices* as a reader. He had left Trinidad to study dentistry and subsequently became a dentist.

Selvon, Samuel. Major Trinidadian novelist and short story writer, born in 1923. He left Trinidad for Britain in 1950, travelling by chance on the same boat as George Lamming. His first novel, *A Brighter Sun*, was published in 1952 while he was working as a regular contributor to, and reader for, *Caribbean Voices*. He published a further nine novels, *An Island is a World* (1955), *The Lonely Londoners* (1956), *Turn Again Tiger* (1958), *I Hear Thunder* (1963), *The Housing Lark* (1965), *The Plains of Caroni* (1970), *Those Who Eat the Cascadura* (1972), *Moses Ascending* (1975), *Moses Migrating* (1983) and a collection of short stories, *Ways of Sunlight* (1957). His plays were broadcast by the BBC and are collected in *Eldorado West One* (1989) and *Highway in the Sun and Other Plays* (1991). He died in 1994.

Senayah, Kobla Emmanuel. Ghanaian radio broadcaster who worked as a vernacular announcer alongside Ben Gadzekpo at Station ZOY.

Setsoafia, H.K. Bidi was a Ghanaian playwright and teacher who worked briefly in broadcasting. Born in the Ewe town of Anloga in 1920, Setsoafia took various jobs to fund his studies until he was able to travel to Freetown, Sierra Leone in 1948 to undertake a degree at Fourah Bay College supported by a Gold Coast Government Scholarship. From 1950 until 1956 he returned to his hometown as a college teacher, during which time he translated and staged Shakespeare productions as well as translations of Chaucer, *Don Quixote*, Booker Washington's *Up from Slavery*, amongst others. Setsoafia wrote his first play, *Fia Agokoli (Chief Agokoli)*, in 1945, and in 1957 his English-Ewe comedy, *I Married a Been-To*, won the Gold Coast Broadcasting Service's radio theatre competition. This made his name as an accomplished playwright. At that time he had gained employment at Broadcasting House and moved to Accra as a Senior Programme Assistant, but he would soon return to teaching in 1958.

Seymour, A. J. Born in Guyana in 1914, Seymour was a pioneering poet, essayist, critic, short story writer, and editor. Notable for the numerous volumes of poetry he published in Guyana well before the London-centred 'boom' in Caribbean writing in the 1950s, he was also responsible for founding the seminal literary magazine *Kyk-over-al* and was a leading figure in the movement to foster a regional literary sensibility. His poetry collections include *Verse* (1937), *More Poems* (1940), *Over Guiana Clouds* (1944), *Sun's in My Blood* (1945), *Six Songs* (1946), *The Guiana Book* (1948), *Selected Poems* (1965), *Monologue* (1968), *Patterns* (1970), *Black Song* (1971), *I, Anancy* (1971), *Passport* (1972), *Song to Man* (1973), *Italic* (1974), *Mirror* (1975), *For Nicholas Guillen* (1976) *The Shape of the Crystal* (1979) and *Time Bell* (1979). *A.J. Seymour Collected Poems 1937-1989* was published in 2000. His works of autobiography such as *Growing up in Georgetown*, and *Pilgrim Memories* warrant republishing. He died in 1989.

Sherlock, Philip. Born in 1902, Sherlock was a renowned Jamaican educator, historian, social worker, poet, and short-story writer. A well-known public figure, his wide-ranging activities spanned many areas of Caribbean social and political life. As a poet, his work has been widely published in anthologies and journals. His collection *Ten Poems* was published in Guyana in 1953, while his dramatic sequence of verse in tribute to Samuel Sharpe – *Shout for Freedom* – appeared in 1976. He had two pieces broadcast on *Caribbean Voices*. He is best known for his work in developing the University of the West Indies and as a historian for his *A Short History of the West Indies* (1968) with J.H. Parry. He died in 2000.

Sibley, Inez K. Jamaican short-story writer and historian, born in 1908. She produced a collection of stories, *Quashie's Reflections in Jamaican Creole*, first published in 1939, as well as the historical works *The Baptists of Jamaica* (1965) and the *Dictionary of Place-Names in Jamaica* (1978). Sibley was a regular contributor to *Caribbean Voices*, her work appearing in multiple broadcasts.

Simmonds, Ulric. Jamaican author, journalist, and political commentator, born in 1920. Simmonds was born in Guantanamo, Cuba of Jamaican parents. He is best known as a political commentator, writing a regular column for the *Gleaner*. But he also produced short fiction, with his stories appearing in *14 Jamaican Short Stories* (1950) and the *Independence Anthology of Jamaican Literature* (1962), as well as on *Caribbean Voices*. He died in 2002.

Simpson, Louis. Jamaican-born poet, editor, translator, and critic. Born in 1923, Simpson moved to the U.S. when he was 17 to study at Columbia University. He subsequently became a highly distinguished poet in his adopted country, but his autobiography *North of Jamaica* underscores his connection to the Caribbean of his childhood. He died in 2012.

Singuineau, Frank. Significant Trinidadian actor, born in 1913, who had a long and successful career in stage and screen from the 1940s to the 1980s, including roles in Jean-Paul Satre's *The Respectable Prostitute* (1954) and Horace Ove's *Pressure* (1975). Born in Port-of-Spain, he travelled to London after WWII and gained early acting experience broadcasting for the BBC's West India service, and appearing with the left-wing Unity Theatre. He served as a reader on *Caribbean Voices* when his acting career was in its very early stages; remarkably, Swanzy was incredibly dismissive of his prospects. He died in 1992.

Small, L. Sylvester. Jamaican writer who had three short stories broadcast on *Caribbean Voices*.

Smith, Michael (M. G. Smith). Jamaican anthropologist, poet, and educator, born in 1921. Smith is perhaps now best known as a distinguished anthropologist, but in the early 1940s he was recognized in Jamaica as one of the outstanding poets associated with the arts journal *Focus*. His poetry featured on *Caribbean Voices* and he also served as a reader on the programme. M.G. Smith's *In the Kingdom of Light: Collected Poems* was published in 2003 and Douglas Hall's biography, *A Man Divided: Michael Garfield Smith, Jamaican Poet and Anthropologist 1921-1993* (1997) is an insightful account of a complex man. He died in 1993.

Soyinka, Wole. Major Nigerian playwright, novelist, poet, and essayist, born in 1934. The first African Nobel Prize laureate, Soyinka is a hugely influential figure in world literature. He submitted his early work for broadcast on *West African Voices*.

Spence, George. Jamaican writer who contributed five pieces to *Caribbean Voices*.

Stephens, Herman. Stephens contributed poetry and a short story to *Caribbean Voices* in 1955. He also acted as a reader on the programme. There appears to be little information available about him. Swanzy refers to him as Antiguan, but Jeremy Poynting, in a brief footnote referencing Stephens' story "Worthless Diamonds," has "a hunch that he is a white Guyanese."

Stewart, MacNeill. Born in Trinidad of mixed African and Scottish ancestry in 1905, Kenneth Donald MacNeill Stewart was sent to England at the age of nine. By the time he was thirteen, he had published poetry in *Pearson's Magazine*, *Time and Tide*, *Pall Mall*, and the *Africa and Orient Review*. At seventeen he moved to the then Gold Coast, where he edited the first daily paper, the *Times of West Africa*, followed by the *Echo*. With the help of J. B. Danquah, he published poetry in 1939 under the title *If I had Wings*, while a collection of war poetry was published by the Government under the title *The Gold Coast Answers*. He was one of only three non-Ghanaians to have their work broadcast on *The Singing Net*, and the only non-Ghanaian to have his work published in *Voices of Ghana: Literary contributions to the Ghana Broadcasting System 1955-57*, compiled by Swanzy.

Sutherland, Efua. Ghanaian poet, playwright, educator, and cultural activist, born in 1924. A hugely influential figure in the development of Ghanaian drama as both a writer and as the founder of various theatres and other national and community projects. She came to Britain in the 1940s where she first met Swanzy and contributed to the BBC's *West African Voices* as writer and reader. Returning to Ghana in 1951, she kept in contact with Swanzy and continued to submit her writing for broadcast by overseas submission. When Swanzy arrived in Ghana in 1954 to head-up the Gold Coast Broadcasting System, Sutherland prepared a list of potential authors for him to contact. Her own poetry and other writings were broadcast on *The Singing Net*. Her published plays include: *Edufa* (1967), *Foriwa* (1967), *Tahinta* (1968), *Odasani* (1969), *The Marriage of Anansewa* (1977). She died in 1996.

Telemaque, Harold. Born in Tobago in 1909, Telemaque was educated in Trinidad and the UK. He was one of the leading poets in Trinidad and Tobago in the 1940s and early 1950s. His first collection, *Burnt Bush*, was published with A.M Clarke in 1947, followed by *Scarlet* (1953) and his work featured regularly on *Caribbean Voices*, where it was also the subject of several significant discussions on Critics' Circle. Telemaque died in 1982.

Thompson, Claude. Jamaican poet, short-story writer, and broadcaster, born in 1907. He worked in the Jamaican civil service and media before moving to London. His short stories were published in the journal *Focus* and in the *Independence Anthology of Jamaican Literature* (1962). His first book, *These My People*, was published in Kingston in 1943. His verse appeared in *A Treasury of Jamaican Poetry*, and he produced an unpublished collection, "Afoot in Jamaica."

Timothy, Emmanuel Bankole. Born in Freetown, Sierra Leone in 1923, Timothy began his career in journalism by writing for the *Sierra Leone Weekly News* whilst at school and college. As a student at the University Tutorial College in London, he also wrote for Ghana's *Ashanti Pioneer* and became involved with the BBC's *Calling West Africa* radio series. Timothy contributed to BBC radio talks on current affairs and submitted poetry for broadcast on *West African Voices*. In the 1940s he became general reporter and then parliamentary reporter for the *Daily Express* until the Mirror Group, despatched him to Ghana as Editor of the Gold Coast's most popular newspapers, the *Daily Graphic*. At independence, the Ghanaian government deported Timothy for his critical standpoint. He then worked in various sectors in both Freetown and London, and continued to write books including two biographical works on Ghana's first President, Dr Kwame Nkrumah.

Treadgold, Mary. English author, literary editor, and producer, born in 1910. In the 1940s, she joined the BBC and worked in various sections of the General Overseas Service. After Una Marson's departure from *Caribbean Voices* in 1946, Treadgold – a close friend of Marson – took over as producer for three months before Swanzy's arrival. She died in 2005.

Vaz, Gloria. Jamaican performer who served as a regular reader on *Caribbean Voices*. She was highly regarded by Swanzy, who consistently used her for what he considered the better literary contributions.

Vaz, Noel. Born in 1920, Vaz was a Jamaican essayist, poet, actor, producer, and teacher. He had a significant impact on the modern theatre of Jamaica. As an Extra Mural Tutor at the University College of the West Indies, he toured the Caribbean promoting local drama. He worked with Louise Bennett on *Bluebear and Brer Nancy* at the Little Theatre in 1949. He arrived in England in the mid-1940s on a British Council Scholarship and worked as a reader on *Caribbean Voices*.

Vincent, Jonathan. Sierra Leonean writer who contributed short fiction to, and served as a reader on, *West African Voices*.

Virtue, Vivian. Jamaican poet, translator, and broadcaster, born in 1911. He was an active member of the Poetry League of Jamaica. His work appeared in the arts journal *Focus* and *The Treasury of Jamaican Poetry*. His collection *Wings of the Morning* was published in 1938. A frequent contributor to *Caribbean Voices*, Virtue was described by Swanzy as a "sensitive, small man, with a touching loyalty to his Gods, Tom Redcam, Langston Hughes." A posthumous collection, *Wings of the Evening: Selected Poems of Vivian Virtue* was published in 2002. He died in 1998.

Walcott, Derek. Major Saint Lucian poet and dramatist, born in 1930. A towering figure in world literature, he was awarded the Nobel Prize for Literature in 1992. His first poetry collection, *25 Poems*, was published in 1948. On receipt of the collection, Swanzy was immediately keen to have Walcott's work broadcast on *Caribbean Voices*, recognizing him even at this early stage as one of the best of the Caribbean poets. Walcott died in 2017.

Walter, Carl. Trinidadian writer who spent most of his life in Colombia. He had two pieces broadcast on *Caribbean Voices*.

Wickham, John. Bajan author, critic, and editor, born in 1923. After a career in the World Meteorological Organisation took him to Europe for several years, he became the literary editor of *The Nation* newspaper. IN 1975, he took over the role of editor of *BIM* from Frank Collymore. Wickham's short stories featured regularly in *BIM*, as well as in many other journals and anthologies. His first collection of short stories, *Casuarina Row*, appeared in 1974 and *Discoveries* in 1992. He had over a half a dozen stories broadcast on *Caribbean Voices*. He published a memoir, *World Without End* (1982) and a collection of columns, *Landings and Landscapes* in 1993.

Williams, Adisa. Nigerian author, critic, broadcaster, and barrister. A frequent reviewer in such journals as *African Affairs, West African Review*, and *Spear*, he was a regular reader on *West African Voices*. He later became producer of the programme. He also served as Programme Organizer for the Western Regional Network of Nigeria Broadcasting Corporation.

Williams, Daniel. Poet and lawyer, born in 1927 in New York of St. Vincent parentage. Together with Shake Keane and Owen Campbell, he was known as one of the 'trio' of St. Vincentian poets, whose work appeared regularly in Caribbean literary journals including *BIM* and *Kyk-over-al*. He was also a regular contributor to *Caribbean Voices*, with a dozen or so pieces broadcast on the programme. He was involved in establishing the literary magazine *Flambeau* (1964-68) and supported socialist and black nationalist causes. He died in a car accident on St. Vincent in 1972.

Williams, Denis. Born Joseph Ivan Williams in Georgetown, Guyana in 1923, Williams was a writer and significant artist who also taught and published in the fields of West Indian and African art and anthropology, and, from 1974, was Director of Art and Archaeology with Guyana's Ministry of Education and Culture until his death in 1998. He published two novels, *Other Leopards* (1963) and *The Third Temptation* (1968), both reissued as Caribbean Modern Classics. He contributed two pieces on Caribbean art to *Caribbean Voices* and also served as a reader on the programme. His own art is documented in Evelyn A. Williams, *The Art of Denis Williams* (2012) and he wrote a ground-breaking study of African art, *Icon and Image: A Study of Sacred and Secular Forms of African Classical Art* (1974) and of pre-colonial Guyana in *Prehistoric Guyana* (2003).

Winful, E. Archie. Born in 1922 at Saltpond, Ghana, he was educated at Mfantsipim School in Cape Coast, Ghana. He then graduated in the Honours School of English at the University College of the South-West, in Exeter, England in 1947. He worked at the School of Oriental and African Studies (SOAS), and trained as a book editor with Oxford University Press. Since 1950, he has been variously employed as editor, schoolmaster, and administrative officer.

Woolford, Gordon. Guyanese writer and a staple reader on *Caribbean Voices*, he was an important figure in the programme's development. Woolford's opinion was highly valued by V. S. Naipaul, who described him as "very important to me... He was an alcoholic, married a shop assistant, a very handsome man. He was a good reader, distinct."

Editors' note: This appendix would not have been possible without the prior research of numerous important Caribbeanist and Africanist scholars, critics, and historians. In particular, we would like to acknowledge the following publications and resources: Glyne A. Griffith, *The BBC and The Development of Anglophone Caribbean Literature, 1943-1958*; *The Caribbean Literary Heritage Project* website; Donald E. Herdeck (ed.), *Caribbean Writers: A Bio-Bibliographical-Critical Encyclopaedia*; the *Caribbean Memory Project* website; Simon Gikandi (ed.), *Encyclopaedia of African Literature*; Janheinz Jahn, Ulla Schild, and Almut Nordmann (eds.), *Who's who in African Literature: Biographies, Works, Commentaries*. It goes without saying that any errors or omissions in the appendix are the fault of the present editors. We would stress that this appendix remains very much a work in progress and we look forward to interested scholars offering corrections, clarifications, and additions in the future.

ACKNOWLEDGEMENTS

First and foremost, we would like to thank the Swanzy family for their incredible generosity in sharing the Swanzy papers and diaries with us. Without the support and understanding of Clare Newton and Martin Swanzy, this project would not have been possible. We are indebted to a long list of colleagues and interlocutors whose insight and scholarship have been invaluable throughout the process of editing these diaries: Stewart Brown, David Dabydeen, Letizia Gramaglia, Philip Nanton, Anne Walmsley, Paloma Mohamed, James Procter, Alison Donnell, Glyne Griffith, Helen Yitah, Audrey Gadzekpo, Bill Schwarz, Thomas Glave, David Killingray, and James Currey. We must also thank former GBC employees who we interviewed, with special mention to Robert Owusu and Cameron Duodu. Thanks, too, to those who contributed to the *Calling West Africa* series in the UK, as well as *The Singing Net* and other programmes from the early days of Radio Ghana, including the late J.H.K. Nketia, the late Atukwei Okai, Frances Ademola (nee Quarshie-Idun), Kofi Anyidoho, and Ama Ata Aidoo. We are also very grateful to the family members who recalled memories of their relatives' engagement with radio in Ghana as programme contributors and broadcasters. Thanks are due to the Arts and Humanities Research Council, Warwick University's English Department and the Yesu Persaud Centre for Caribbean Studies, and the BBC's Written Archives Centre in Reading (with special mention to Jeff Walden). Finally, we would like to thank the brilliant Peepal Tree Press and the incredible work of Jeremy and Hannah.

INDEX

Aarons, R.L.C., 51, 197
Ablack, Ken, 37, 39, 64, 92, 144
Ablack, Robert, 197
Abrahams, Dorothy, 38, 41
Abrahams, Peter, 12, 77, 102, 110, 121, finds Ghana "xenophobic", 152; *Wreathe for Udomo*, 192
Adali-Mortty, Geormbeeyi, 17, 183, 184, 188, 189, 191, 192, 197
Adamafio, 93
Adams, Grantley, 44
Addams, Ishmael, 193, 194, 195
Addow, 193
Adjei, Ako, 189
Adoki, G.E., 51, 63, 197
African Affairs, 9, 13, 16, 25, 30, 38, 50, 68, 76, 100, 103, 153, 157, 160, 169, 172, 198, 202, 210, 211, 214, 222, 223, 227, 240
African Society, 14, 105
Agbadja, Adolph, 178, 180, 182, 189, 190, 198
Agbonkonkon, Peter, 110, 126, 130, 142, 151, 198
Aggrey-Smith, J, epic drama, 184
Agodzo, Roland, 175, 190
Aikins, Archibald, 184
Aiyedun, Gbola, 83
Akar, John, 92, 93, 107, 128, 160; has to flee from a sexual proposition from a British TV producer, 163; 198
Akinsemoyin, Kunle, 94, 101, 124, 129, 142, 150, 151, 161, 198
Akintola, S.L., 37
Akiwowo, Akinsola, 49, 198
Akuro, Doris, 99
Akyem, Owusu, 190
Allen, Walter, 127, 159
Aloba, Lennard, 80
Aluko, Tim, 49, 51, 55, 72, 88, 125, 169, 199
Amarteifio, Sam, 101, 176, 195, 199

Anfom, Dr & Mrs, 189
Ankrah, Edward, 42, 188
Antubam, Kofi, 56
Arena, 66, 70, 173
Arlott. John, 28, 29, 35, 41
Arthur, James, 172, 175, 190
Arthur, William S., 81, 199
Athill, Diana, 7, 9-10, 166-167, 185
Atlee, Clement, 52
Auguste, Rose, 108, 199
Baako, Kofi, 179, 190, 194, 195
Babalola, Solomon Adeboye, 12, 75, 78, 81, breakdown and confinement, 107; 133, 160, 199
Badu, Osei, 174
Baffour, Robert, 175, 183, 193
Baker, Flora, 43, 200
Bannerman, Sam, 187, 189, 191
Baptiste, Mona, 64
Barima, Twum, 34, 49
Barrow, Raymond, 43, 200
Barsoe, Elsie, 73, 115, 200
Bassir, Olumbe, 162, 200
Bawden, Edward, 27, 89, 105
BBC and government views on colonial role, 19; anti-communist propaganda, 41; closeness to government edicts and a single "British view", 44-45
BBC and programme skills training, 16
Beachcroft, Tom, 97
Bedward, Alexander, 118
Beier, Ulli, 192, 193
Bell, Gordon, 29, 161, 200
Bello, Martha, 156
Benjamin, Elsie, 116
Bennett, Louise, 33, 74, 83, 94, 96, 101, 105, 107, 200
Bennett, Wycliffe, 27, 57, 201
Berger, John, 76, 84
Betjeman, John, 104
Bim, 11, 26, 49, 79, 88, 110, 128, 136,

167, 199, 204, 205, 209, 212, 217, 227, 232, 233, 234, 240
Bing, Geoffrey, 186
Binyon, Helen, 39
Black Orpheus, 153, 170, 192, 193, 197
Black, Clinton, 115
Blackman, Hugh, 98
Blackman, Peter, 33, 58, 201
Blavo, Ralph, 189
Boateng, Oto, 175
Bolton, Valerie, 73, 201
Bowles, Vincent, 97
Boyce, Edgar, 82, 94, 126, 129, 209
Braithwaite, E.R., 201
Braithwaite, Lloyd, 155
Brathwaite, E. Kamau, 13, 134, 142, 143, 147, 155, 159, 161, 168; novella "The Boy and the Sea", 169, reads a portrait of F.R. Leavis, 170, in Ghana, 178, unhappy at Technical Institute, 179-180, 201
Brathwaite, R.B.E., 36, 54, 201
Brew, Osborne Kwesi, 184, 189, 202
Brown, Enitan, 49, 160, 202
Brown, Marjorie, 12, 94, 116, 202
Browne, Michael, 67, 202
Bunting, J.R. 32, 43, 202
Burgess, Guy, 94
Burke, Ivanhoe, 118
Burke, Terry, 70, 74, 76, 116, 119, 203
Busby, Bill, 172
Bustamante, Alexander, 116, 121
Cain, Henry, 44, 203
Calder-Marshall, Arthur, 26, 27, 30, 31, 33, 35, 38, 40, 47, 48, 59, 72, 74, 75, 78, 87-88, 95, 96, 104, 107, 110, 121, 122, 124, 125, 126, 130, on *In the Castle of My Skin*, 139; 203
Calling East Africa, 158
Calling Mauritius, 29, 105
Calling the West Indies, 10, 224
Calling West Africa, 37, 59, 168, 181, 192, 208, 213, 222
Cameron, James, 155
Campbell, George, 27, 39, 203
Campbell, Owen, 67, 105, 127, 137, 204

Campbell, Roy, 66
Carberry, H.D., 47, 66, 70, 204
Carew, Jan, 71, 77, 78, 93,.95, 99, 100, 102, 129, 134, 140, 143, 155, 159, 166, 170, 204
Caribbean Federation, 143
Caribbean Quarterly, 131, 200, 217, 222
Caribbean Voices programme, 7, 8, 10, Swanzy's concern over "metropolitan interference", 11; local colour and universal interest, 11; women's representation, 12; symposium on West Indian Culture, 76; party, 78; economics of and fees, 86
Carr, Ernest, 32, 39, 66, 204
Carstairs, C.Y., 96
Casely-Hayford, Archie, 182
Catholic Herald, describes Africa as "very heart of Satan's Empire", 93
Cattouse, Nadia, 137, 171, 204
Cezair-Thompson, Margaret, 200
Chalk, Peggy, 95
Chancellor, Sir John, 26
Chang, Carlisle, 93, 105, 108, 205
Chapman, Esther (*West Indian Review*), 115
Charles, Cyril, 137, 155, 205
Chen, Bryan, 141, 143, shocks Swanzy's father-in-law, 144, 205
Chijioke, 106, 127, 131, 133
Chilver, Sally, 97
Christian, Angela, 95, 129, 150
Claridge, W. Walter, 165
Clark, Jack, 35
Clark, Noel, 151
Clarke, Lloyd, 162, 205
Clarke, Sheila, 76, 96, 125, 205, 217
Close connections between BBC and Colonial Office, 40
Cohen, Andrew, 31, 38
Cola Rienzi, Adrian, 39
Collingwood, R.G., 45
Collymore, Frank, 55, 56, 74, alias Eric Codling, 127; 128, 167, 205
Collymore, George, 84, 206
Colonial Exhibition, 1949, and rac-

ist stereotypes of Africa, 55; improved 1950, 69
Colonial Review, 51
Colonialism, postwar ameliorations, 14
Commonwealth and Empire (BBC programme), formerly *Experiment in Freedom*, 42
Connor, Edric, 13, 27, *Calypso*, 36; 57, 85, 86, 88, 159, 169, 206
Connor, Pearl, 169
Conton, Willy, 92, 94, 206
Coronation of Elizabeth II, mixed feelings among colonials, 144-145
Coulthard, G.R., 113
Crabbe, Neville, 35, 45, 51, 62, 68, 129, 206
Craig, Harry, 30, 51
Crowley, Alestair, 88, 95
Crozier, E.L. 79
Cudjoe Club, 94, 102
Cummings, Ivor, 182
Cunard, Nancy, 102, 134
Currey, Ralph, 49, 54, 71, 88, 124, 156, 206, 254
Cust, Archer, 100
Dadson, Isaac, 186, 187, 207
Daily Worker, 101
Dako, O.K., 184
Danquah, J.B., 30, 187, 237
Danquah, Moses, 80, 94
Davenport, John, 66
Davidson, Basil, 150, 187
Davidson, Karl, 45, 207
Davis, Kathleen, 55, 142, 207
Dawes, Neville, 34, 100, 105, 108, 110, a regular Thursday nighter, 124, critiques Michael (M.G.) Smith, 126, 134, 154; "Ta Ta Small", 161, 207
Day Lewis, Cecil, 40
De Chazal, Malcolm, 168
De Graft, J.C., 176, 192, 207
De Paiva, Lennox, 59, 63, 68, 208
Dei-Anang, Michael, 16, 182, 187, 193, 208
Delaney, David, 129
Delano, Isaac Oluwole, 142, 150, 208
Deutch, Andre (company), 7, 166, 185
Dickinson, Patric, 40
Djabanor, Rose, 60, 186, 188, 208
Djoleto, Amu, 176, 209
Donnell, Alison, 12
Dougherty, Ronke, 95
Dover, Cedric, 102, 134
Drayton, Geoffrey, 88, 129, 209
Dunbar, Rudolph, 13, 64, 85, 143, 209
Duncan, Patrick, 50
Dunham, Katherine, 41
Duodu, Cameron, 17, criticism of Swanzy's unilateral editing but praise for his role, 18, 187, 189, 196, 209
Easmon, Mrs, 189
Editorial principles in selection from the diaries, 19-20
Edmett, Willy, 32, 37, 38, 43, 68, 82, 135, 169, 210
Ekpunobi, 166
Ekwensi, Cyprian, 7, 8, 12, 60, "Sharro", protest against its broadcast, 62; 63, 67, 83, 99, 101, 103, 108, 110, 126, 129, 131, 134, 135, 137, 142, 143, 154, 160, 210
Eliot, T.S., 104
Elliott, A.K., 163, 210
Empire Day, the *Times* on, 73
Empson, William, 132-133, 134
Enahoro, Tony, 130
Enwonwu, Ben, 13, 36, 54, 67, 147, 210
Epelle, Kiea, 97, 127, 135, 142, 160, 210
Escoffery, Gloria, 34, 81, 87, 89, 92, 210
Ewart, Gavin, 70, 106
Eweka, U., 49, 211
Eytle, Ernest, 51, 54, 142, 211
Fabian Society, 26, 27, 30, 36, *Compass Points* (Swanzy contributes to), 48
Fagwuna, D.O., 125, 141-142, 145, 146, 211
Ferland, Barbara, 151

Festival of Britain, HS sees it as having written off the empire and commonwealth, 100
Fforde, Daryll, 100
Figueroa, John, 11, 12, 13, 24, 29, 32, 34, 36, 37, 50, 51, 62, 78, 80, 82, 88, 102, 104, 106, 109, 113, 121, takes over the Thursday club, 131, 136, 140, 146, leaves UK for Jamaica, 150, finds UWI "shallow", 152, 211
Fitzgerald, Alex, 96
Focus (Jamaica), 47, 49, 11, 203, 224, 237, 238, 239
Foot, Hugh (Governor Jamaica), 120
Forde, A.N., 105, 147, verse play, "The Plot in the Garden", 151, 162; 212
Fortune, Felix Ramon, 66, 212
Foster Davis, Noel (Ena), 60, 63, 212
Fraser, A.G., 34
Fraser, Byron, 108, 116, 212
Fredericks, Eva, 56, 57, 63
Frost, Victor, 80
Fuller, Roy, 35, 52, 54, 71, 73, 74, praises Wilson Harris, 131; 155, 212
Gadzekpo, Ben, 16, 66, 74, 124, 172, 173, 175, 176, 179, 181, 183, 186, 187, 212, 213
Gardiner, Robert, 167, 182, 186, 193, 194
Garwood, Tirzah, Swanzy married to, 10, 25, 27, 33, 50; illness, 37, 62, 64-65, 76, 77, 82, 88, 89; as artist, 84, 89; death and funeral, 90-91
Gayeux, Richard, 171
Gbedemah, Komla, 174, 195
Gbeho, Philip Comi, 79, 124, 174, 177, 193, 195, 213
General Overseas Service, gives a spot to *Caribbean Voices*, 139
Ghana, 8, 13,
Ghartey, Joseph, 16, 64, 66, 79, 172-173, 180, 185, 186, 190, 213
Gibbins, Naomi, 162, 163, 213
Gibbs, Egbert, 38
Gilmore, John, 205
Giuseppe, Undine, 42, 213
Giwa-Osagie (Moru Yesufu-Giwa), 49, 214
Gold Coast Broadcasting Service, 8, 10, 13, 14, 15, 170, 199, 217, 221, 225, 226, 229, 231, 233, 235, 238
Gomes, Albert (Bertie), 72, 74, 142-143, 169, 214
Goveia, Elsa, 113, 126, 213
Grant, Cy (C.E.L.), 57, 60, 84, 92, 214
Grason, Doreen, 74, 76, 214
Gray, James, 25
Green, Henry, 95
Grenfell, Stephen, 55
Grenfell-Williams, John (JGW) 13, 27, 31, 37, 38, 39, 40, 43, 44, 45, 46, 47, 55, 56, 58, 61, 68, 69, 70, 72, 74, 76, 82, 83, 84, 88, 92, 93, 96, 98, 100, 103, 107, 108, 109, 114, 123, 127, 128, 131, 132, 133, 138, 140, 141, 142, 144, 145, 146, concerned about Caribbean Voices writers meeting Cheddi Jagan, 153, 158, 159, 160, 162, 163, 164, 166, 167, 169, 171; sudden death, 174; 215
Grimes, John E., 132
Haig, Milner, 59
Hailey, Lord, 36, 50
Hall, Stuart, 171, 215
Hamilton, Rostrevor, 40
Hammond, John, 188
Harris, Wilson, 13, 84, 85, "Closets of Sunset", 85; 87, 93, 127; 129; "The Fabulous Well", 130, 131, 137, 138; "Canje, the River of Ocean", 153; HS meeting with, 165, 166; 168, 169, 171, 215
Harrison, J., 82, 83
Hassan, Mallam, 47, 49
Hastings, Lewis, 28, anti-communist broadcasts, 88, 92, 94
Haweis, Stephen, 46, 215
Hazell, Vivian, "Ballad of the White Wife", 151, 215
Hearn, D. 76

Hearne, John, 135, 137, 140, 216
Hendricks, A.L. (Micky), 115, 123, 216
Hendricks, Vivette, 33, 34, 43, 54, 65, 76, 144, 216
Hennessy, Spike, rude about Nigerian writers, 146; 156
Henriques, Fernando, 113
Henriques, Pauline, 13, 26, 29, 31, 35, 37, 40, 43, 50, 52, 53, 56, 68, 85, 96, 99, 129, 163, 216
Henry, A.E.T., 29, 30, 42, 44, 51, 64, 68, 77, 84, 88, 92, 134, 140, 159, 216
Herbert, C.L., 29, 51, 217
Herring, Robert, 27, 144
Hewitt, J.M., 168, 217
Hill, Errol, 59, 63, 64, 65, 66, 73, "Pingpong", 81, 82; adapts Walcott's *Henri Christophe* for radio, 85, 107, and at the Hans Crescent Hotel, 108; 100, 103, return to Trinidad, 127; 131, 217
Hill, Sydney, 67, 73, 82, 83
Hodson, Arnold, 15
Hoh, Israel Kafu, 180, 181, 187, 191, 192, 193, 217
Holder, Boscoe, 73, 75, 76, 159, 205, 217
Hope, G.M., 123
Howard, O.M., 110, 122, 218
Howerd, Frankie, cannibal turns on his review show cut after protests, 107
Hughes, Langston, 39, 98, 225, 230, 239
Hutton, Albinia, 62, 218
Hutton, Elsie, 53, 68, 218
Huxley, Elspeth, 166
Ichabod, why diaries named as, 7, 18
Ingrams, Ken, 117
Itayemi, Phebean, 53, 57, 60, 62, 110, 156, 160, 218
Jack J. Gordon, 77
Jacob, Ian, 44
Jacob, Major General Sir Ian, 27
Jagan, Cheddi, wins Guyanese elections, 1953, 142, Pilgrim and Kempadoo sent by Labour Party to wean Jagan from communists, 153
Jahn, Janheinz, 153, 170
Jakes, Bob, 93, 102, 218
James, C.L.R., 148-149
Jarvis, Euton, 146, 218
Javabu, Noni, 49
Jectson, Seth, 93, 97, 104, 129, 130, 145, 157, 166, 218
John, Errol, 98, 104, 108, 123, 129, 132, 218
John, Macaulay, 80
Jones, Evan, 131, 147, 150, 219
Jones, Marcus, 93
Jones-Quartey, Gilly, 182
Jones-Quartey, K.A.B., 48, 49, 58, 219
Jour de Fete, Jacques Tati, 71
Kayper-Mensah, Albert, 16, 17, 176-177, *The Rescue*, 184; 189, 190, 191, 193, 219
Keane, Ellsworth McG (Shake), 66, 87, 88, 98, 130, 133, 134, 137, 138, 139, 141, 148, 151, 153, 155, 219-220
Kempadoo, Peter Lauchmonen, 153, 220
Kennedy, Joyce, 31
Kent, Lena, 62, 220
Kenyatta, Jomo, 27, 136
King, James A., 54
Kirkwood, Kenneth, 164
Kitch, Lord Kitchener, 64
Kittermaster, Michael, 145
Kraal, Felhoen, *West Indische Gids*, 156
Kriel, Louis, 126
Kykoveral (Guyana), 49, 204, 217, 221, 225, 233, 240
Labat, Madeleine, 31
Labour Party and failure to support colonial nationalism, 35
Lambert, Calvin, 37, 38, 39, 44, 52, 53, 58, 220
Lamming, George, 7, "A Way of Seeing", 8; 12, 13, 24, "Growing Up in the Village", 47; 48, 57, 69, criticises *Caribbean Voices*, 71, 72;

argues politics with Mittelholzer, 71; discusses seminal books with Swanzy, 72, 84-85; 72, 74, 83, successful reading at ICA, 87; tea with Spender, 88; 92, 94, 98, 102, "Birthday Weather", 102; Lorca but not Betjeman, 104; 104, 105, 106, 108, reads an extract from *Farewell to the Land* [*In the Castle of My Skin*], 108; 109, 110, *Castle* accepted by Michael Joseph, 123; 125, 127, 128, 131, 134, 135, 137, reviews of *Castle* 139; 146, 151, reads from *The Emigrants*, 152, good reviews from Walter Allen and Joyce Cary, 159; 159, 166, 220
Larteh, Tetteh, 193
Laryea, Susana, 176, 221
Lasebikan, E.L. (Tunde), 47, 48, 58, 81, 160, 221
Laski, Marghanita, 92
Lawton, Jack, 172
Le Page, R.B. (Bob), 97, (on Walcott), 98, 221
Lee, Laurie, 40
Lee, Margaret, 154, 221
Lehman, John, 147
Leigh-Fermor, Patrick, *Traveller's Tree*, 92; review of *In the Castle of My Skin*, 139
Levy, Eric, 44, 221
Life and Letters, 27; Jamaica number, 33
Lincott, P.D. [Patrick Chookolingo], 48, 55, 221
Lindo, Archie, 115, 167, 221
Lindo, Cedric, 11, 44, 61, 111, 112, 117, 118, 119, 121, 122, 141, writes that the Jamaican consensus is that Lamming's *In the Castle* is tedious, 149; 154, 222
Lindo, Gladys, 11, 26, 42, 44, 50, 54, 111, 222
Little, Kenneth, 28
Livesey, Ted, 151
Lloyd, Harrison, 104, complains about vivisection of his story, 105, 222

Locke, W.J., 95
Lockhart, Emily, 63, 222
Loewenthal, Enid, 222
London Calling, 165, 167
Lotbiriere, S.J. de, 53
Low, Gail, 11
MacJajah, Prince (N.O.M.), 42, 52, 58, 68, 69, 88, 99, 222
Mackay, Mercedes, 51, 54, 62, 64, 67, 69, 81, 95, 100, 107, novel Black Argosy, 147, 162, 170, 221
Mais, Roger, 33, 37, 40, 50, 63, 115, 131, 133, "Something for a Wedding", 133; 135, 137, "Atalanta at Calydon", 140; *The Hills Were Joyful* published, 140; 141, 145, 149, 223
Majekodunmi, N.C., 49, 223
Manley, Carmen, 33, 36, 39, 223
Manley, Edna, 47, 57, 73, 111, 121, 122, 203, 204
Manley, Michael, 7, 47, 92, 118, 119, 223
Mansfield, John, 29
Marsh, Probyn, 178
Marson, Una, 7, 10, 110, 117, 119, 120, 223
Martins, Orlando, 13, 32, 54, 58, 224
Marvell, Andrew, 104
Maxwell, Ken, 139, 224
McAlpine, Warren, 110
McBurnie, Beryl, 13, 80, 105-106, 224
McDonald, Malcolm, 53
McFarlane, Basil, 74, 75, 224
McFarlane, J.E. Clare, 27, 42, 70, 81, 115, 141, 155, 224, 229
McFarlane, R.L.C., 162, 225
McGlone, Tony, 26, 38, 67, 79
McGlurg, Bill, 121, 123
McKay, Claude, 42
McTurk, Connie, 157
Meikle, Rupert, 101, 225
Melville, Edwina, 12, "Fishing on the Rupununi", 148, 161; "The Voice", 164-165, printed in *London Calling*, 167; 225
Mendes, Alfred, 65, 72, 74, 225
Millar, James, 14, 15, 60, 69, 134, 141,

164, 166, 167, 169, 172, 179, 185, 225
Milner, Harry, 33
Milner-Brown, A.L., 60, 225
Milton, Beau, 51, 53, 57, 66, 80, 83, 85, 136, 226
Mitchell. Joseph, 49, 50
Mittelholzer, Edgar, 7, 12, 32-33, "The Burglar", "Island Tints", 33; 36, 39, 45, "Sorrow Dam and Mr Millbank", 48; 52, 60, success of *A Morning at the Office*, 70, 71; "The Sibilant and the Lost", 74; 80, 83, *Children of Kaywana*, 88, 123, liked by Marghanita Laski, disliked by Gloria Escoffery, 92; 89, 106, *Shadows Move Among Us*, 98; its success, 106; on Selvon's *A Brighter Sun*, 108; *The Weather in Middleshot*", 133, admires Mais's *The Hills*, 149; 154; 159, 224, 226
Mittelholzer, Neville, 154
Moorfoot, Rex, 103
Morgue, Theodora, 34
Morris, Sam, 30, 33, 45, 54, 86, 88, 93, 97, 136, 147, 185, 226
Morrison, Hugh, 146, 150, 226
Morrison, Nancy, 57
Moses, Addio, 34
Muir, Edwin, 104
Mulira, Eridadi, 52, 226
Mullings, Aston, 167, 226
Murphy, Richard, 131
Naipaul, Seepersad, 66, 76, "Gratuity", "brilliant, funny", 71; 78, "The Engagement", a "brilliant little story", 84; 96, "Ramdas and the Cow", "gentle humorous art", 148, 150; 227
Naipaul, V.S., 7, 13, poems, 80; "This is Home", 95, 98; 99, "Mourners", 109; 125, "Old Man", 142, reads his father's story, 148; "Epicurean Service", 152, "A Family Reunion", 160; "My Aunt's Gold Teeth", 167; rejections and poverty, 170, 227
Nanton, Philip, 13

Nchami, V.C., 57, 58, 62, 71, 79, 104, 131, 134, 143, 152, 160, 166, 227
News of the Colonies, 30-31
Newton, Kenneth P., 104, 135, 137, 228
Nicol, Davidson, 12, 28, 33, 36, 42, 49, 102, 136, 227-228
Nketia, J.H.K., 47, 48, 176, 177, 178, 228
Nkrumah, Kwame, 7, 15, 16, 27, 34, 35, 86, 95, 172, 174, 182, 183, 184, 186, 187, 188, 193, 194, 195, 208, 226, 230
Nwokedi, Francis, 85
Nyaku, Frank Kofi, 186, 187, 228
Ofori, Henry, 17, 179, 182, 183, 191, 193, 228
Ogundere, J.D., 160
Ogunsheye, Fidelis, 34, 38, 66, 81, 83
Okai, Atukwei, 17
Olivier, Laurence, 42
Onwuegbuzia, Christopher, 67, 68, 71, 76, 79, 229
Opoku, Andrew Amankwa, 175, 178, 181, 185, 229
Ormsby Cooper, Eileen, 45, 63, 132, 166, 229
Ormsby Marshall, Helen Violet, 115, 229
Orwell, George, 26
Osadebay, Dennis Chukude, 48, 49, 230
Otoo, Samuel, 178, 182, 230
Owusu, Charles, 170
Padmore, George, 32, 35, 44, 49, 75, 89, 169, 182, 194
Paget, Hugh, 160
Parkes, Frank Kobina, 17, 175, 176; begins work with Swanzy, 177, 178, 180, 182, 185, 193, 230
Pasuka, *De Prophet*, 26
Patterson, Vic, 108, 126
Pearce, Andrew, 55, 131
Perham, Marjorie, 139
Perowne, Leslie, radio broadcast on West Indian culture, 67; in Ghana, 179

Philip, Prince, 52
Phillipp Fumbles (Golding), 45
Phillips, George, 79, 92, 230
Pilgrim, Frank, 108, 133, 138, 151, 153, 163, 231
Pioneer Press, 117
Ponsonby, Sir Charles, 28, 150, 166, 231
Pool, Rosey, 102, 105, 170
Pope-Hennessy, Richard James, 161, 231
Potter, Stephen, 40
Prah, Florence, 16, 100, 101, 177, 231
Prempeh, Owusu, 188
Presence Africaine, 24, 36, 39, 47, 77
Price, Keith Hamilton, 31
Primus, Pearl, 102
Pritchett, V.S., excellent review of *In the Castle of My Skin*, 141
Public Opinion (Jamaica), 44, 81, 122, 119, 203
Quansah, John, 83
Quarshie-Idun, Frances, 16, 151, 156, 161, 166, 172, 176, 231
Raine, Kathleen, recommending Lamming as poet to 3rd programme, 126
Ramkeesoon, Mrs, 39
Ramon-Fortune, Barnabas J., 32, 60, 83, 96, 106, 127, 138, 161, 232
Rattray, R. Carl, 43, 232
Rattray, R.S. *Religion and Art in Ashanti*, 177
Raven, Simon, damns *In the Castle of My Skin*, 139
Ravilious, Eric, 10
Ray, Norman, 109
Reckord, Barry, 89, 93, 132, 136, 140; *Adella*, 161, 232
Reckord, Lloyd, 89, 93, 95, 106, 130, 131, "Back o' Wall Boy", "brilliant and sick", 132, 137; 140, 147, 148, 151, 161, 232
Redfern, John 187
Redhead, Eula, 12, 33, 55, 133, 136, 152, 232
Rees, Goronwy, 95

Rees-Williams, David, 30
Reid, Victor S., 47, 66, 72, 115, 144, 233
Reith, Lord John, 15; lectures, 46, 50, 189
Ricardo, Peter, 105
Richardson, Willy, 41, 43, 51, 65, 78, 95, 97, 142, 152, 155, 165, 169, 233
Rilke, Rainer Maria, 39
Roach, E.M. (Eric), 58, 65, 72, 78, 87, 92, 98, 138, "Coronation Verse", 144, 147, "In Mango Shade", 149, 154, 159, 161, 233
Robeson, Paul, 50, 119
Robinson, R.O.A., 161
Rose, Edgar, "Fedon's Camp" (cut for anti-British sentiments) 132, 233
Ross, Emory, 135
Royal African Society (RAS), 13, 26, 31, 67, 100, 134, 150, bankers and influence sought, 151; 164, 166, 231, 252
Royal Empire Society (RES), 100
Rozan, Georges, 29, 95
Rudette, Ken, 152
Russell, Bertrand, 41, 46
Sabine, Noel, 27
Sackey, Joseph H., 176, 233
Sadji, Abdoulaye, 24
Salkey, Andrew, 13, 54, 80, 124, 125, 128, 137, 140, 143, 154, 161, 233
Sam, Albert, 180
Sam, Albert, 183
Sassoon, Victor, 127, 170
Saunders, Gil, 185
Savonnet, 24
Scott, Michael, 50
Sealy, Clifford, 94, 137, 234
Sealy, Karl, 95, 168, 234
Sealy, Theodore, 115
Sekyi, Kobina, 16, 174, 184, 234
Selvon, Dennis, 144, 156, 234
Selvon, Sam, 12, 13, 30, 35, 39, 41, "Behind the Hummingbird", bowdlerisation of, and protests against its frankness, 43; 52, 59, 67, 69, 70, 71, 76-77, 78, 94, 96;

"Cane is Bitter", 62-63; sells *A Brighter Sun*, 96, its success, 108, 109, 126 (2000 copies sold); "Gussy and the Boss", 125; "The Mouth Organ", 134, "The Calypsonian", 136, 137; diagnosed with TB, 143, 152, 153, 156; "Foster and the Coronation", 144; 165, 168, sends Swanzy second novel, *An Island is a World*, 178; 234

Senayah, Kobla, 100, 101, 107, 172, 235

Setsoafia, H.K. Bidi, 183, 184, 193, 235

Seunarine, Pandit, 62, 66

Severn, Merlyn, 135

Seymour, A.J., criticism of *Caribbean Voices*, 61; 66, 97, 235

Sharp, Stanley, on Derek Walcott, 136

Sherlock, Grace, 116

Sherlock, Philip, 111, 236

Sibley, Inez, 12, 26, 36, "The Terror Bull and the Taunt Song", 56, 58; 60, 76, 115, "Maroon Defence" 148; 150, 236

Siggs, Olive, 52

Simmonds, Ulric, 49, 54, 236

Simpson, Louis, 82, 87, 236

Singuineau, Frank, 33, 236

Small, L. Sylvester, 148, 154, 237

Smith, Michael (M.G.), 36, 39, "Testament", 42, "Madonna and Child", 147; 237

Smith, Reggie, 103

Smith-Mensah, Marian, 16, 100, 101, 172

Soyinka, Wole, 154, 237

Spence, George, 61, 237

Spender, Stephen, 27, 61, 87, 88, 97, 98, 103, 104

Springer, Hugh, 115, 116, 146

St Vincent School (see Keane, Owen Campbell and Daniel Williams), 87, 98, 127, 130

Stalin, Joseph, death of, 138

Stanley, Keith, 49

Stephens, Herman, 167, 237

Stevens, Siaka, 34

Stewart, MacNeill, 62, 64, 83, 129, 144, 153, 176, 182, 188, 193, 237

Stradling, Sheila, 42, 45, 98

Straker, Henry, 190

Strong, L.A.G., 40

Sutherland, Efua, 7, 16, relationship with Swanzy, 46, 59, 60, 62, 79, 101, 102, 101, 131, 156; announces marriage, 162-163; 189, 190, 193, 238

Swanzy, Henry, self-description, 8, 18, 25; family background, 9; marriages, 10; work after *Caribbean Voices*, 10; interest in working class lives and culture, 11; attitude to middle-class women's writing, 12; editorial gatekeeping and editorial decisions, 10, 11, 17; awareness of contradictions in his editorial position, 18-19, 35, 41; at-homes for writers, 12-13, 38; support for "young nationalism" in Africa, traditional regionalism and national identity, 15; radio work in Ghana, 16-17; monetary support for writers, 8, 17, 69, 84, 109, 110, 125, 152; as a questioner of himself and British orthodoxies, 19; poem about Gandhi, 28-29; in trouble over article on Gold Coast riots, 30, 31, 36, 40; frustration over British attitudes to *Caribbean Voices*, 36; political self-conflict over the Malay emergency and British atrocities, 41; encouraged by plans for a West African literary programme, 43; as moderate socialist, 44; self-contempt over his own moderateness, 45; takes on *West African Voices*, 45, 46; relationship with Efua Sutherland, 46, 59, 60, 79, 163; excitement over "discovery" of George Lamming, 47; on "pretentiousness" of *Focus*, 47; excitement over Walcott's *Twenty Five Poems*, 48; proto-feminist instincts, 49; bowdlerisation, 43, 49; writes "Prolegomena to a Caribbean Culture", 51; applies for a British passport, 53; resigns from Royal Institute of International Affairs, 53; criticised for patronising tone, 54; sees parallels between Orwell's *1984* and BBC, 56; not really a convinced socialist, 61; attempts to expose *Caribbean Voices* on other BBC channels rejected, 62; meets Lamming and Selvon, 69; personal finances, 69-70; resigns from West African Society because of its eurocentrism, 70; talks with Selvon, 71; takes Lamming home, 71-72, 73, 74, finds Lamming much deeper than himself, 84; enjoys *A Morning at the Office*, 72; meets Jan Carew, 77; reads Walcott's *Henri Christophe*, 77; infuriated by the poor quality of a West Indian poetry anthology edited by J.E. Clare McFarlane, 81; agony over Tirzah's illness, 82; argues with Mittelholzer about religion, 83; told about Wilson Harris's remarkable poetry, 84, and writes a poem inspired by it, 85; discussions with Jan Carew and Denis Williams, 93-94, 100; sees parallels between himself and Guy Burgess, 94; takes V.S. Naipaul to tea, 99; votes Conservative, 101; holds parties to try to mix Africans and West Indians, 102, 128; encourages his Thursday literary at-homes (the *causerie*) with the addition of gin, discussions of T.S. Eliot and antisemitism, 104; 105, 108, 109, 110, 124, 125, 127; worries about Calder-Marshall's acerbic criticism, 104, 105; works on memoir of Tirzah and knows it cannot be published, 105; feels *Caribbean* and *West African Voices* are falling into a routine, 105; has to deal with Jonathan Vincent's arrest and breakdown, 106, 107, 109, 110; hears of Babalola's breakdown and confinement and wonders "What are we doing to them?", 107; learns he is being sent to Jamaica, 110; visit to Jamaica, 111-121; Bahamas: whites served by blacks, 111, meets the Lindos and confirms who is the author of the letters, meets Philip Sherlock, 111; meets Derek Walcott, 112; meets J.H. Parry and Elsa Goveia, 113; attempts to promote interests of John Figueroa, Fernando Henriques and Lamming rebuffed, 113; meets G.R. Coulthard who points out total lack of interest in Caribbean writing in the English department, 114; European theatre at the Garrison Theatre, 114; meets a hostile Mickey (A.L.) Hendricks, and Archie Lindo at JBC, 115; experiences Jamaican colour/class divides, 115; meets PEN club, middle-brow and middle class, 115-116; meets Vic Reid and Inez Sibley, 115-116; incompetence with recording devices, 116; meets Una Marson, 117; visits poverty of August Town, ignored by the university, 117-118; meets Michael Manley, learns about Ras Tafarians, 118-119; gets to know the Lindos better, 119; visits British Council and spends day with Una Marson, 120; gives what he thinks is an over-optimistic Governor Hugh Foot benefit of his impressions, 120-121; visits John Figueroa's family home, 121; visits Edna Manley and makes peace, 122; concludes that he is not attached to Jamaica at the deepest level, 122; moves from BBC Oxford Street to Langham, 123; discovers that much of Jamaican recordings are useless, 123; complaint from McLurg, JBC, on Swanzy's attitude to commercial radio, 123; tea with V.S. Naipaul, 124; shares Calder-Marshall's criticism of Mittelholzer's *Kaywana* and its selling as soft porn, 126; lunch with Mittelholzer, 126; JGW tells him the literary programmes are under attack, 127; plans marriage to Henriette [Van Eeghan], and is investigated by future father-in-law and defended by JGW, 127-128; marriage, 129; feels he is scraping the barrel for the *Voices* programmes, but intrigued by what he thinks are Jan Carew's imaginative versions of himself, 129, 139; visited by Shake Keane, 130; instalment sent by the Lindos of includes stories of wishful sex and the rape of white women; meets Roger Mais, 131; underpaid for Notes for the Royal African Society's *African Affairs*, 132; lunch with Mais, "silly, sweet and violent", reads proofs of *In the Castle of My Skin*, and Mittelholzer's *The Weather in Middenshot*, and supper with Shake Keane, 133; supper with Lamming who ribs him; attends a party at the Carews – "What a man!", 134; views on metropolitan writing about Africa; meets John Hearne, 135; gives a paper on the "Caribbean imagination and meets Edward Brathwaite; dismayed by EKB's attitude to Roach, 136; pleased that *In the Castle of My Skin* acknowledges the BBC in the blurb, but puzzled that Walcott is not acknowledged for the title, 137; thinks about posts in Africa and needs to get out, but Henriette pregnant; thinks Roach is the best current Caribbean poet, 138; his essays rejected by Faber; pleased by Lamming's sales, 139; shares V.S. Naipaul's finals traumas, 142; sceptical about whether *Caribbean Voices* has aided the federaln spirit, 143; implication that the anti-imperialist sentiments of Eric Roach's "Coronation Verse" were toned down for broadcast, 144; reads *The Hills Were Joyful Together* and is disgusted by its violence but wonders if this is the response of a Colonial Made Gent, 145; Figueroa an "aimiable badger", 146; visited by Eddie Brathwaite thinking about going to Africa and carrying "rather bad" poems by Thom Gunn, 147; an "aristocratic" V.S. Naipaul comes to supper, he admires Saki, 148; meets and is impressed by C.L.R. James, 148-149; Mittelholzer writes from Canada about nudity, 149; John Figueroa comes to say goodbye, 150, 151; supper with Nchami, 151; a racist incident in the studio, 151; wonders whether Lamming should be a philosopher rather than a novelist, 152; tries to help Vidia Naipaul distressed by the death of his father, 152; visits Sam Selvon in the sanatorium, 152-153; first child with Henriette, 153; writes "notes" on Mau Mau atrocities, and on "the brilliant sick mind of Barry Reckord", 154; notes British atrocities in Kenya and racism in Bermuda, 155; makes a visit to East and Central Africa to inspect radio services, comments on belatedness of late colonial efforts, and signs of the emergency in Kenya; idea of an East African Voices dismissed, 157-158; attends Willie Richardson's West Indian party, 159; V.S. Naipaul comes for supper, 160; gives a talk on African writing to the Circle, 160; writes the half-yearly *Caribbean Voices* report lamenting the death of Seepersad Naipaul and attacking Pope-Hennessy's ignorance of Caribbean writing; notes focus on race in recent writing and wonders about his response, 161-162; reflects on BBC career, 163-164; invited to take post of head of programmes in Gold Coast, 164; Vidia Naipaul discussed as a replacement editor, 164; lunch with Sam Selvon, 165; reads up on the Gold Coast and notes family connections, 166; meets Wilson Harris and talk about Martin Buber, 166; leaves Royal African Society, 166; gives Vidia Naipaul a homily on *agape*, 167; Wilson Harris and Malcolm de Chazal most interesting minds he has met, 168; visits home of Cyprian Ekwensi, 168-169; reads *The Emigrants*, 169 and goes to farewell party for Lamming; Naipaul, "no friend of the Negro race", not present, 169-170; VSN for drinks, 170; his final *Caribbean Voices* recording, with Harris; sees Salkey, Selvon, Barry Reckord, Eddie Brathwaite, Nadia Catthouse and VS Naipaul as among the writers and performers the world will hear from, 171; meets his Gold Coast radio staff in London and recognises the unfairness of their pay differential in comparison to his and thinks about the challenges of five languages, 171; last programme involves Stuart Hall; leaves for Accra, 171; meets some old acquaintances and learns of a political crisis, 172; on programme exchanges between language groups; plans literary programme, *The Singing Net*, 173; visits Efua and new husband and baby, 173-174; meets Nkrumah and finds him charming, 174; hears of and regrets JGW's death, 174; first edition of *The Singing Net* criticised for "too much Swanzy", 176; Henriette and son arrive, 176; hears from Sam Selvon and Eddie Brathwaite turns up, 178; outdoor broadcasts revolutionised by midget recorders; political tightropes to be walked, 179; Eddie Brathwaite visits with Efua and he stays the night, 180-181; religious and language tensions at programme meetings; thinks Andrew Opoku's poem is one of finest things from West Africa, 181; programme meeting too European, 182; writing a paper on the 19th C Swanzy family in Africa, 183; back in London meets Diana Athill and hears talk of publishing mergers, 185; back in Ghana, problems over regional balance and adjectives to be derived from the country's name, 185-186; programmes for the eve of independence, 186; what is the independent broadcasting company to be called?, 186; meets the Duchess of Kent, 187; the independence day celebrations, 188; new government orders that no BBC news to be broadcast, 189; trying to recruit Cameron Duodu, 189; replaced by a Ghanaian, 190 and station put under direct government control and first hints of censorship, 190; daughter born; writes to Figueroa and Vidia Naipaul to congratulate on *The Mystic Masseur*, 190; plans an anthology drawn from *The Singing Net*, accepted by ministry, 190-191; thinks of working with Efua on the anthology but thinks she only likes people who write like her (cf Naipaul when he took over CV) and she proposes to compete with her own anthology, 191; is hurt that *Black Orpheus* contains material unacknowledged from *Calling West Africa*, 192; starts planning his exit, 192, Henriette not well, 192; meets

Efua who is conciliatory about the anthology; helps choose the words for the national anthem, and proofs *Voices of Ghana*, 193; meets the Ghana cabinet with the anthem shortlist and is part of a panel to refine it, 194; thinks about whether he wants to leave Ghana (in two months), 194; final deliberations on the anthem, 195; presents a copy of *Voices of Ghana* to Nkrumah, 195; farewell party and embarrassment by generous press coverage of his departure, and sung a farewell by Ishael Addams choir on board ship; feels he has not been a total failure, 196

Taylor, Tom, 112

Telemaque, Harold, 39, 54, 56, 58, 161, 238

The Listener, 30

The Singing Net, 16-17, 20, 170, 173, 175, 176, 177, 178, 179, 180, 181, 182, 183, 185, 186, 188, 190, 197, 210, 213, 217, 228, 229, 230, 233, 237, 238

Third Programme, takes an anthology of poems from Caribbean Voices, 147; heard by around 40,000, 149

Thomas, Dylan, 40, 48, 103, 154

Thompson, Claude, 126, 129, 238

Timothy, Emmanuel Bankole, 176, 238

Toynbee, Arnold, 36

Treadgold, Mary, 11, 27, 35, 38, 40, 45, 49, 76, 84, 103, 239

Tribune, 61

Tudor, Cameron, 39

Tukur, Mallam, 49

Turner, George, 31

Tutuola, Amos, *The Palm Wine Drinkard*, 124-125; denigrated by educated West Africans, 125; 142, 145, 149, 160, 166

Tuvari, Ramjass, 127

Tynan, Kenneth, 78

Uganda Broadcasting Service, 14

Uhlman, Fred, 76, 104, 126

Ukeni, 140

Ustinov, Peter, 34

UWI, Mona, 112

Van Eeghan, Henriette, Swanzy married to, 10, 127-128, pregnant, 138

Vaughan Thomas, Wynford, 53, 82; reports meeting Amos Tutuola in Nigeria, 149

Vaughan, H.A., 65

Vaz, Gloria, 66, 106, 110, 147, 164, 239

Vaz, Noel, 103, 124, 148, 239

Vincent, Jonathan, 92, 93, 104, breakdown and arrest, 107, 109, 110; in prison, 124, repatriated, 130, 145, 239

Virtue, Vivian, 27, 74, 97, 98, 102, 105, 109, 113, 115, 239

Voices of Ghana: Literary Contributions to the GBS 1955-57, 8, 17, 18, 194, 195, 196, 198, 207, 229, 230, 237,

Vowden, Michael, 42

Walcott, Derek, 13, *Twenty-Five Poems* sent to *Caribbean Voices*, 48; 52, 58, 63, 65; *Senza Alcun Sospetta* (broadcast verse play), 73; 74, *Henri Christophe*, 77, adapted for radio, 85, despair over poor quality of performance and recording, 86, performed live directed by Errol Hill, 108; 78; *Harry Dernier*, 103, 106; 110,113, "The Hermit and the Circus", 125; 239

Walter, Carl, 35, 240

Ward, Ida, 46, 59

Waterton, Charles, 60

Weatherhead, Rev. Leslie, 59

Wedgwood Benn, Tony, 67

Weidenfeld, George, 9, 30, 38, 50, 60, 102, 185; on Swanzy, 9

West Africa (journal), 44, 51, 156

West African Broadcasting Unit, 177, 186

West African Diary, 51

West African Society (UK), 42, 47, 48, 60, 70, 94

West African Voices, 8, 46, 47, preliminary discussion, language issues, 47; launched, 47-48; 49, oral literature, 52; 56, 63, 66, need to deal with tribal/ethnic sensitivities, 71; 81, 94, garden party, 95-96; 105, 107, 162, 164, 193, 197, 198, 199, 200, 202, 210, 211, 213, 214, 218, 221, 222, 223, 225, 226, 227, 229, 230, 231, 237, 238, 239, 240

West African Writers and Artists Club, 99

Westmoreland, Rusty, 194, 195

Whettam, Graham, 85

Whitehead, A.N., read by Lamming, 80, 84, 152

Whitley, Oliver, 40, 41, 58, 59, 61, 70, 80

Wickham, John, 54, 59, 95, 240

Williams, Adisa, 101, 106, 110, 130, 140, 240

Williams, Basil, 26

Williams, Daniel, 96, 240

Williams, Denis, 56, 84, 100, 127, promoting Wilson Harris, criticising Jan Carew, 130; no longer a disciple of Harris, 169; 241

Williams, Eric, 169, 170

Williamson, Hugh Ross, 88

Wilson, Helen, 92

Wilson, Willie, 53

Winful, Archie, 174, 183, 189, 193

Woolford, Gordon, 30, 39, 45, 47, 54, 61, 62, 63, 67, 80, 81, 84, 87, 88, 93, 96, 97, 104, 106, 108, breakdown, 124; 127, 146, chapters of an autobiographical novel, "On the Rocks", 166, 169; 241

Wright, Richard, 25, 97

Wyne, Ruth, 129, 131

Yoruba poetry, 58, 78, 133, 221

You and I (interracial magazine), 138

Zaire, 51

WRITERS WHO FEATURE IN HENRY SWANZY'S
DIARIES AND ARE PUBLISHED BY PEEPAL TREE
PRESS

Kamau Brathwaite
Strange Fruit
ISBN: 9781845233082; pp 124; pub. 2016; £12.99; poetry

Arthur Calder-Marshall
Glory Dead
ISBN: 9781845235314; pp. 208, pub. 1938, 2022; £12.99; non-fiction.

George Campbell
First Poems
ISBN: 9781845231491; pp. 180; pub. 1945, 1981, 2012; poetry

Jan Carew
Black Midas
ISBN: 9781845230951; pp. 200; pub. 1958, 2012; £9.99; fiction

The Wild Coast
ISBN: 9781845231101; pp. 240; pub. 1960, 2009; £8.99; fiction

Episodes in my Life: The Autobiography of Jan Carew
ISBN: 9781845232450; pp. 324; pub. 2015; £19.99; non-fiction

Neville Dawes
The Last Enchantment
ISBN: 9781845231170; pp. 332; pub. 1960, 2009; £9.99; fiction

Fugue and Other Writings
ISBN: 9781845231095; pp. 372; pub. 2012; £17.99; poetry, short stories, criticism

Gloria Escoffery
Mother Jackson Murders the Moon
ISBN: 9781900715249; pp. 60; pub. 1998; £7.99; poetry

John Figueroa
The Chase: Collected Poems
ISBN: 9780948833526; pp. 152; pub. 1992; £9.99; poetry

Wilson Harris
Heartland
ISBN: 9781845230968; pp. 96; pub. 1964, 2009; £7.99; fiction

The Eye of the Scarecrow
ISBN: 9781845231644; pp. 112; pub. 1965, 2011; £8.99; fiction

The Ascent of Omai
ISBN: 9781845233549; pp. 134; pub. 1970, 2018; £8.99; fiction

The Sleepers of Roraima and the Age of the Rainmakers
ISBN: 9781845231651; pp. 200; pub. 1970, 1971, 2014; £9.99, fiction

John Hearne
Voices Under the Window
ISBN: 9781845230319; pp. 145; pub. 1955, 2005; £7.99; fiction

Stranger at the Gate
ISBN: 9781845234546; pp. 287; pub. 1956, 2020; £12.99; fiction

Errol Hill and Errol John
Interviewed in Olivier Stephenson, *Visions and Voices: Conversations with Fourteen Caribbean Playwrights*
ISBN: 9781845231736; pp. 436; pub. 2013; £19.99; interviews

Peter Kempadoo
Guyana Boy
ISBN: 9781900715560; pp. 184; pub. 1960, 2002; £8.99; fiction

George Lamming
Of Age and Innocence
ISBN: 9781845231453; pp. 436; pub. 1958, 2011; £14.99; fiction

Water With Berries
ISBN: 9781845231675; pp. 278; pub. 1971, 2016; £11.99; fiction

Roger Mais
The Hills Were Joyful Together
ISBN: 9781845231002; pp. 342; pub. 1953, 2017; £12.99; fiction

Black Lightning
ISBN: 9781845231019; pp. 164; pub. 1955, 2015; £8.99; fiction

Una Marson
Una Marson: Selected Poems, ed. Alison Donnell
ISBN: 9781845231682; pp. 164; pub. 2011; £10.99; poetry

Edgar Mittelholzer
Creole Chips and Other Writings: Short Fiction, Poetry, Drama and Essays, 1937-1954
ISBN: 9781845233006; pp. 448; pub. 2018; £19.99; fiction, poetry

Corentyne Thunder
ISBN: 9781845231118; pp. 248; pub. 1941, 2009; £8.99; fiction

A Morning at the Office
ISBN: 9781845230661; pp. 210; pub. 1950, 2010; £9.99; fiction

Shadows Move Among Them
ISBN: 9781845230913; pp. 358; pub. 1951, 2010; £12.99; fiction

The Life and Death of Sylvia
ISBN: 9781845231200; pp. 366; pub. 1953, 2010; £12.99; fiction

My Bones and My Flute
ISBN: 9781845232955; pp. 206; pub. 1955, 2015; £9.99; fiction

A Swarthy Boy
ISBN: 9781845235550; pp. 195; pub. 1963, forthcoming 2023; £12.99; memoir

Seepersad Naipaul
Amazing Scenes: Selected Journalism 1928-1953
ISBN: 9781845235635; pp. 450; pub. 2023, forthcoming; £24.99; non-fiction

Gurudeva and Other Indian Tales: Collected Short Stories
ISBN: 9781845235543; pp. 180; pub. 1943, 2023, forthcoming; £9.99; fiction

Victor S. Reid
New Day
ISBN: 9781845230906; pp. 360; pub. 1949, 2016; £13.99, fiction

E.M. Roach
The Flowering Rock: Collected Poems 1938-1974
ISBN: 9781845232078; pp. 230, pub. 2012; £12.99; poetry

Andrew Salkey
Escape to an Autumn Pavement
ISBN: 9781845230982; pp. 218, pub. 1960, 2009; £8.99; fiction

Hurricane
ISBN: 9781845231804; pp. 102; pub. 1964, 2011; £6.99; children's fiction

Riot
ISBN: 9871845231819; pp. 172; pub. 1967, 2011, £7.99; children's fiction

Earthquake
ISBN: 9781845231828; pp. 106; pub. 1965, 2011; £6.99; children's fiction

Drought
ISBN: 9781845231835; pp. 122; pub. 1966, 2011; £6.99; children's fiction

Samuel Selvon
Eldorado West One
ISBN: 9780948833069; pp. 156; pub. 1991, 1998; £7.99; drama

Highway in the Sun and Other Plays
ISBN: 9780948833076; pp. 215; pub. 1991; £8.99; drama

Derek Walcott
Jean Antoine Dunne, *Derek Walcott's Love Affair with Film*
ISBN: 9781845233655; pp. 213; pub. 2017; £19.99; criticism

Jean Antoine Dunne, ed. Interlocking Basins of a Globe : Essays on Derek Walcott
ISBN: 9781845232207; pp. 224; pub., 2013; £17.99; criticism

Denis Williams
Other Leopards
ISBN: 9781845230678; pp. 200; pub. 1963, 2009; £8.99; fiction

The Third Temptation
ISBN: 9781845231163; pp. 108; pub. 1968, 2010; £8.99; fiction

Evelyn A. Williams, *The Art of Denis Williams*
ISBN: 9781845231934; pp. 180; pub. 2012; £27.99; art criticism